Barnes & Noble Critical Studies

General Editor: Anne Smith

The Plays
of D. H. Lawrence:

A Biographical
and Critical Study

Barnes & Noble Critical Studies published and in preparation:

E. E. Cummings: A Remembrance of Miracles
The Fiction of Sex: Themes and Functions of
Sex Difference in the Modern Novel
Henry James: The Ibsen Years
The Historical Novel and Popular Politics
in Nineteenth-century England
Margaret Drabble: Puritanism and Permissiveness
The Silent Majority: A Study of the Working
Class in Post-war British Fiction
Wyndham Lewis: Fictions and Satires

The English Sickness: A
Secret History of Modernism
George Gissing
Günter Grass
New Essays on Carlyle
Reaching into the Silence: A Study
of Twentieth-century Visionaries

THE PLAYS
OF D. H. LAWRENCE:

A Biographical
and Critical Study

Sylvia Sklar

BARNES & NOBLE
BOOKS
10 East 53d St., New York 10022
(a division of Harper & Row Publishers, Inc.)

Barnes & Noble Books
10 East 53rd Street
New York

ISBN 06–496333–0

For Eric, Hilary and Ian

First published in the U.S.A. 1975
© 1975 Sylvia Sklar

Printed and bound in Great Britain
MCMLXXV

Contents

Editorial Note

The authors of the *Barnes & Noble Critical Studies* apply the critical theory and techniques of the seventies to the literature most relevant to our own age, but with the aim of the best critics of every age: to stimulate in the reader what T. S. Eliot called 'a development of sensibility'; to enlarge, and challenge, his own perceptions of the original work, and to make him want to go back to it, with a deepened sense of engagement.

A.S.

Author's Note

In order to reduce the number of footnotes to an acceptable minimum, references to the two most frequently cited secondary sources are inserted in the text in parentheses immediately following the relevant quotation, the two sources concerned being abbreviated as follows:

CL   *The Collected Letters of D. H. Lawrence*, 2 vols., ed. H. T. Moore (London and New York, 1962)

      D. H. Lawrence: A Composite Biography, 3 vols., ed. Edward Nehls (Madison, Wisconsin, 1957, 1958 and 1959)

N.I	Volume I	1885–1919
N.II	Volume II	1919–1925
N.III	Volume III	1925–1930

Acknowledgements

For the interest that led to the undertaking of this study, I am grateful above all to Peter Gill's productions which, in 1967 and 1968, brought Lawrence's plays to life at the Royal Court Theatre, London.

I am also greatly indebted to the introductory essays on Lawrence's drama by Keith Sagar, Michael Marland, and Raymond Williams, which led me to the sources of Lawrence's dramatic work. Among those sources, I owe particular gratitude to the work of Edward Nehls, editor of *D. H. Lawrence: A Composite Biography*, and Harry T. Moore, editor of *The Collected Letters of D. H. Lawrence*.

Invaluable, too, have been the collections of Lawrence's letters to S. S. Koteliansky and to Louie Burrows, edited respectively by George J. Zytaruk and James T. Boulton. I also owe particular thanks to Professor Boulton for his pilot work on the Young Bert Lawrence Exhibition in Nottingham in 1972 which gave such prominence to Lawrence's interest in the theatre.

I wish also to thank Laurence Pollinger Ltd., The Viking Press Inc., and the Estate of the late Mrs. Frieda Lawrence for permission to quote from Lawrence's published work.

Introduction

In introducing the plays of so well known a writer as D. H. Lawrence, one is immediately faced with the problem of avoiding repetition. Known not only for his novels, but also for the details of his life story, Lawrence has been given such thorough critical and biographical attention that to go over the familiar ground once again would obviously be redundant. Yet to omit the background altogether would be to do less than justice to the difficulties that Lawrence overcame in writing plays in the face of continued indifference—amounting in some cases to outright hostility—even on the part of those who most energetically encouraged him to write in other forms.

Out of the rich material provided by biographers, I have therefore selected only those details that relate to the hitherto neglected aspect of Lawrence as a writer of plays. Gathered together, and supplemented by the invaluable testament of Lawrence's own letters[1], these details provide here a background for a close analysis of the plays that Lawrence wrote, not merely—as has often been suggested—as diversions from the more strenuous business of writing in the mode of narrative fiction, but as dramas which he above all visualised as being produced on the stage.

The evidence for the order of composition of the early plays is confused and conflicting, and Lawrence's habit of repeated revision makes the task of accurately dating these plays a particularly difficult one. The difficulty is, of course, compounded by

[1] *The Collected Letters of D. H. Lawrence*, edited by Harry T. Moore. Copyright © 1962 by Angelo Ravagli and C. M. Weekley, Executors of the Estate of Frieda Lawrence Ravagli. All rights reserved. Reprinted by permission of The Viking Press, Inc., and Willian Heinemann Ltd.

the fact that the plays have been the last of Lawrence's works to receive scholarly attention. During his lifetime, only three of the eight plays were published: *The Widowing of Mrs. Holroyd* in 1914, *Touch and Go* in 1920, and *David* in 1926. After Lawrence's death, these three were published in 1933 in a collection entitled *The Plays of D. H. Lawrence*, and, in the following year, *A Collier's Friday Night* received its first publication, with an introduction by Edward Garnett. As interest in Lawrence grew during the years after his death, the remaining plays were successively rediscovered, *The Fight for Barbara* appearing in the December issue of *Argosy Magazine* in 1933 (under the title, *Keeping Barbara*), followed by *The Married Man* in the Autumn Number of *The Virginia Quarterly* in 1940, and *The Merry-go-Round* in the Christmas number of the same periodical in 1941. One scene of the fragment, *Altitude* was published in the 'little' magazine, *Laughing Horse* in the summer of 1938, the other fragment, *Noah's Flood* having been published in 1936 in the collection of miscellaneous writings by Lawrence, edited by Edward D. McDonald and entitled *Phoenix*.

Finally, the collection of Lawrence's dramatic work as we now know it in *The Complete Plays of D. H. Lawrence*[2] was published in 1965, and it is in this edition that *The Daughter-in-Law*—arguably among the most striking of all Lawrence's plays—makes its first appearance. The available evidence for dating this, and the other five plays which Lawrence wrote between 1906 and 1914 has been considered in conjunction with the discussion of the plays themselves.

In view of the still imperfect chronology, I have decided to group together the three naturalist plays, *A Collier's Friday Night, The Widowing of Mrs. Holroyd* and *The Daughter-in-Law*, both because of their thematic preoccupations and because the mode in which they are written exemplifies Lawrence's exploration of the possibilities of naturalism.

Although *The Merry-go-Round* may have preceded *The Daughter-in-Law* in actual date of composition, this play has

[2] *The Complete Plays of D. H. Lawrence.* Copyright © 1965 by The Estate of Mrs. Frieda Lawrence. All rights reserved. Reprinted by permission of The Viking Press, Inc. and William Heinemann Ltd.

been taken, together with *The Married Man* and *The Fight for Barbara* in a second group which finds Lawrence exploring a quite different mode of tragi-comedy, in which the discoveries drawn from naturalism are set to work in creating formal distance.

All too little is known about the dates of alternative versions of many of Lawrence's plays, and there is virtually no work at all as yet on the relationship between versions in the several cases where variant manuscripts and typescripts exist. For the purposes of this introductory study therefore I have simply pointed out where such work remains to be done, and have briefly suggested the ways in which variant readings might provide interesting sidelights on our responses to the plays as we have them in the standard collected edition of 1965.

It is above all with the texts, as they exist in *The Complete Plays of D. H. Lawrence* that this book is concerned. However much further information research may yet discover on the subject of Lawrence's drama, it has seemed to me that there is a great deal already to be done in analysing the currently authoritative versions of the plays, and in giving them their rightful share of critical attention as an important part of Lawrence's work as a whole.

Ideally in analysing these plays, I would have liked to adopt the method used by Professor J. L. Styan in his commentary on the four major plays in *Chekhov in Performance* (1971), not only because Lawrence's early drama has so much of the Chekhovian about it, but also because Professor Styan's method of approaching the plays is, as he himself writes, 'also the method of the director in the theatre'. Since, however, there are eight plays to be dealt with here, in addition to the placing of Lawrence's drama in the perspective of his life and other work, the method has had to be considerably adapted and compressed. Even so, it is hoped that the approach made here remains recognisably closely related to that which might be made by a director in the theatre; an approach, that is to say, which pays attention to those aspects of the plays which make their several effects on an audience in a theatre as a result of Lawrence's stagecraft.

Anyone in the least acquainted with the major novels and some, at least, of Lawrence's prolific output of short stories, will at once discover parallels between them and the plays, both in the

11

straightforward matter of content and in the more elusive concerns of theme. In plays like *A Collier's Friday Night* and *The Fight for Barbara* in particular the literary parallels are made even more complex by the relation between the fictions and the episodes in Lawrence's life upon which we commonly speak of them as being 'based'. These treatments in different forms of the same 'source material' from life, deserve a comparative study of their own. Here the dramatic treatment has been singled out for special attention in order to demonstrate how Lawrence consciously selected, shaped and ordered his material with stage production in view.

After an overall survey of the part played by drama in Lawrence's life, I have then devoted a chapter to each of the plays—with the exception of the two fragments, the likely proximity of which in time of writing made it seem appropriate for for them to be considered together. Each of these chapters begins with an account of the circumstances in which Lawrence wrote the particular play, and continues with an analysis of that play as *dramatic literature*; that is to say, as a play in its own right, without special reference to any interest that we might take in it as a 'document' of its author's life. In this way I hope to have provided an introduction to further study both of the important function of dramatic form in Lawrence's work as a whole, and of the plays themselves as viable texts, worthy of inclusion in the classic repertoire of twentieth-century English drama.

Even more importantly, I hope to have contributed in some small way to the growing interest in Lawrence as a writer of plays. It has certainly not been any part of my purpose to establish 'definitive' interpretations of plays which are remarkable largely for the way in which they elude such unambiguous final judgements! A complete edition of the plays has been amongst us now for a decade, and, though there are hopeful signs that they are now being given attention by those men of the theatre who alone can realise them on the stage where they belong, the plays are still virtually ignored as the important works of literature that they so clearly are. It has for too long been taken for granted that the plays are interesting only as a gloss on the novels—or even on the life—of their author. This state of affairs can only be remedied if more readers will take a direct look at the plays themselves, as they exist in all their variety in the pages of *The Complete Plays of D. H. Lawrence*. It is principally in the hope of encouraging more readers to take that direct look—and form their own judgements and interpretations of those plays, that this book has been written.

1

Lawrence and the Theatre

As readers or critics, we perhaps too readily categorise writers as 'dramatists' or 'novelists' or 'poets' in response to the form in which they preponderantly work. But how meaningful are these categories to the writers themselves? Should we not rather recognise that 'dramatist', 'novelist' and 'poet' are elements that are concurrently present in any literary artist whose work compels our attention? These seem to me to be crucial questions to ask when considering the plays of a writer whom we generally think of as 'a novelist'.

The categories are after all, when we come to think about it, only meaningful in relation to the completed works. We can say without hesitation that Lawrence wrote *more* novels than plays, and, in that sense, confidently and properly describe him as a novelist rather than a dramatist. But the judgements that we base on such convenient distinctions must not even then be projected so as to exclude the dramatic aspect of Lawrence's writing. Nor, as has so often been the case, should we proceed from the evidence of the proportions in which each of the forms are to be found in his completed works to the verdict that Lawrence was, absolutely and innately, a novelist first and foremost, then a poet, and only in the smallest measure a dramatist.

The fact of the matter is that most artists do not see themselves in such hard and fast terms. Circumstances, rather than 'natural' or 'given' talents often determine the form that comes to predominate in any writer's work. Among those circumstances, the predominant form of a particular historical or cultural period obviously plays an important part, as do all the other influences and pressures—both literary and non-literary—of living, as a writer, in a particular time and a particular place.

Lawrence, at all events, did not see himself as categorically 'a novelist', or 'a dramatist', or 'a poet', but as a writer. At the age of twenty-three, when the idea of becoming a writer had already taken a powerful hold upon him, he wrote: 'I put out my hands passionately for modern verses and drama—and, in less degree, novels.' (CL p. 44) Though, with the advantage of hindsight, we know that the balance was changed in his own writing; that the novel actually came to dominate to the highest degree in Lawrence's work, we must not therefore simply overlook the impulse towards poetry and drama that was equally operative in the creative drive that brought those novels into existence.

To think of becoming a writer at all was, as we know, a most extraordinary thing for Lawrence to have done, given the time and place in which he was born, and much has been written to account for the way in which he overcame circumstantial odds and rose to become a major novelist of the twentieth century. In re-dressing the balance here, I will concentrate on those aspects of Lawrence's personality and early experience that most closely relate to the dramatic element in his writing; *not* in order to re-categorise him as a dramatist in any arbitrary way, but to suggest that the dramatic—both as a form in the shape of plays and as a particular way of rendering an attitude to life and the world into literary art—was intrinsic to Lawrence's total creativity as a writer.

As a young man, Lawrence loved the theatre. His was not merely a literary interest in plays as books, but a passionate enthusiasm for acting, for producing, and even for the designing of sets—in short for the full experience of drama in performance. Opportunities for formal theatre-going must have been rare enough for the youngster who grew up in Eastwood, 'a mining village of some three thousand souls, about eight miles from Nottingham'.[1] At the turn of the century, Nottingham itself could hardly be described as a centre of any kind of cultural or artistic activity, but it was the nearest to the 'bright lights' of city life that Lawrence was to know right up to his early twenties.

---

[1] 'Nottingham and the Mining Countryside', *Phoenix: The Posthumous Papers of D. H. Lawrence*, ed., Edward D. McDonald (London and New York, 1936), p. 133.

Money, as we know from Lawrence's own factual and fictional accounts of his early life, was not easily come by in the Lawrence household, though his mother always managed somehow to scrape the necessary pennies together for her spoilt darling 'Bert'. Some of the earliest of those pennies may well have been spent revelling with the other village lads in the bloodthirsty histrionics of Teddy Rayner's travelling company of actors. Years later, and a world away from his Eastwood boyhood, Lawrence was to recall those gory productions in a theatre which he describes in *The White Peacock* as being 'gloriously nicknamed the "Blood-Tub" ', when he saw 'Amletto who is Hamlet with an Eyetalian hat on' (CL p. 177) during the Carnival celebrations at Christmas in Gargagno in 'a cast-off church (that) made a good theatre.'[2] Two pennyworth of *Sweenie Todd the Barber* or *The Murder in the Red Barn*, goggled at from a rough plank seat in the 'much worn old tent . . . lighted by coal oil flares' (N.III p. 746) that served the Rayner family of showmen as a theatre, made a lasting impression on the delicate and imaginative youngster who (to our great benefit) was so alert to all the details of his small world.

From all that we know about that frail boy, so prone to illness from babyhood that his mother feared she would never 'rear' him, it seems incredible that he was able to survive the years of travelling to and from Nottingham every day, first to attend the High School where he enrolled as a Scholarship boy, three days after his thirteenth birthday, and later to serve the brief apprenticeship to the firm of Haywood's which was brought to an abrupt close by his near-fatal attack of pneumonia in the winter of 1901–2. Next came the arduous life of a pupil teacher, travelling again every day to Ilkeston for the studies that were to take him on to Nottingham University College Day Training Section, where he spent yet a further two years gaining his professional qualifications as a teacher.

But the daily commuting that must have put such a strain on the already damaged health of the student Lawrence seems not at all to have prevented him from joining in—and indeed more

[2] 'The Theatre', *Twilight in Italy* (Penguin edition), p. 62. Originally published London and New York, 1916.

17

often leading—the activities of the group of local friends who called themselves the 'Pagans'. We owe the most vivid pictures of Lawrence's formative years (other than those which Lawrence himself has left us) to members of this group which included Jessie Chambers, George Neville and Louie Burrows, all of whose memoirs—as well as many more, written by friends and acquaintances Lawrence made later in life—bear witness to his 'genius' for charades; those improvised theatricals in which, throughout his life, Lawrence loved to exercise his celebrated talent for mimicry and play-acting.

Representative of those many accounts is that given by William Hopkin whom Lawrence later immortalised—as he had always threatened to do—as the socialist leader, Willie Houghton, in *Touch and Go*. Hopkin, who knew Lawrence from babyhood and recollects his first sight of the delicate infant being pushed along the streets of Eastwood in a three-wheeled pram, recalls that 'Bert was a positive genius at charades and his love for them lasted through his life. In his later school and college days before he went to Croydon, he was our most constant visitor, and if a party collected, charades would certainly come on. The house looked like a second-hand clothes shop afterwards.'[3]

Similarly impressed by Lawrence's talent for play-acting was Jessie Chambers' younger brother David who 'as a mere child', privileged to join in the fun and games of his elders, remembers the eighteen year old Lawrence as 'the most exciting person I had ever met'. Of all the things that Dr. Chambers recalls—after a gap of forty years—about that exciting person, it is the passion for improvised theatre that obviously created the most lasting impression. 'But to me . . . he was at his greatest in charades. There have never been such charades since.' (N.I p. 47)

As Hopkin rightly observed, it was not only the young 'Bert' Lawrence who loved informal play-acting, but the mature man who, in the dark days immediately after the first World War, is remembered for his staging of charades in the Berkshire countryside, and for the 'great fun at which he and Frieda excelled'. (N.I p. 506) In his introduction to two of Lawrence's plays, Michael Marland also cites Derek Patmore's memory of Lawrence in the

[3] 'Recollections of D. H. Lawrence', *The Nottingham Guardian*, 2 March 1936, p. 6.

mid 1920's when the latter was still entertaining his friends with his remarkable talent for mimicry and his fondness for acting, as he continued to do in New Mexico, where he not only exercised these informal gifts, but also began to dramatise the events of the period in the unfinished *Altitude*—while at the same time planning the more ambitious *David*, the leading female role of which was designed for the actress Ida Rauh, herself dramatised in the fragment. At that time, Andrew Dasburg (Ida Rauh's artist husband) also found it most notable, among Lawrence's many remarkable characteristics, that 'No one enjoyed himself more playing charades than he'. (N II p. 197) So enduring an enthusiasm in the man must surely be reflected in the writer, as has indeed been well understood by critics of the dramatic aspects of Lawrence's novels and stories. In the playwright too the 'genius' for capturing the essence of a situation and presenting it in dramatic form can be seen to play no small part.

Lawrence's inclination towards dramatic form became channelled by a variety of forces into directions other than that of writing plays. That the talent went, so to speak 'underground' and was subsumed in the creation of novels is a matter of history; that the gift for drama was, nevertheless, very much 'there' is testified to, at least in part, by the stream of dramatisations of Lawrence's novels and stories that have been made for the theatre, for film and for television in recent years. Since it was thus diverted though, it has been less widely recognised that a passion for drama, as drama, can be seen as a constant factor in Lawrence's work.

To the organisers of the Young Bert Lawrence exhibition, held in Nottingham in 1972,[4] it was apparent that this aspect of their subject would come as something of a surprise to his present day admirers who, though accustomed to thinking of the 'dramatic' qualities of his narrative fiction, would be less familiar with Lawrence's positive engagement with the drama as such. In true theatrical style, they filled the gap left by so many biographers and critics by designing a life-size 'toy' theatre to house mementoes of the years when Lawrence and the 'Pagans' got up amateur

---

[4] The exhibition was organised by Lucy I. Edwards, David Phillips and Arnold Rattenbury, and mounted at the Castle Museum, Nottingham Castle, under the auspices of the Nottingham Festival Committee with the assistance of the Arts Council of Great Britain.

theatricals, play-readings and visits to the theatre, as well as writing, painting and singing together in the intervals between their work and studies. Among these mementoes were strikingly displayed posters featuring the plays that Lawrence and his friends could have seen, as well as the entertainments that they devised for themselves. In this context, imbued as it was with the heady atmosphere of the live theatre in the early years of the twentieth century, the comment in the catalogue that 'it was Lawrence's whole early intention to be a playwright' carried considerable conviction.

Once the force of that 'intention' is acknowledged, there is no shortage of evidence to support a belief in its existence. Writing to Blanche Jennings during his time at University College, for example, Lawrence excitedly anticipates a chance to see Sarah Berhardt in *La Dame aux Camelias*: 'As Camille I think she will be thrilling . . . and if you are good I will tell you all about *la divine* Sarah in my next letter.' (CL p. 14) True to his word, he writes ten days later, 'Sarah Bernhardt was wonderful and terrible', and goes on to 'review' the performance with the appreciative eye for what 'works' on the stage that one associates only with the rare 'Phoenix' among drama critics. At the same period in his life he expressed a willingness to write 'crits' if anyone would print them, and we can measure something of what was lost when no one came forward to accept his offer, in the mature criticism—of drama in particular—in the essays on 'The Theatre' (in *Twilight in Italy*) and on 'Indians and Entertainment' (in *Mornings in Mexico*).

For a fictionalised rendering of Lawrence's early passion for the theatre, we have only to turn to *The White Peacock* (itself described in the letters to Blanche, under its original title of *Laetitia* as 'almost the sole result of my coll. career'), where we read of George and Meg's response to the Carl Rosa Company's production of *Carmen* at the 'Royal' theatre in Nottingham:

> They stared on the stage fascinated. Between the acts they held each other's hands, and looked full into each other's wide bright eyes, and, laughing with excitement, talked about the opera. The theatre surged and roared dimly like a hoarse shell. Then the music rose like a storm, and swept and rattled at their feet. On the stage the strange storm of life clashed in music towards tragedy and

futile death. The two were shaken with a tumult of wild feeling. When it was all over they rose bewildered, stunned, she with tears in her eyes, he with a strange wild beating of his heart.

Only a man who cared deeply and passionately for the theatrical experience could, one feels, have captured the essential quality of its atmosphere and excitement as accurately as that.

In connection with Lawrence's response to particular dramatists, Jessie Chambers' memoir interestingly tells us of the play-reading evenings among the Pagans when Lawrence introduced his companions to the work of Ibsen. 'Going to the theatre was the same as reading, he identified himself with the play and for the time being lived in its atmosphere,' Jessie begins, giving us further confirmation that 'drama' and 'literature' were, for the young Lawrence at least, obviously indivisible. 'He admired Ibsen tremendously' she continues, 'so we read *Rosmersholm* which was Lawrence's favourite and *The Lady from the Sea* of which he gave a full description in advance saying that it was the most poetical of Ibsen's plays that he had read. Finally we read *Hedda Gabler* which he thoroughly disliked.'[5]

Lawrence had already revised the views reported here by 1909, when he sent Louie Burrows two volumes of Ibsen for her twenty-first birthday. The first, sent in advance of the birthday because 'there is generally a blank before a long awaited day', contained 'the Pretenders', 'the Vikings' and 'Lady Inger' which Louie was instructed to read in that order 'so that the first may be best. The Pretenders is by far the best of the three—I will say no more that you may form your own judgements.' Louie must have jibbed at the second volume since Lawrence teases her about her reaction to it. 'Why do I send you Rosmersholm and Hedda Gabler? But really, my dear, you must be on bowing acquaintances with these people. You in happy thoughtless—in your comparative jolly savagery of leopard skins and ox-hide buskins—well, I sent you The Vikings;—you will only stare in young, tawny wonder at the pale spectre of Rosmersholm, and the new-fangled madness of Hedda Gabler.'[6]

[5] Jessie Chambers, *D. H. Lawrence: A Personal Record by 'E.T.'*, ed., J. D. Chambers (2nd. ed. London and New York, 1965), pp. 208–209.

[6] *Lawrence in Love: Letters to Louie Burrows*, ed. with intro. and notes by James T. Boulton (Nottingham, 1968), pp. 26–28.

21

Ibsen indeed seems to have been something of a favourite author in regard to the young Lawrence's relations with women. Not only did he introduce both Jessie and Louie to the 'difficult' Norwegian, but also took a volume to Alice Dax (the model, we are told, for Clara Dawes in *Sons and Lovers*, and, according to Emile Delavenay, the mature woman who gave Lawrence his first sexual experience). Mrs. Dax, being an 'advanced' and emancipated woman, had already read the plays that Lawrence gave her, but the gesture was evidently appreciated nevertheless.

During the next phase of his life as a schoolteacher in Croydon, Lawrence kept up the interest in matters theatrical which had been so close to his heart in Eastwood. It was in Nottingham that he saw Galsworthy's *Strife* which was then considered *avant garde*, though not, it would appear, by the literary circle gathered around Lawrence's first mentor, Ford Maddox Hueffer (now better known under the name he later adopted of Ford Maddox Ford). But in London too he writes often to his then fiancée, Louie Burrows, of the extensions to his theatre-going that were made possible—even on a junior teacher's meagre salary—by big city life.

From the very beginning of his life in London, it is evident that Lawrence enjoyed taking advantage of these increased opportunities to frequent the theatre, opera and concerts. Often, however, Lawrence's remarks about these activities are quoted as demonstrating his hostility to drama—and it is easy to see why that impression has come to be formed when one considers the direction subsequently taken by his creative genius. If, for example, we read a particular letter to May Chambers Holbrook in the light of that later development, we can see how open it is to misinterpretation. Comforting one of his friends, left behind in the provincial obscurity of Eastwood, Lawrence writes: 'Do not lament a town so much. Truly, there are meetings, and, better, theatres and concerts. But meetings are places where one develops an abnormal tone, which it takes some time to soften down again, and theatres and concerts have not much staying power. The true heart of the world is a book; there are sufficient among your acquaintances to make a complete world, but you must learn from books how to know them. . . . Read, my dear, read Balzac and Ibsen and Tolstoi, and think about them.' (CL p. 38) Taken at its face value, this advice could only confirm the prevalent belief in Lawrence's preference for the more rewarding pleasures of reading over the ephemeral delights of theatre and concert-going.

But we note with some amusement that, after giving his advice, the young writer has the grace to apologise for 'preaching'. After all, he himself was only twenty-three at the time and not given then to the pompous and avuncular tone of these comforting 'words of wisdom'. What has to be remembered here is that May Chambers must have heard of the delights of London from Lawrence himself—as well as from more general sources. The cultural and political interests of the Pagans were certainly topics prominent in the letters that passed between members of the group. Though Lawrence plays down in this particular letter, the intellectual stimulus of meetings, theatres and concerts, it is quite plain that he is doing so partly out of compassion for May who was too far away to enjoy them with him. At all events, the letter continues in a more buoyant vein, much more typical of the young Lawrence's letters in its description of Davidson Road School and in particular of some of its boys who lived in the nearby Actor's Home. 'They are delightful boys,' Lawrence writes, 'refined, manly and amiable. The other week we had Beerbohm Tree and Cyril Maude and other big actresses and actors round to see them in school.' Try as he would to keep May from feeling envious of his luck in rubbing shoulders with the 'great', it seems that he was unable for long to contain his own pleasure in being close to the hub of artistic life in London.

His headmaster at Davidson Road School, Philip T. Smith, also recalls Lawrence's interest in the 'actor' boys, some of whom 'bore well-known names connected in the past with the English stage'. (N.I p. 87) For a school dramatic performance, Lawrence painted all the scenery, revised and added to the text of the play, and, after the initial rehearsals remarked, 'These actor boys know more than we do about this kind of thing. We can't teach them the beginnings of play acting. Let them run the show as they see fit.' Frank W. Turner (one of Lawrence's pupils at the school) also remembers that school production, of which he writes, 'The visionary artist in him showed itself when the school produced *Ali Baba and the Forty Thieves* in the school hall. Leaning over

23

canvas material covering a large part of the floor, he painted with a whitewash brush, from a bucket of colour, a backcloth of an Eastern bazaar, and another of palm trees in the desert.' (N.I pp. 91–92)

From the Croydon school days too comes the story of Lawrence's anger when a visiting schools' inspector disturbed his class during a 'dramatic reading' of *The Tempest*. Undaunted by the Ministerial visitor, Lawrence is reported to have rushed at him with outstretched arms bidding him 'Hush! Hush! Don't you hear? The sea chorus from *The Tempest*.' (N.I p. 86) As Philip Smith who recalls the incident comments: 'Those were the days of conventional methods of instruction, and Lawrence's excursions into dramatic expression were not likely to meet with full approval.' Another Shakespeare class which seems to have been just as lively—though, in this case mercifully uninterrupted by visits from 'higher powers'—was devoted to *As You Like It*, and must have given Lawrence great pleasure for, in the letter to Louie[7] in which he describes it, he speaks affectionately of teaching and of the boys in his care. Chafing as he did against the restrictions imposed on the kind of teaching he would have liked to have been able to give to these boys, Lawrence seems to have found his greatest comfort in the release from educational drudgery provided by these 'excursions into dramatic expression'.

During his convalescence at Eastwood in the April of 1912, after the attack of pneumonia that eventually put an end to his teaching career, Lawrence received from his colleagues at Davidson Road School a present of two books, one of which was a volume of Chekhov's plays. Thanking Philip Smith for this present, Lawrence writes, 'the plays are exceedingly interesting. I hope you read them. Tchekhov is a new thing in drama'. (CL p. 108) Most probably the version in which Lawrence first encountered Chekhov's plays was in the translation by George Calderon of *The Seagull* and *The Cherry Orchard*, published in England early in 1912. Calderon's introduction to this volume remains one of the most perceptive and interesting critiques ever made of Chekhov's mode of drama, and, to the aspiring dramatist of 1912, must have been of the greatest interest. Certainly Lawrence felt that Chekhov's plays themselves had a close affinity with his own

---

[7] *Lawrence in Love*, pp. 86–88.

first ventures into dramatic form, the earliest versions of which had been completed by the summer of 1911.

This sense of an affinity is firmly established in Lawrence's clearest statement of his views on the drama of his own time, conveyed in a letter to Garnett written in the February of 1913:

> I believe that, just as an audience was found in Russia for Tchekhov, so an audience might be found in England for some of my stuff, if there were a man to whip 'em in. It's the producer that is lacking, not the audience. I am sure we are sick of the rather bony, bloodless drama we get nowadays—it is time for a reaction against Shaw and Galsworthy and Barker and Irishy (except Synge) people— the rule and measure mathematical folk. But you are of them and your sympathies are with your own generation, not with mine. I think it is inevitable. You are about the only man who is willing to let a new generation come in. It will seem a bit rough to me, when I am 45, and must see myself and my tradition supplanted. I shall bear it very badly. Damn my impudence, but don't dislike me. But I don't want to write like Galsworthy nor Ibsen, nor Strindberg, nor any of them, not even if I could. We have to hate our immediate predecessors, to get free from their authority. (CL p. 182)

Lawrence's enthusiasm for Chekhov's drama has been cast into doubt by his opinions of Chekhov in later years, particularly in his much-quoted view of the Russian as 'a second rate writer and a willy wet-leg', expressed in a letter to Rhys Davies in 1928. (CL p. 1109) What is seldom taken into account when this dismissive opinion is quoted is the reason for Lawrence's apparent later contempt for Chekhov—which, perhaps has more to do with his troubled relationship with Katherine Mansfield and J. M. Murry than with any radical revision of his own views on Chekhov as an important new influence in drama.

The Chekhov cult of the post-war years was largely the making of Katherine Mansfield and her set, and, as has been remarked, it was this cult 'which almost succeeded in reducing the universality of that dramatist to a clique worship by intellectuals'.[8] At all events, in 1919 Lawrence was eagerly enquiring of S. S. Koteliansky about a new work on Chekhov, and was disappointed when the work turned out to be Koteliansky's own essay on

[8] Rex Pogson, *Miss Horniman and the Gaiety Theatre Manchester* (London, 1952), p. 47.

25

Chekhov which he had already read. Throughout the correspondence with Koteliansky there is evidence of this continued interest in Chekhov and of the co-existing difficulty in approving wholeheartedly of a writer so much cried up by people of whom Lawrence did not entirely approve. The conflict is epitomised in a letter written in 1927 in which Lawrence concedes: 'I'll read the Tchekhov book next. But Tchekhov, being particularly a pet of Murry and Katherine, is rather potted shrimps to me.'[9]

Whatever Lawrence's later views on Chekhov might in fact have been, the evidence of his own early plays, so close in feeling and form to those of Chekhov in their intense realisation of lived experience, illustrates a profound affinity between the modes of the two dramatists which will be examined in detail in the chapters concerned with the specific plays. Strange as it may seem that, (as a reviewer of the first production of A Collier's Friday Night in 1965 remarked) 'of all the giants of his time, Lawrence should have chosen the gentle and little known Chekhov as his model',[10] the affinity is nevertheless obviously there—though, as we have seen, the dates of composition of Lawrence's 'Chekhovian' plays must make us cautious about the extent to which he could be said to have 'chosen . . . Chekhov as his model'. Clearly too, Lawrence did *not* model himself as a dramatist on Ibsen, whom he had earlier so much admired, nor yet on Strindberg whom he describes in the letters of a period (1911–1913) in which he was much concerned with his own plays as '. . . unnatural, forced, a bit indecent—a bit wooden, like Ibsen, a bit skin-erupty.' (CL p. 152) Though latter-day critics have drawn parallels in reviews of productions of Lawrence's plays between Strindberg and Lawrence, with headlines like 'A Strindberg of our Own', the resemblance seems only superficially related to the concern with the 'sex-war' shared by both dramatists.

Towards Shaw, Lawrence's feelings were always mixed. 'Do not think because I rave at Bernard Shaw I don't like him. He is one of those delightful people who give one the exquisite pleasure of falling out with him wholesomely', he wrote in 1908. (CL p. 44)

[9] *The Quest for Rananim: D. H. Lawrence's Letters to S. S. Koteliansky 1914–1930*, ed. and intro. George J. Zytaruk (Montreal and London, 1970), p. 311.
[10] The Economics of Affection', *The Times* (London), 8 August 1965, p. 5.

Later his feelings were to be conditioned by personal circumstances. At the height of Lawrence's difficulties over the prosecution of *The Rainbow*, Shaw was among the few who contributed—though only to the extent of £5—financial assistance. Against this it has also been recorded that Lawrence had been greatly disappointed when Shaw, who had declared that he thought *The Rainbow* the best book produced by his fellow writer, had not publicly uttered any protest against its being banned.

There is no space here to go again into the well-known history of Lawrence's interest in, and subsequent rejection of, the Fabian ideals for which, as a young man at any rate, he more or less admired writers like Wells and Shaw. Restricting the link with Shaw only to the matter of plays, it is interesting to note that, though Lawrence put Shaw among the 'rule and measure mathematical folk', he was nevertheless delighted with a compliment paid by Shaw to the dialogue in *The Widowing of Mrs. Holroyd*. Rolf Gardiner reports this compliment when he writes to Lawrence: 'I have just come back from seeing *Mrs. Holroyd*. It was a very good performance and Esmé Percy had produced it in the right way . . . Bernard Shaw, who was there, said the dialogue was the most magnificent he had ever heard, and his own stuff was "The Barber of Fleet Street" in comparison!' (N. III p. 121) In her memoirs Frieda Lawrence recalls this incident, and remembers how pleased Lawrence was by Shaw's praise. 'He should know about dialogue', she reports Lawrence as saying. 'It's very generous of him.'[11]

As late on in his life then, as 1926, there is evidence that Lawrence continued to take an interest in dramatists and drama, though—as with other literary forms contemporary to him—he was never entirely satisfied with the work that other people were doing. As has been seen in the letter of 1913 he felt that an audience for his 'stuff' could be 'whipped in' if the right producer could be found. At that time certainly there was no such producer. The English stage was just not ready for Lawrence's stuff. Though promoted by a few perceptive spirits—Bernard Shaw and Arnold Bennett notably amongst them—Chekhov's own plays did not gain acceptance until the 1920's, and then, as has been

[11] *Frieda Lawrence: the Memoirs and Correspondence*, ed., E. W. Tedlock Jr. (London and New York, 1961), p. 147.

seen, under the rather hot-house conditions fostered by the Chekhov 'cult'. A more general understanding of the nature of Chekhov's 'new thing' in drama did not filter through into English theatrical circles until the late 'twenties', by which time Lawrence's dramatic interests had taken an entirely different 'new' form, quite alien to that of Chekhovian naturalism.

Before the first World War, at the time when Lawrence might have had an opportunity of 'breaking in' on the contemporary scene, there was already a strong *avant garde* movement in the English theatre, represented by the Vedrenne-Barker management at the Royal Court, where Shaw was the major dramatist, and where the plays of Granville-Barker and Galsworthy received their first showings. Inspired by what was then known, and, under Shaw's influence, understood as 'Ibsenite' drama, this group of playwrights was sufficiently ahead of its time to encounter severe opposition from the reactionary forces of censorship. Lawrence's drama, far more experimental and tentative in form than the socially 'shocking' drama of Shaw, Galsworthy and Granville-Barker could obviously hope for little support in such a climate.

There was, however, a theatre in Manchester which might have offered him a foothold. From 1908 the Gaiety Theatre, (bravely pioneered by Miss A. E. Horniman, who had also helped Yeats to get started in Dublin and had anonymously—and unknown to Shaw—financed Florence Farr's production of that revolutionary young dramatist's plays as long before as 1889) had set itself the task of bringing a new and authentic form of repertory theatre before an English audience. Among the dramatists that Miss Horniman's courageous venture helped to establish was Galsworthy, whose *Silver Box* gave the Gaiety its first major success in February 1908. The life of this fascinating theatre, described by Rex Pogson in *Miss Horniman and The Gaiety Theatre Manchester* (1952), was cut short by the war of 1914–18, but its history is fundamental to an understanding of repertory theatre in this country, and also clearly illuminates the kinds of realism and naturalism that were acceptable to the British and American publics in the years before the first World War.

By the thirties, when a reaction against naturalism had begun to set in, the term 'Manchester Realism' had become rather derogatory, as can interestingly be seen in the reviews of *My Son's My*

Son,[12] the version of Lawrence's *The Daughter-in-Law* adapted by Walter Greenwood and presented in London in May 1936. But in 1911 the plays staged at the Gaiety must have seemed daring indeed to audiences reared on the then popular West End fare. Though Miss Horniman was the guiding spirit and also the financial benefactress of the venture, it was Iden Payne who, as artistic director of the Gaiety company, put the ideas into theatrical practice between 1908 and 1913. In connection with Lawrence's own plays, it is the name of Iden Payne which is particularly significant, since it was through him that Lawrence almost achieved a production of one of his plays right at the outset of his writing career.

In 1911 Lawrence had first met Edward Garnett whose support and guidance were to be of such great assistance to him. Among the works that Lawrence first offered Garnett (after the latter had made the initial approaches) was a play which had been submitted by Lawrence's earlier supporter, Ford Maddox Hueffer, to Granville-Barker who had returned it to Lawrence with a 'read it with much interest but afraid I don't want it'[13] note. Thanks to this rejection, Lawrence had the play by him when he first submitted his work for Garnett's opinion. That opinion was so favourable that Garnett offered to get a volume of three plays published in the spring of 1912 on the basis of the one play that Lawrence had been able to submit to him. Much to Lawrence's distress, he was unable to get back the two other plays he had submitted to Hueffer in time, and so that project fell through.

Nevertheless, Garnett was so much impressed by the one play he had seen; a play which, on all the evidence, seems most likely to have been a version of *The Widowing of Mrs. Holroyd*, that he submitted it to Iden Payne who was sufficiently interested in it to arrange a meeting with Lawrence in the April of 1912 to discuss a possible production. Nothing ever came of the meeting, though Lawrence's excitement at the prospect of it remains to indicate how he would have liked things to have turned out. In April 1912, however, Lawrence's personal life was in a crucial

---

[12] The production was reviewed by A. V. Cookman in *The London Mercury*, Vol. XXXIV, No. 201, July 1936, pp. 249–250, and by the Drama Critic of *The Times*, 27 May 1936, p. 14.

[13] *Lawrence in Love*, p. 130.

phase. He had met and fallen deeply in love with Frieda, then married to Ernest Weekley, Professor of French at the University of Nottingham and among Lawrence's teachers when he had been a student there. At the time of the proposed meeting with Payne, Lawrence was also making plans to go away with Frieda to Germany. Indeed the letter, in which he thanks Garnett so excitedly for making the contact with Payne, ends with his description of Frieda as 'the woman of a lifetime'; a prophetic phrase as the future was to prove.

Why the play was never produced must remain a matter for conjecture. In anticipation of the meeting with Payne, Lawrence had written to Garnett, 'It is huge to think of Iden Payne acting me on the stage: you are like a genius of the *Arabian Nights* to get me through. Of course I will alter and improve whatever I can, and Mr. Payne has fullest liberty to do entirely as he pleases with the play—you know that. And of course I don't expect to get money by it. But it's ripping to think of my being acted.' (CL p. 107)

From the joyous and exultant tone of this letter much can be gathered of the zest and enthusiasm that Lawrence felt for his play. From its contents too it could hardly be supposed that the meeting with Payne failed for want of willingness to adapt on the author's part. As was the case with Hueffer's disastrous mislaying of the two plays that might otherwise have been available to be published together with *The Widowing of Mrs. Holroyd* in the spring of 1912, it seems much more likely that the meeting with Payne failed to produce results for reasons that had nothing at all to do with Lawrence's ambitions for his play. That meeting was due to take place in the last week of April 1912. By the first week in May, Lawrence was in Germany, having staked all on the strength of his love for Frieda: sufficient grounds, one might feel, for the neglect of those arrangements that would have been necessary in order to 'nurse' his play towards its first production.

Although that particular opportunity for being 'acted on the stage' was lost, Lawrence by no means gave up hope for his play, continuing to revise and recast it right through 1913, and thereafter making repeated attempts to secure a production for it. In 1915 hope was again revived by the interest of Esmé Percy. Back in England that year, Lawrence wrote in August to Percy: 'Never

mind about Manchester. Yes, do the play in Glasgow and Edin-
boro, if you will. Let me know beforehand, because I think I can
help you quite a lot in both places—have connections with newspapers there, and know people. As a matter of fact, a good many
people in Manchester care about my work. But no matter.' (CL
p. 363) Once again, nothing came of the project, though it was
Esmé Percy who eventually gave the play its first professional
production in 1926.

Before that time though, *The Widowing of Mrs. Holroyd* was
presented for the very first time by a company of amateurs in the
north of England. Here at last was the opportunity to see 'what
the thing looks like on the stage' that Lawrence had envisaged
as such 'good fun' when he wrote to Koteliansky about the plans
for production in 1915. Five years later, he was still keenly interested, even though by that time his experiences with the
theatre had taught him not to hold out high hopes of success.

Shattered in health and spirit by his experiences in post-war
England, Lawrence had decided in the autumn of 1919 to go once
more into voluntary exile, and, by the end of the year had managed—after a long and exhausting winter journey across Europe—
to reach the 'wondrous fine' climate that he so much needed in
the south of Italy, moving on from there to Sicily where he remained until the April of the following year. Quite unable to
contemplate a return journey to England at that time, Lawrence
made as sure as he could that he would get first-hand reports
from friends of how the production of his play went. Three months
in advance of the event, he wrote to Koteliansky, 'I have a letter
from the Altrincham Stage Society—they are acting *The Widowing
of Mrs. Holroyd* on March 10–13 inclusive. I wish somebody saw
it. . . .' Just in case his friend 'Kot' failed to take the hint,
Lawrence adds to the letter the precise address of the Altrincham
Society together with the information '—the place is near Manchester'.[14]

Douglas Goldring, on whom Lawrence's hopes of a production
for his latest play, *Touch and Go*, then hinged, was also urged
to make the journey to Altrincham and report on the performance
to the anxious dramatist. On March 9 1920, when the first staging to be given to any of his plays was, at long last, imminent,

[14] *The Quest for Rananim*, p. 200.

Lawrence wrote to Goldring: 'I am so curious to know what they do with Mrs. Holroyd at Altrincham.' (N.II p. 38) Goldring did take the trouble to make the journey, and was 'greatly impressed' by what he saw. As will be described in greater detail in the chapter concerned with *Touch and Go*, Goldring's object at that time was to persuade the committee of his People's Theatre Society that Lawrence's plays were eminently well worth staging under that Society's auspices. After his visit to Altrincham he 'hurried back to London, in triumph, to report to my colleagues. At last it seemed certain that we should be able to justify our existence, and keep faith with our members, by producing a play by Lawrence. If a company of amateurs could put on the play successfully in the provinces, surely, with all the professional talent at our command, we could do the same in London.' (N.I p. 495)

But Goldring's scheme did not, in the event 'come off', and there was great bitterness between him and Lawrence when the publication of *Touch and Go* followed that of Goldring's own *Fight for Freedom* in the Plays for a People's Theatre Series, instead of preceding it as had been promised. Lawrence's views on *The Fight for Freedom* were outspokenly hostile—at least in the privacy of his letters to Kotsliansky—and though the breach between Lawrence and Goldring was subsequently patched over, nothing ever came of the project to produce *Touch and Go*.

When the play finally came out in book form, Lawrence took little notice of it or of the reviews that appeared at the time. To his great friend Catherine Carswell he wrote simply: 'I see *Touch and Go* is out. Have you got a copy? I ordered you one. If they haven't sent it, I'll send one.' (CL p. 631) Catherine Carswell too had been among the trusted friends appealed to by Lawrence to make the trip to Altrincham and report to him on *The Widowing of Mrs. Holroyd*. Of all his friends, she was the one who took Lawrence's plays most seriously, and comes closest to doing them justice in the pages of her memoir, *The Savage Pilgrimage*. Wittily she 'puts down' Katherine Mansfield's objection that *Touch and Go* was 'black with miners' as 'hardly enlightened as a criticism of a play that concerns itself with miners',[15] and herself offers a much more positive critique of

[15] Catherine Carswell, *The Savage Pilgrimage: A Narrative of D. H. Lawrence* (rev. ed. 1932; rpt. London, 1951), p. 133.

Lawrence's dramatic skills. A professional critic of drama, Mrs. Carswell got into serious trouble over her review of *The Widowing of Mrs. Holroyd* which, she confesses, was much too long. But, when the review appeared—severely cut and distorted—she was much more distressed about the pain it might cause to Lawrence than about the consequences to herself. It is a bitter irony then, that it is Mrs. Carswell's remarks that have so often been quoted as evidence that Lawrence 'hated' the theatre.

When we come to look at what she actually wrote on the subject of Lawrence and the theatre, we see that she has once again been made the victim of cutting and distortion. We must, of course, make certain allowances in the light of the theatrical context (of the early 1930s) in which *The Savage Pilgrimage* was written, but even in that respect it is remarkable how well Mrs. Carswell has overcome any topical predilections in order to give Lawrence's drama a fair showing. After a sensitive and thoughtful consideration of the plays themselves, and of the performances she loyally made a point of seeing, Mrs. Carswell concludes in regard to Lawrence and the theatre generally:

> Of contemporary productions, opera with its lighthearted formality and transparent artifice was probably most to his taste. He was not interested in "problems", effective situations, or any of the sophisticated trickery of the modern theatre. I question indeed whether he found any enjoyment in witnessing a play, unless it might be one of the older classics. Once and only once I was so ill-advised as to book seats for him and myself to see—what he thought might be interesting—the translation of Tolstoi's *Living Corpse* at the St. James Theatre, with Henry Ainley and my friend Athene Seyler in the leading parts. And *how* he hated it and everything about it, so far as the theatre was concerned! The more the germ of the thing appealed to him, the more he was appalled by what he considered to be the falsity and ineptitude of its stage appeal.[16]

Taken out of context, parts of this report of a disastrous visit to the theatre—which ended with Mrs. Carswell and Lawrence having to crawl out over the knees of their neighbours while the performance was still in progress, because Lawrence could not bear to see any more of it!—could well, of course, appear to support

[16] *The Savage Pilgrimage*, p. 143.

the traditional view of Lawrence as a man who had no time for the theatre or for plays. But which of us has not, at some time, felt the urge to leave a theatre during a performance which *we* felt to be particularly abysmal? Looking at Lawrence from an unprejudiced and quite different point of view, this account of his behaviour in a theatre actually supports the argument that he felt a serious and continued concern for drama as a form of literary art. He *did* hate the 'falsity and ineptitude' of the theatrical conventions of his time, just as he was to despise the 'fools' who, he was given to understand, 'nimble-pimbled' at the dialogue of his *Mrs. Holroyd* in the production of 1926. As Mrs. Carswell evidently understood, and as a fairer selection from her memoir than is generally made would excellently illustrate, Lawrence cared deeply for the fate of the theatre, and passionately desired to replace its false and inept conventions—all the 'sophisticated trickery of the modern theatre'—with the true and appropriate values that he felt to be embodied in his own plays.

Much has also been made of Lawrence's 'reluctance' to attend the few performances of those plays that were given during his lifetime. Reluctant he was; but chiefly out of a despairing certainty that his plays would inevitably be falsified by the then prevailing modes of production. Such a reluctance can hardly be put down to plain lack of interest—as, however, it categorically is by Arthur E. Waterman in his essay on 'The Plays of D. H. Lawrence', when he writes: 'Lawrence didn't take his dramatic work very seriously, and when two of his plays were given stage performances, he didn't bother to see them.'[17] The correspondence around the time of the staging of the plays absolutely refutes such a statement. In the case of *David*, the evidence (assembled here in Chapter 10) demonstrates incontrovertibly that Lawrence would dearly have loved to be present, both at rehearsals and at performances of that play, had the delays in mounting the production and the deteriorating state of his own health not prevented him. Around the time of the 1926 pro-

---

[17] Arthur E. Waterman, 'The Plays of D. H. Lawrence', *D. H. Lawrence: A Collection of Critical Essays*, ed., Mark Spilka (Englewood Cliffs, N.J., 1963), p. 142. Appearing as it does in a collection that aims to present 'the best in contemporary critical opinion on major authors', this essay may be felt to have had a wide influence on current views of Lawrence's plays.

duction of *The Widowing of Mrs. Holroyd* too, Lawrence's letters are full of interest as to how the play would go, and express deep disappointment with the hostile reviews that it received.

Without doubt Lawrence was right in feeling that the theatrical establishment of his time was totally unreceptive to the innovations he successively tried to make. His nomadic existence, moreover, deprived him of those opportunities for building a connection with a living theatre that might have persuaded producers and audiences that he had something important to contribute in his radically reforming ideas of what the drama ought to offer. As Michael Marland has observed, 'an exile, for that was what Lawrence virtually was after 1918, can hardly be a dramatist'.[18] While this might be qualified by pointing to Ibsen's persistence as a dramatist 'in exile', it would also have to be allowed that, before going into exile, Ibsen had been for many years a practical man of the theatre. Lawrence did not even have that kind of experience to build on. In essence then, the condition of voluntary exile might be held to account to some extent for the way in which Lawrence appeared to turn his back on the theatre in favour of other forms of literary creation.

His achievement as a dramatist can, of course, only be assessed on the evidence of the plays he actually wrote—in persistent defiance of the hostility and indifference with which they were received. The account given in this chapter of that reception, and of Lawrence's response to it, can only serve as a perspective in which to look at the plays in something of a new light. Above all, the facts that substantiate Lawrence's 'whole early intention to be a playwright' would seem firmly to repudiate the widely held opinion that drama and the theatre were beneath his contempt. Clearly this was not the case.

It has been suggested (also in the essay by Arthur E. Waterman) that Lawrence's delight in writing in dramatic form, so spontaneously expressed in the letter to Garnett in which he writes, 'I enjoy so much writing my plays. They come so quick and exciting from the pen' (CL p. 175) indicates that he re-

[18] *The Widowing of Mrs. Holroyd* and *The Daughter-in-Law*, with an introduction by Michael Marland (London, 1968), p. xix. This very useful edition of two of the 'colliery' plays provides a helpful glossary of the dialect words.

garded the writing of plays as a relaxation from the more serious business of writing novels. Although much of that early delight was to be crushed by repeated rejections, it does not seem at all justifiable to conclude that Lawrence felt the existence of any such hierarchy of seriousness in alternative literary forms. His feelings about writing that came freely to him remained as constant throughout his life as did the interest in drama. As late as 1925, Frieda's daughter Barbara records that 'His writing flowed off the end of his pen', and recollects Lawrence himself saying that 'If it doesn't, my writing is no good'. (N.III p. 24) Far from suggesting that the ease and pleasure with which he wrote his plays marks Lawrence's opinion that they were less 'serious' than his other works, it would appear, on the contrary, that their coming 'so quick and easy' to his pen was a measure to him of how good they were—as well as of the pleasure he took in writing them.

In this study of his plays therefore, Lawrence has not been regarded as a mere 'Sunday' dramatist, dashing off plays in his leisure hours while storing up the energy to give to more 'important' work, but as a writer to whom all forms were equally serious. While the biographical background accounts, to some extent, for the channelling of the major part of Lawrence's creative energy into the writing of novels, it is by no means suggested either that this re-direction of the 'whole early intention to be a playwright' took place somehow against Lawrence's will. Obviously there were complex forces at work directing him to that form in which he was best equipped to achieve his greatest work: the form of the novel.

It is in this balance that Lawrence's dramatic work has to be considered. As things turned out, it would be as ridiculous to cry him up as a dramatist *manqué* as to dismiss the plays that he did succeed, against all the odds, in writing as negligible. That they are overshadowed by the novels—though not eclipsed by them in Lawrence's own mind—is a fact of history, but that they are not at all negligible as plays, designed to be produced on the stage, becomes abundantly clear when prejudices about Lawrence's views on drama are set aside, and the plays he wrote are approached as the work of a writer who fully understood the particular nature of drama as a literary form.

2

A Collier's Friday Night

Although it was certainly among the three plays that Lawrence had completed by July 1911, A Collier's Friday Night lay neglected until 1934, when it was published with an introduction by Edward Garnett who quotes the note pencilled on the MS by Lawrence telling us that the play was written 'when I was twenty-one, almost before I'd done anything. It is most horribly green.' Though Garnett goes on to praise the 'sureness of touch and penetrating directness of this dramatic chronicle of family life', it is evident that he had not felt much confidence in the play's stageworthiness when Lawrence first submitted it to him, after Hueffer had belatedly managed to find it. In April 1912—too late for publication in the spring of that year—Mrs. Hueffer had returned the two mislaid plays to Lawrence with the comment that 'They might have taken quite well, while collieries are in the air'. Lawrence reports that the Hueffers found the plays 'very interesting, but again formless', (CL p. 107) and for all his enthusiasm, Garnett can be seen to share this view in his confession in the 1934 introduction that he finds the play 'a bit too artless and diffuse, too lacking in concentration and surprise' for a theatre piece.

This opinion was not shared by the practising dramatist Sean O'Casey who reviewed the 1934 publication and declared: 'Here is a play that was worth production when it was first written, and it is worth production now. Had Lawrence got the encouragement the play called for and deserved, England might have had a great dramatist.'[1] Even if the play had not remained hidden away,

[1] Sean O'Casey, 'A Miner's Dream of Home', review of 1st edition of A Collier's Friday Night, The New Statesman and Nation, 28 July 1934, p. 124.

O'Casey claimed that no one would have produced it, 'for the play is too good in essence to ensure a shower of gold into a manager's lap', and this pessimistic view of the English stage from pre-war days up to the mid thirties was borne out by the fact that no producer rushed in to prove O'Casey wrong.

It was indeed only by the merest coincidence that *A Collier's Friday Night* came to be the first of the Lawrence plays so brilliantly and vividly brought to life by Peter Gill. Intrigued by a report he had heard of a television production of *The Widowing of Mrs. Holroyd*, Gill sent off for a copy of that play, but received instead a copy of the 1934 edition of *A Collier's Friday Night*. The error was a fruitful one, resulting as it did in the well received Sunday night production without décor of Lawrence's first play which was followed in 1967 by a full-scale production of *The Daughter-in-Law* and in 1968 by the D. H. Lawrence Season in which the two earlier productions were joined by *The Widowing of Mrs. Holroyd*.

Lawrence may have been exaggerating a little in order to excuse the play's 'immaturity' when he told Garnett that it had been written in 1906. It was in the September of that year that he had begun his life as a student at University College Nottingham, and, like Ernest in the play, had soon, 'lost forever my sincere boyish reverence for men in position' as he expresses the experience in a letter to Blanche Jennings written in May 1908. (CL p. 9) The letter continues, 'Professors and the rest of great men I found were quite small men', and we hear an echo of the same sentiments in Ernest's lament 'I used to think men in great places were great. . . .' Echoed too is the phrase in Lawrence's letter, 'having lost my reverence for men, my religion rapidly vanished', which, in Ernest's mouth becomes: 'By Jove, if you once lose your illusion of "great men", you're pretty well disillusioned of everything.' The thoughts could, of course, have been with Lawrence consistently throughout his two disillusioning years as a student, but the similarity of the terms at least suggests that the play, like so much of Lawrence's work, was constantly undergoing revision and was still being worked upon in 1908.

Though Lawrence is reported to have shown Jessie Chambers the completed manuscript of a play which she describes as being about his home on a Friday night, when she came to London to see him in 1909, it is also possible that Lawrence went on re-working and revising as was his usual habit right up until the play's first formal submission to Hueffer which was made, as Lawrence reminds Louie Burrows, 'before the holiday'[2] that he took in July 1911. It is in September 1910, for example, that Lawrence writes excitedly to Louie: 'I've got Baudelaire's "Fleurs du Mal"—got them for 9d in Charing Cross Road on Friday: it was a fine capture. I'll read some to you when there is an oppor-tunity. They are better than Verlaine.'[3] While there is no proof that this was Lawrence's first encounter with Baudelaire, his enthusiasm suggests the excitement of a new discovery, and it is the poems of Baudelaire that Ernest reads to Maggie in *A Collier's Friday Night*.

The letters Lawrence wrote to Blanche Jennings during his years at college most often mention *Laetitia*—the earliest version of *The White Peacock*—as the work on which he was principally engaged. Indeed, as we have already seen, he describes that novel as 'almost the sole result of my coll, career', '—except, of course,' he goes on to add, 'loss of my mental and moral boyhood and gain in scepticism'. While he does not specifically mention the writing of a play, we have seen too that he avowed more generally to Blanche 'I put out my hands passionately for modern verses and drama—and, in less degree, novels', and this, together with the pain of growing up which is a constant theme of these letters, could well lead us to suppose that *A Collier's Friday Night* was taking shape side by side with *Laetitia*, while ideas were also germinating for the earliest version of *Sons and Lovers* which Lawrence began in 1910.

Thematically, there can be little doubt that the first play is concerned with that pain of growing up which Lawrence described to Blanche as 'a frightful experience' which 'hurts horribly; but when you have got over it is delightful'. In *A Collier's Friday*

[2] Lawrence's feelings about the missing plays, and towards Hueffer for mislaying them are clear in this letter, written on 10.x.1911: 'I sent them to Hueffer as you know, before the holiday. And last night I had a letter from Hueffer to say he'd never had them and that he didn't know any-thing about them . . . I hope the dramas will turn up. I should be angry if they were lost. It is just like Hueffer.' *Lawrence in Love*, pp. 139–140.
[3] *Lawrence in Love*, p. 55.

Night, written, one would judge, with the hindsight of one who had 'got over' the painful experience and begun to know the delight of having it in the past, Ernest takes the first important step towards breaking from his mother by asserting his right to a relationship with Maggie. This point of view, together with all the circumstantial evidence to be found in letters and records of Lawrence's life between 1906 and 1910, leads us fairly to conclude that the play occupied more of Lawrence's time than the note on the MS was designed to have Garnett believe. Indeed we might justifiably conjecture that the play in the form in which we now have it was not finalised much before Lawrence submitted it to Hueffer in the summer of 1911.

Like *The Widowing of Mrs. Holroyd* and *The Daughter-in-Law, A Collier's Friday Night* is characterised in production by the extent to which it persuades spectators that it is a 'copy' of real life. To an extraordinary degree, audiences to these plays seem to feel that what they are watching is 'transcribed' or 'recorded' or 'photographed' from an episode in real life, rather than created as dramatic literature. Those who do not care for the mode usually object to it as 'mere photographic realism', while those who admire it do so for the authenticity with which it seems to reproduce the forms of life as we commonly experience them in our everyday existence.

People seem to have this feeling about Chekhov's plays too. In Moscow, for example, audiences to *Three Sisters* speak of 'spending an evening with the Prozorovs', as if they were visiting friends instead of attending a performance in the theatre. This kind of naturalism is different from the 'realism' of Ibsen or Shaw in that it does not appear to carry a thesis or 'message'. It is just about the way that people live and 'that's that'. Sometimes called 'high', 'strict', or 'close' naturalism, this mode of drama is most distinctively characterised by the way in which the dramatist appears merely to be a passive recorder of events as they actually happen. The fact that plays like these are consciously structured according to a system of dramatic conventions seems completely to escape the audience's notice.

Moreover, the strangeness and remoteness to their own lives of the life that they see being 'lived' in the plays appears also to escape spectators' attention. Without any experiential knowledge of what it was like to live in Chekhov's nineteenth century Russia, or in the mining midlands of the first decade of the twentieth century, an audience finds no reason to question the authenticity of the life it is being shown in the plays of Chekhov and Lawrence. 'Yes,' we tend to say, 'that is just how it was.' But how do we know? What makes us so sure that the dramatist has so exactly captured the quality of life at a particular time and in a particular place, when we have no personal knowledge ourselves of that particular time or place? Critics do not seem to feel the need to ask these questions when they talk about the plays being 'filmed' from the life as with 'a hand-held camera' thus suggesting even more strongly the sense in which this kind of drama is felt to be 'documentary'. Some approve of the truth to life; some find it 'undramatic', but all subscribe to the view that, in some curious and unexplained way, the plays draw them in to participation at an occasion in life rather than a performance in the theatre.

When a play deals, as *A Collier's Friday Night* does, with material from the author's own life, the impression that he is merely recording or setting down an unmediated account of what he has himself experienced becomes even stronger. Yet we can see soon enough when we read the text of the play (just as we can, for example by comparing *Sons and Lovers* with the life experience on which, as we usually say, 'it is based'), that the real life events have had to be chosen, ordered and arranged in a particular way in order for us to be persuaded that they really were experienced.

The clearest example of this now widely recognised truth that literature, however 'realistic', cannot copy 'reality' but can only *persuade* us that it copies 'reality', can be found in the matter of dialogue. No less eminent an authority on the use of language than Randolph Quirk makes this abundantly clear when he writes: '. . . our reading habits tend to persuade us that the dialogue of contemporary plays, and the pieces within quotation marks in novels, are precisely what speech is actually like; we forget that such dialogue is synthetic and is *written* before it is spoken or read. It is an imaginative attempt by a *writer* to represent speech, and even a writer like Pinter with a talent for capturing colloquial structures cannot forget that the

41

primary function of the dialogue is to be the vehicle for his plot.'[4]

In these days of the easy accessibility of tape recorders, many of us have experienced the surprise of finding that our own voices do not sound 'natural' to us. More generally we will find that transcriptions of conversations are immeasurably more hesitant and disjointed than any of the written 'naturalistic' dialogue that we are persuaded, when we hear it on television, in the theatre, or in the cinema, to experience as being accurately 'life-like'. Similarly we all know how 'unlike' our own image of ourselves most photographs are. Yet we persist in feeling that a play or film which 'looks real' must 'merely' be photographed from life.

It is evident, therefore, that what we must look for in these plays of Lawrence's that appear so accurately to reproduce the forms of life, are the dramatic techniques by means of which this appearance of reality is created, rather than for the biographical 'facts' which we are made so strongly to feel that they are recording. Since, however, there are those of us who know about the biographical facts—and they are so well known that they are bound to impinge on the consciousness of most spectators to the plays —it is worth looking first at the biographical material presented in A Collier's Friday Night in order, as we move through the play, to see how the author has arranged it so as to *compose* a life-like synthesis.

We have already seen that Lawrence's experience of disillusion at college (1906–1908) becomes part of Ernest's 'character' in A Collier's Friday Night. In Jessie Chambers' memoir of D. H. Lawrence we are told, however, that the Friday night French lessons in the Lawrence home ended before Lawrence entered college. In that memoir too we find a vivid description of the young woman on whom Lawrence's character, Beatrice Wild, is based, in the girl who used to revel in taunting courting couples and whose teasing was so painful to Jessie when it interrupted her precious Friday night tutorials with Lawrence. In the play, Ernest's sister Nellie teases him about a girl friend called Lois; close enough, we might guess, to the real-life Louie

---

[4] Randolph Quirk, 'Speech and Communication' in *The English Language and Images of Matter* (London, 1972), p. 99.

Burrows to whom Lawrence became engaged in 1910—though he had known her as a friend and fellow student long before that time. Much more accurately datable is the announcement, read out by Ernest as his mother turns the loaves, of the death of Swinburne which took place in 1909. Whenever Lawrence wrote the play then, it immediately becomes clear that it does not mechanically record the events of one Friday evening as they actually occurred in life. What we find rather is an artistic arrangement of experiences spread over several years but combined in dramatic form so as to give the impression of intensely accurate 'lived experience'. The hand-held camera metaphor begins to falter!

What Lawrence has done as a dramatist in this play is to telescope the experience of many evenings into a shape that gives them the unity of one single representative evening. Every incident therefore seems to fall 'naturally' into place, and there is no awareness of symbolic 'nudging'. Once we have discovered that the biographical material is drawn from a span of some four years in Lawrence's life, we are more prepared to ask ourselves whether indeed it is all that 'natural' to suppose that the events of this particular evening could 'really' have happened in precisely the order shown in the play. Could it 'really' have been on the same evening, or indeed on any evening at all, that the mother's bread was neglected and burned by the son who chooses that particular evening to stand up for his adult right to love another woman as well as his mother? Examined like this the coincidence is evidently dramatic in a conscious, designed way. This becomes even more obvious when we look at the confrontation scene between mother and son and find Ernest drawing on the central baking motif when, explaining to his mother that he can love both Maggie and her in different ways, he protests, 'If I like apples, does it mean I don't like—bread?' The slight pause marked by Lawrence before the word 'bread' emphasises the extent to which our view of the quarrel is designed to be controlled by the natural domestic activity of the son's failure to watch over his mother's baking.

So important is this particular activity to the way in which we understand the relationship between mother and son that we find the acts themselves to be divided in accordance with the stages in the baking process. Act I sees Mrs. Lambert preparing her loaves and setting them to bake. As she leaves the men to get on with their business of dividing the week's money (a business at which, as Lawrence's stage directions indicate, it is not considered proper for wives to be present), her last words are a reminder to Ernest to 'look at the bread'. On her entry in Act II, Mrs. Lambert goes straight to the oven to see how her bread is progressing. Preoccupied as she is with the need to go out to market, to buy, it will be noted, provisions to feed her family, she is equally concerned that her preparations at home shall not be neglected. Her concern and reluctance are intertwined here with the extent to which she feels resentment about Maggie's relationship with Ernest. Her resentment of Maggie's visit is only indirectly conveyed; we are made to feel it by her insistence that Ernest take care of the loaves. Ernest is shown to be upset when he neglects the duty imposed on him by his mother; the token of her authority over him while she is absent. 'Won't Ma be wild though!—What a beastly shame!' he exclaims as the cinders are pulled out of the oven. He soon recovers his spirits though, among the joking of the admiring girls, and here too the conflict between the son's duty to his mother and his natural urge to be independent is firmly underlined by the *action* of the play.

Ernest knows too that his mother will blame Maggie for distracting his attention from that duty to his mother, and his expectations (as well as ours) are fulfilled when Mrs. Lambert returns, wearily humping the week's shopping, to discover the ruined loaves which spark off the climactic Act III quarrel between mother and son.

The thematic function of the bread baking becomes even more evident when we notice how much of the play's realistic detail is devoted to illustrating Mrs. Lambert's nourishment of her family. When we first meet her she is preparing tea. Returning from a hard day at school, the teacher daughter, Nellie complains that there are no apricots for tea. Her mother explains that there aren't any because Ernest is sick of them. First and foremost Mrs. Lambert caters to her son's tastes, but, after a pause, she fetches apricots for Nellie. This way of indicating that Nellie comes second in her mother's affections is repeated in Act III in the distribution of the delicacies that are brought home specifically for Ernest, though Nellie is allowed to sample them when she insists on doing so. Very far behind both children in the matter of the mother's affections comes her collier husband who snatches the tea-table away from his daughter when he comes home from work. Evidently he feels—and rightly as the play shows—that he must shift for himself. Unlike Nellie, he is refused an alternative when he asks for something other than what his wife offers him for 'tea', and the contrast is made even more marked by Mrs. Lambert's willing attention to her son's appetite when he in his turn comes home from 'coll'. Ready-buttered toast and a smiling mother to pour his second cup of tea are the measure of the superiority that Ernest enjoys in the hierarchy of family affections established by the naturalistic details which, at first sight, appear only to be there because they featured in the experience of life on which Lawrence has drawn in the writing of his play.

It is, of course, the most 'natural' thing in the world for a mother to be concerned about feeding her family; so natural that, in this most naturalistic of plays, we scarcely notice the way in which these details are used to bind the play together, giving it a structural and thematic unity so indissolubly connected that the resultant picture appears to be a seamless rendering of life.

Having examined some of the contributory details in the dramatic pattern, we can now see that the life-like quality of the play does not depend on its closeness to biographical fact, nor on the passive gift for observation for which Lawrence is so often praised, but on his ability to impose a particular kind of design on his experience. We see too that the details of domestic life are not as random as they at first appear, but are carefully chosen in order to fit in with the design that will make them *seem* naturally random in the context of the play.

The way in which incidents from life are combined in this dramatic fiction clearly shows that *A Collier's Friday Night* is no straightforward 'diary' account of a single evening in Lawrence's own early life. Indeed we see that, even if we did not happen to know the biographical 'facts' from other sources, the shape of the play would still persuade us that what happens in it 'actually happened' in life. Chekhov, with whose dramatic mode I have suggested Lawrence's naturalist plays have much in common, described the process by which the artist transposes life experience into literature as one of selection, arrangement and synthesis. It is this conscious shaping which makes of the raw material of life a story or play which appears to copy the reality of 'life as it actually is'.[5] For Lawrence too this Chekhovian process was obviously well and consciously understood.

Like Chekhov in *Three Sisters* and *The Cherry Orchard*, Lawrence in his 'colliery' plays selects a setting which implies the existence around itself of a world from and to which the characters we meet in the plays come and go. The part of that world which we see in the play stands for the larger world in which it is thus placed as existing. It is important to note, however, a distinction which is being made here between 'setting' and 'set'. When *A Collier's Friday Night* was first produced in 1965, it was observed by one critic that the impression of real life created by the play was textually governed by the comings and goings of characters from and to a world around the one in which the events of the play were seen to take place. This observation was made to a production *without décor*. It cannot therefore be a matter of production, or a question of the designer's skill in building a set, which accounts for the impression of 'real' life produced by this play, but of the way in which the action of the play *as written* itself establishes this relation between the world it shows us and the wider world of which it is a representative part.

The shape of Lawrence's 'autobiographical' play is determined by the comings and goings which define the situation, in which the presented action is taking place, as part of the wider life of the mining community at large. We have this sense of a 'life' around the play from the moment when the curtain rises on Act I to find Mrs. Lambert in the detailed setting of the collier's kitchen. Crowded as the room is with these details—many of which will come to be seen as relating to the social lives of the characters whom we will meet during the course of the play—it is the window through which the rain can be seen dripping onto a garden to which Lawrence's stage directions give prominence. Mrs.

[5] The letters in which Chekhov most clearly states his aims and methods in these terms can be found in *Letters of Anton Chekhov*, ed. and intro. Simon Karlinsky (London and New York, 1973), p. 62 and p. 117.

Lambert is obviously waiting for someone to arrive. 'The table is laid for tea with four large cups.' Attention is drawn to her waiting by her impatient movements and her looking out of the window, and the first hint of an encounter with another character comes when, 'someone passes the long, narrow window, only the head being seen, then quite close to the large window on the left'.

It is Nellie who is first to arrive and we can see the technique for establishing the existence of a life outside the cottage at work in her lively account of her day at school. Coming home to her mother, she brings with her the 'reality' of the life she has lived during the day out in the community. We get a convincing sense of the way in which Nellie, as a person formed and shaped by the family life inside the cottage, contributes to, and in her turn forms, the life that goes on in the village of which the cottage is a part. We can then contrast this interaction with the outside experience of her collier father whose work is, most fundamentally of all, linked with the very existence and survival of the mining families. This again is contrasted with the life of which Ernest tells when he comes home from college. Between them, daughter, father and son represent the separate strands that are woven together in creating the whole fabric of life within the Lambert family. Mr. Lambert toils at digging the coal. Despised and looked down upon by his genteel wife, he is nevertheless the source of the family's basic income, just as his work is representative of the economy of the whole community. The importance of this work is signified in dramatic terms by the gathering of his colleagues for the weekly share-out. As has already been seen, the mother— the emotional 'heart' of the household—plays no part in this share-out, and has no real say in the portion of her husband's earnings that are handed out to her.

Nellie, the schoolteacher, maintains the quality of life as it presently exists in the world in which she lives. From her account we gather that she does her work conscientiously, but does not take it too deeply to heart. She is quick to throw off the cares of the workaday week in the enjoyment of her weekend's relaxation, and we see too, in her failure to help her mother bring home the marketing, that she is not deeply involved in the emotional ties of the household. Nellie has won her independence.

Her mother is ready to accept the fact that she will leave home and marry. Good-hearted and well-intentioned, Nellie is shown, in her relationship to the context of her home, to be pretty much content with what she has made of her life. We feel that, for her, to have become a schoolteacher is to have made the best of the circumstances into which she was born, and we draw this conclusion not so much from what she says as from how she *acts* in the situations that are developed within the play.

The same dramatic patterning of the relation between character and context makes us aware that Ernest's life outside the home represents aspirations to a wider sphere of life than that which satisfies Nellie. We may feel that this is because he is the 'Lawrence figure' in the play, but we will also note that the Lawrentian identification is made on the basis of the kind of information that Ernest brings home from the outside world. He tells about the books he has to buy; the restaurant he has visited; and, more importantly, about the horizons that are being opened for him in the literature that he is discovering for himself—almost in spite of the 'mechanical' efforts of his teachers at college.

Outside the home in which we see them then, Mr. Lambert, Nellie and Ernest lead lives that characterise them as 'working-class', 'middle-class' and 'intellectual'. While we watch the play, we feel no inclination to reduce the characters, so vividly rendered as living beings, to these abstract categories. But we can see, nevertheless, that it is in the way in which they fully represent these aspects of a socio-cultural world that they appear to be rounded and life-like. What is important is that we do not have to make the abstraction, so necessarily and naturally are the essential facts about each of the characters integrated into the flow of domestic incident.

At an emotional level, one could similarly separate out the thematic abstraction of the Oedipal element in the conflict between mother and son. Again we would find that to do this would be reductive of the sense of full and experienced life characteristic of the play, because the abstraction is not so much symbolised in the play as re-produced in its action. The burning of the bread does not, for example, stand out from the play as a metaphor for Ernest's rejection of his mother's love. When we see, or even read, the play, the whole incident is rather received as a part of the family's life which 'actually happened'. From Lawrence's stage directions it can be seen how careful he was to build up this impression that the baking of the bread is simply a part of the normal Friday night activity of the household. Its significance as representative of the emotional situation is submerged into the detailed portrayal of family life, so that we do not notice the way in which it directs our response until, as here, we look at the play analytically in order to discover how the life-like impression is built up.

Most important of all to the success of this naturalist mode; most essential, that is, to the effect of reality which it creates, is the way in which events and impressions are controlled so that the reader or spectator appears to discover meanings for himself—without the direct guidance of the dramatist. In this particular play, for example, we see that our impressions of character are built up from our observations of how each person relates to the milieu in which he or she is shown. Established as a 'real' place by the means already described, this milieu becomes a standard against which we measure an individual's behaviour. In life, of course, it is by observing the interaction between people and the setting in which we encounter them that we form our judgements of what they are like; of what kind of people they are. Lawrence's play re-produces this situation by withholding direct comment on character. What we learn about the Lamberts we appear to learn ourselves by observing their attitudes to their home and to the other people in it.

What one will want to do then in a production or in a 'productive' reading of this and the two other naturalist plays will be to concentrate on the interplay between person and place. This is precisely what Peter Gill did in his brilliant realisations of the plays in the naturalist 'trilogy' in the D. H. Lawrence Season at the Royal Court Theatre, London in 1968. Some measure of the success of his achievement can be gained from a cross-section of comments made by dramatic critics on that season as well as on the production a year earlier of *The Daughter-in-Law*. Of the latter Frank Marcus (himself a practising dramatist) wrote: 'The most remarkable thing about this production is its realism. The characters are as rounded as figures from a canvas by Courbet. The household tasks, preparing, cooking and eating meals, the miner washing off the grime after a day in the pit, his clothes drying over the oven, have an absolute versimilitude.'[6] Of *A Collier's Friday Night* Herbert Kretzmer observed, 'This is a production dedicated to the truth, to the way people live, to reality' and pointed out that the play, and Peter Gill's direction of it, 'is packed with such minute detail, such accurate observation, that one is gradually sucked into the slow, humdrum world of the collier'.[7] B. A. Young described Lawrence's plays as 'still-life studies in which the reactions of a group of people are examined in relation to a strong central situation',[8] and the importance of such interaction was also remarked upon by Benedict Nightingale who, however, counteracts the 'still-life' impression with his opinion that, 'There is continual action, reaction and re-reaction; they are the least static plays one could imagine'.[9]

Sensitive to Lawrence's mode of naturalism, Irving Wardle declared, 'It would be a big mistake to dismiss the plays as artless', and perceptively observed that 'one is left to discern the complex family bond under the daily traffic of eating, washing, gossiping and sharing out the pay packet'.[10] It is this sense of the spectator being 'left to discern' the deeper meanings for himself that causes commentators to attribute objectivity to Lawrence as a dramatist in these plays, just as has been the case with the plays of Chekhov—particularly *Three Sisters* and *The Cherry Orchard* in which the method for creating an effect of life in dramatic terms is so strikingly similar to the method Lawrence employs in his 'colliery' plays. Indeed there are remarkable affinities to be found between the critical comments quoted above and reviews of productions of Chekhov's plays in English.

It is obviously not the business of reviewers to account for how the impression of reality comes about, but Ronald Bryden came

[6] Frank Marcus, 'The Dominant Sex', *Plays and Players* (May 1967), p. 19.

[7] Review of *A Collier's Friday Night* in the *Daily Express*, rpt. in *The Critic*, 8 March 1968, p. 10.

[8] Review of *The D. H. Lawrence Season* in *The Financial Times*, rpt. in *The Critic*, 22 March 1968, p. 11.

[9] Benedict Nightingale, 'On the Coal Face', *Plays and Players* (May 1968) pp. 18–19, 21 and 51.

[10] Review of *A Collier's Friday Night* in *The Times*, rpt. in *The Critic*, 8 March 1968, p. 12.

very close to locating what is proposed here as the source of the life-like effect when he wrote, of *The Widowing of Mrs. Holroyd*, that 'you can see how he (Lawrence) does it if you attend to the unobtrusive detail of washing, cleaning and ironing'.[11] As I have suggested, these homely activities are not included in the plays in the naïve hope that, because we know such things happen in life, we will therefore believe that the plays are life-like—though it is perhaps this aspect of some kinds of naturalism that has earned the mode a bad name! In contrast to what Shaw contemptuously called 'cup and saucer' naturalism, the naturalist mode of Chekhov and Lawrence is based on the selection of particular activities from life which lend themselves to the structural design of particular plays, as we have seen to be the case with the bread-baking activity around which Lawrence builds the structure of *A Collier's Friday Night*.

Bearing this structural technique in mind, we can return to an analysis of *A Collier's Friday Night* which follows the dramatist through his disposition of the real-life elements into a dramatic pattern, and discover that, in spite of the fact that he has so well covered his tracks, the shaping artist is just as present in these plays as in others in which we feel authorial direction more strongly; the plays of Ibsen, Strindberg or Shaw, for example, or those of Galsworthy or Granville-Barker, in all of which, at one level or another, there is a tendency for an audience to feel that the author is 'telling them something'. Again we may note that it is by the apparent absence of any such transmission of a 'message' that Lawrence's naturalist plays are characterised.

Yet, although there is no sense in which these plays can be felt to carry a thesis or even direct us to see a situation—as we might feel for example happens in the plays of Strindberg—from the dramatist's point of view, there is an important sense in which we feel that they do enlarge our awareness of the way in which life is lived. Certainly not blandly or objectively amoral, these plays obliquely imply that some ways of living are 'better' than others. As has frequently been remarked, again both of Chekhov's plays and Lawrence's, they show us no villains and no heroes, but, among the people that they do show us, some can be seen to have

[11] Review of *The Widowing of Mrs. Holroyd* in *The Observer*, rpt. in *The Critic*, 22 March 1968, p. 10.

51

come to better terms with the society in which they live than others.

In *A Collier's Friday Night* we see in Mrs. Lambert a woman who has compensated for what she feels to have been a mistaken marriage by indulging her children and by setting them on paths which she hopes will enable them to escape from the life in which she is trapped. Tragically for herself she is unable, especially where Ernest is concerned, to leave them free to take flight. The deadlock of her relationship with her husband is shown to be much of her own making. We see, in Lambert's warm response to Gertie Coomber's polite conversation how readily he responds to being treated as a human being, and we sense his sufferings at the hands of a wife who feels herself a cut above him in his aggressively masculine pride on the occasion of the share-out.

Tragically for Ernest too, his mother's resentful feelings towards his father have created in him a hatred which is almost murderous. At the climax of the quarrel in which Ernest has risen to his mother's defence he says: 'I would kill him, if it weren't that I shiver at the thought of touching him.' It is all very well at this late stage for Mrs. Lambert to protest: 'Oh, you mustn't! Think how awful it would be if there were anything like that. I couldn't bear it.' But, even in this shocked reaction to Ernest's threat, we hear the social rather than the personal note of shame. Although he is not overtly presented as sympathetic, the details of the play actively endorse Lambert's view when he berates his wife for making the children detest him. 'You teach 'em to hate me. You make me like dirt for 'em: you set 'em against me,' he accuses, and, in the dispensation of food, in the matter of the money for Ernest's books and little 'treats' bought out of the meagre budget which will not stretch to the kind of pudding that Lambert prefers to eat, we have seen the truth of his accusation enacted.

In the central episode of Maggie's visit we see too how the mother's inability to let her son get on with living his own life inflates a boy-and-girl friendship into a passion that threatens family unity. Ernest is well enough satisfied with Maggie's admiration. He enjoys patronising her, teasing her about her fractured French and despairing of her unfamiliarity with the foreignness of a name like Baudelaire which to him is as familiar as

'Pearson'. He is flattered when Maggie compares him to Shelley and delighted to impress her with his careless dismissal of his own talent in the attractive and well-turned phrase: 'I tell you I have got nothing but a gift of coloured words.' But, though he gallantly protects Maggie from the teasing of Beatrice and Nellie, it is made very plain that she is not the only girl in his life. In fact most of her importance in Ernest's eyes is seen to derive from Mrs. Lambert's disapproval. Nellie says that Ernest generally forgets to watch the bread when Maggie is there. Maggie hotly denies the accusation. Because Nellie bases her remark on her mother's opinion about the extent of the hold Maggie has over Ernest, we are made to feel that it is Maggie who is speaking the truth. Moreover, it has also been made clear that Nellie is teasing and trying to 'get a rise' out of Maggie, so that she can join with the spiteful Beatrice and the shamefaced Gertie Coomber in the discussion of Maggie's discomfiture which takes place after the latter's departure with Ernest.

The connection between Maggie's presence and the burning of the bread is not then, one of simple cause and effect. On the contrary, it is Beatrice and her teasing interruptions that cause him to forget his charge. Deep as he has been in conversation with Maggie up to the time of Beatrice's arrival, Ernest has not till then neglected his task. While Maggie reads his verses, we see him go through the routine of transferring the dough from one pan to another, and he continues to remember his duty well enough to build up the fire. Maggie, it is clear, while she is interesting to Ernest, does not absorb the whole of his attention.

It is interesting in this play to notice how the dramatic form enables Lawrence to externalise the autobiographical elements in what seems to be a less biased assessment of his relationships with his father and mother and with Jessie Chambers than was possible for him in the narrative form of Sons and Lovers. Frieda Lawrence records in her memoir that, years after writing the book, Lawrence's attitude to his parents changed and he said, 'I would write a different Sons and Lovers now; my mother was wrong and I thought she was absolutely right.'[12] In A Collier's Friday

---

[12] Frieda Lawrence, "Not I But The Wind . . ." (New York, 1934: London, 1935), p. 52. See also Keith Sagar, 'D. H. Lawrence: Dramatist' in The D. H. Lawrence Review, Vol. 4, No. 2, Summer 1971, pp. 158–159.

Night, at a time when, biographically, Lawrence still felt that his mother was 'absolutely right', he was nevertheless capable of presenting a character (whom we take to represent his mother) in such a way that the degree to which she was 'wrong' becomes clearly apparent. In the character of the father too, we see evidence of fair-mindedness and sympathy on the part of the dramatist in the criticism that the action makes of the treatment meted out to Lambert by his wife, son and daughter. Ernest, as a character in the play, like Paul Morel as a character in the novel *Sons and Lovers*, cannot preserve this dispassionate distance. The difference for us is that we see the situation from Paul's point of view in the novel, but are left to discern for ourselves the 'truth' of the situation as it is presented to us in the play. Evidently it is the dramatic form itself which allows Lawrence—whether or not he was aware of it—to present a view of the family situation which he only came personally to recognise as 'true' for himself very much later in life.

For realist writers, at all events, it would appear that dramatic form offers a readier way to the achievement of aesthetic distance than does the novel. From his continuing struggle to achieve that distance—to 'keep himself out of the book'—we know how important a goal Lawrence felt this to be. Yet, in these early plays, it seems to come quite spontaneously to him. Biography is at least a useful guide here in helping us to distinguish between the controls imposed on any writer by his choice of form. In the case of Lawrence, the evidence of these early plays exists to illustrate how dramatic form freed him from the personal and emotional constraints from which he found it so difficult to escape in the writing of his novels.

In the plays, authorial direction of our response is provided by the formal techniques which render place by means of a particular kind of setting (one which is a representative part of the wider world for which it stands), and those for presenting character in interaction with that setting. It is out of these relationships that we build up our system of meaning for the plays. It therefore follows that there is no need for dialogue which explicitly expresses these meanings. It has been said of Chekhov, for example, that we understand that his characters are thinking something quite different from what they are saying, and that we understand their unspoken thoughts very well. The same is true of these naturalist plays of Lawrence's.

When, for example, Mrs. Lambert talks to Ernest about buying Christmas presents for 'little Margaret', we know that she is apologising to her son for her unpleasant remarks about Maggie and asking him not to be pushed by her animosity into an even closer relationship with the girl. How though do we come to be so sure that this is what is 'meant'? Again it seems to me that these 'sub-textual' meanings derive from the relationship between context and character, so firmly established by the forms of the play that we refer to it as a standard against which everything else is measured.

We have seen Mrs. Lambert in her straitened, but by no means poverty-stricken circumstances putting what she can aside to provide little extra comforts for Ernest. In this context, such small indulgences become the currency of the 'economics of affection'; the coinage with which the mother 'pays' for her son's continued affection and love. She is, as we have already remarked, less ready to expend that coinage on Nellie, and completely resistant to the idea of 'wasting' it on Lambert, by whom, incidentally, the real money to pay for the treats is shown to be earned. Knowing that she has over-stepped the mark in her scornful allusions to Maggie's willingness to tramp over muddy fields in order to see Ernest, Mrs. Lambert tactically redresses the balance by discussing treats for the 'little thing', referring obliquely to the generosity of her nature of which Ernest has himself received so many tokens. He 'takes' her meaning, but rejects the concealed apology by reminding her 'You gave our things to the lads, didn't you?' Affection, he implies, cannot be bought, directly or indirectly, and the 'sound of failure' that Lawrence indicates for the tone of Mrs. Lambert's following remarks underlines the extent to which her attempt at conciliation has failed.

Such undercurrents to the actual dialogue give us, as audience, the sense of being particularly intimate and privileged onlookers to the play in performance. We are not merely eaves-droppers who hear only the words that are spoken, but intimate confidantes of the innermost thoughts of these people. We are privileged to be able to interpret those thoughts, even beneath the disguise of the words that are actually spoken, and we are enabled to do so because the signs by which the characters interpret the hidden meanings are equally available to us in the realistic context of the setting.

These undercurrents can be found throughout the play amplifying our understanding of the words that the characters are actually given to speak, and consistently making us feel intimate with their unspoken thoughts. And we find, as we read or watch the play, that it is by the sub-text rather than the given dialogue that we follow the play's meaning. It is worth emphasising again here that it matters not at all whether we consider this particular design for the structure of dialogue as a conscious dramatic device of the dramatist's or not. Either intuitively or deliberately, Lawrence has here hit upon a way of presenting meaning which effectively reproduces the way in which meaning is generated in the experience of everyday life. We do not expect ordinary conversation to be fully informative. Indeed we are well aware that most conversation is hesitant, allusive, and full of gaps which have to be filled in in the light of the particular context surrounding that conversation. The more familiar we are with the people to whom we are speaking and with the situation in which we are speaking to them, the less we rely for understanding of what is meant on the words that are actually spoken. It is the impression of this kind of real experience that Lawrence's naturalist mode recreates. So we see how important it is that the setting makes us feel from the outset that we are in a solid, real place which has a vital and demonstrable connection with the world around it. And we see too how crucial it is that our notions of the kind of people that the characters are, is conditioned by the way in which they relate to that substantially realised 'real' place.

By Act III of *A Collier's Friday Night* we have become so thoroughly conditioned by these methods of presentation that we are scarcely conscious of the amount of extra information that we are ourselves providing in order to fill in the gaps between what the characters say and what they mean. The climactic scene between Ernest and his mother is a good example of the way in which we make such amplified 'readings', both when we are actually reading the play and when we are watching it on the stage.

Taken at its face value, this scene is a word-for-word 'copy' of a typical row between a possessive mother and an adolescent son. We have all, we feel, either experienced or heard first-hand reports of such scenes in life, and we may assume that it is this 'accuracy of observation' which makes us feel that the scene is so life-like. We tend to believe that what we are doing is comparing the quarrel with similar quarrels experienced or overheard in our lives outside the theatre, and that we therefore understand the emotional undertones because we know what we have, or would have, felt in a comparable situation.

But, if we examine the scene in detail, we will see that we are basing this assumption on a very particular case. The conflicts that underlie the situation are not as generalised as they seem. What we are doing therefore is not so much comparing this situation with a similar situation in life, but using the same perceptual approaches to understanding it as we would do in life. We are assembling all the information that has been provided for us by the context in order to understand the underlying meaning of what is being said, just as Mrs. Lambert and Ernest are themselves doing in the dialogue within the play. There is an important difference here, it will be agreed, between the way in which the play can be seen to persuade us that it is copying reality and the way in which it is certainly not a 'copy' in the sense of 'a mere photographic reproduction' of reality.

In order to arrive at the general or universal cause for Mrs. Lambert's having 'taken against' Maggie as she evidently has, we, like the characters in the play, have to work through the concrete particulars of the given situation.

The quarrel begins with Mrs. Lambert's concern for the burned bread. Left alone with her son, she asks him 'quietly', 'What did you do with that other loaf?' Knowing quite well the direction that her recriminations are going to take, Ernest tries to treat the matter lightly. He looks up smiling from his book and blandly admits, 'Why, we forgot it and it got all burned.' The exchange cannot remain for long in this light-hearted key. Mrs. Lambert's enquiries become more searching and bitter, and her anger is reflected in Ernest's changed expression from smile to frown. 'It's always alike though. If Maggie Pearson's here, nobody else matters. It's only a laughing matter if the bread gets burnt to cinders and put on the fire,' his mother continues, and 'bursts into a glow of bitterness' as she approaches the real core of her complaint. 'It's all very well, my son—you may talk about caring for me, but when it comes to Maggie Pearson it's very little you care for me—or Nellie— or anybody else.'

Ernest tries to battle his way out of the situation by distinguishing between the topics he can discuss with Maggie and those suitable for discussion with his mother. Again, from the sacrifices she has been seen to have to make in order to be able to take an interest in the Impressionism and pre-Raphaelism that he thinks would only bore her, we know that Ernest's argument will only fan the flames of his mother's anger—as it effectively does. Attempting another diversion Ernest confronts her with the charge, '. . . you wouldn't care if it was Alice, or Lois, or Louie. You never row me if I'm a bit late when I've been with them. . . . It's just Maggie, because you don't like her.' Frankly admitting, '(with emphasis): No, I *don't* like her—and I *can't* say I do', Mrs. Lambert stubbornly refuses to yield up any reason for her dislike. Ernest returns to the question of it being possible to care in different ways for his mother and for Maggie, but she refuses to concede the possibility, insisting that, though he may care for Maggie, he gives no sign of caring for her. '(*Pathetically*)' Ernest tries a further tactic by drawing a parallel between the different ways in which his mother loves Nellie and himself, and draws the admission from her that 'she (Nellie) doesn't mean the same to me. She has never understood—she has not been—like you. And now—you seem to care nothing—you care for *anything* more than home: you tell me nothing but the little things: you used to tell me everything: you used to come to me with everything; but now—I don't *do* for you now. You have to find somebody else.'

Into the pauses textually provided for by the punctuation of this passionate accusation we insert the information that has been provided by the 'real life' action of the play. We have watched Mrs. Lambert channelling her own frustrated hopes and aspirations into her son and realised that whatever he may achieve will, for her, be an achievement of her own. Now we see her confronting the truth that, having made his escape from the oppressive milieu possible, she must inevitably be left behind. Beneath this too we recognise the even deeper level of the over-intense relationship between a woman whose relationship with her husband has failed, and the son onto whom she has projected the passion unfulfilled in her marriage. We feel too the sense in which Ernest is subject to that bondage of love for his mother which remains more powerful than his affection for Maggie.

In this context there is no way of speaking about these underlying feelings, and indeed for the characters in the play, as for us, there is no need to speak of them, so concretely are they made present in the undercurrent to the words that are actually spoken. This impasse is recognised in Ernest's appeal, 'Well, my dear, we shall have to let it be, then, and things will have to go their own way.' Speaking with difficulty (as Lawrence indicates in the stage direction), Ernest continues, 'You know Mater—I don't care for her—really—not half as I care for you. Only, just now—well, I can't help it, I can't help it. But I care just the same—for you—I do.' Here, as suggested by the 'difficulty', Ernest is trying to say what cannot be put into words. There is some truth in his reassurance. As we have observed in the acting out of the bread burning incident, Ernest is not completely committed to Maggie. Yet, as has been seen too in the scene in which Maggie and Ernest are alone together, the potential for a complete passionate involvement is a latent possibility. Latent in this final scene too is the sexual commitment between mother and son which stands between the latter and his capability of 'growing up'; something he knows he has to do, but wants to accomplish without wounding his mother. That she too accepts the impossibility of finding a way to resolve their conflict is implicit in Mrs. Lambert's acceptance of the truce under which she and Ernest tacitly agree to leave unsaid the facts about their relationship of which it is impossible to speak. '(With great gentleness having decided not to torment him)' Mrs. Lambert brings the encounter to a close with her soothing 'Yes, I understand now', the incomplete truth of her statement being drawn attention to by Lawrence's further stage direction, '(*She bluffs him*)'.

The truce is a fragile one. Peace has been declared for this Friday night, but it does not promise to last much longer. The gentleness between mother and son is in itself a sign of the fragility of their pact, as we see at the very end of the play, in

Lawrence's demanding stage direction 'There is in their tones a dangerous gentleness—so much gentleness that the safe reserve of their souls is broken'. We do not, of course, feel that this direction requires a particular degree of subtlety for its interpretation since the emotional tension that it indicates has been written in throughout the play. We do not have to be told by any extra stage 'business' that this state of tension exists and is, in a very important sense what the play is 'about'.

We have been persuaded to come to this conclusion because our way of seeing the play has been imposed upon us by Lawrence's chosen form; that form in which we assess the setting as real in a concrete and naturalistic way, and thence feel as real the emotional truth underlying the surface 'reality'. Proceeding from the particularity of the life in the miner's home—so 'real' that we feel the need to identify it with circumstances in the author's own life—we arrive at an understanding of the more generally human reality motivating the characters whom we are persuaded to feel that we know as well, and indeed perhaps better, than they know themselves. All this we appear to do without any direction or guidance from the dramatist, whose function seems to have been merely to set down an account of the life he himself experienced.

Aptly described as 'A Poet's Realism' by Desmond MacCarthy in a review of *The Widowing of Mrs. Holroyd*[13] this naturalist mode manifests the element of artistic selection in the specific choices that it makes from the available material of real life. At this moment in time we happen to know that the play portrays something very like Lawrence's own experience, and we are inevitably influenced by that knowledge. But, if we could imagine an audience to whom Lawrence the man was completely unknown, we would surely not feel that an experience of the play in production would be any less life-like for that audience than it is for us. As has been seen, the choice of a particular physical milieu and of the objective details within it is in no way arbitrary, but has been dictated by considerations of characterisation and theme. The bread is baked and allowed to burn, not simply because this was a common Friday night occurrence in the Lawrence household, but because of the way in which this actual physical process

[13] In the *New Statesman*, 18 December 1926, p. 310.

interacts with the emotional crisis between mother and son. Similarly with all the other objective details, we can see that they are not 'simply' there in the play because they were there in life, but because of the dramatic function they have to perform in persuading us to attend to the reality at both its surface and submerged levels. If we attend to these details we will know, as has also been said of these plays in performance, 'without Freudian hinting or nudging symbolism',[14] why the characters must behave as they do, and we will know also that Lawrence the *dramatist*, though apparently absent from his play, is, through his choice of these details, directing our response in a particular way.

[14] The comment occurs in Ronald Bryden's review of *The Widowing of Mrs. Holroyd* cited above (Note 11).

3

The Widowing of Mrs. Holroyd

For us today *A Collier's Friday Night* enjoys the distinction of being the first play Lawrence wrote, but *The Widowing of Mrs. Holroyd* must, for its author have enjoyed the even greater distinction of being the first to secure recognition of his talent as a dramatist. Hueffer, like Garnett after him, evidently found *Mrs. Holroyd* the most promising of the three plays submitted to him in 1911, since it was this play that he chose to send to Granville-Barker. Lawrence was obviously disappointed when the latter sent it back to him with the conventional 'read it with much interest but afraid I don't want it' rejection slip, and, after that rebuff, it is not surprising that he re-submitted the play to Garnett in rather apologetic terms. 'I send you this, the one play I have at home', he writes. 'I have written to Mr. Hueffer for the other two. This is the least literary—and the least unified of the three. I tried to write for the stage—I tried to make it end up stagily. If I send it to you at once, you can read it at your leisure. The first scenes are good.' (CL p. 81) As has already been seen, Garnett was so delighted with the play that he offered to publish it, together with the two plays he had not even had an opportunity to read, in the spring of the following year, and, when those plays failed to turn up in time, continued to be interested enough in *Mrs. Holroyd* to submit it to Iden Payne.

Hueffer's preference for this among the three 'colliery' plays submitted to him by Lawrence may, in part, be accounted for by the similarity of its subject to that of *Odour of Chrysanthemums*, the short story which had so much impressed him with Lawrence's talent and which he had published in *The English Review* of June 1911. But Garnett's preference for this same play (when he was eventually able to compare it with the other two) and Payne's willingness to meet the author to discuss a possible production suggest that Lawrence had been more successful in this particular case in his aim to 'write for the stage'—at least insofar as the tastes of the time were concerned.

Certainly the structure of *The Widowing of Mrs. Holroyd*, as we know it, bears a closer resemblance to what might have been felt to be 'dramatic' in the English theatre of 1911 than do the more innovatory structures of Lawrence's other 'colliery' plays. But the play seen and approved by Hueffer, Garnett and Payne underwent many modifications before it emerged as the published version of 1914. Lawrence was in Germany when the offer of this publication was made, and he writes to Garnett, 'I have been very busy reading the play to Frieda. It wants *a lot* of altering. I have made it heaps better. You must by no means let the MS. go to the printer before I have it—neither here nor in America. What a jolly fine play it is, too, when I have pulled it together. . . . Must I find another title? *The Widowing of Mrs. Holroyd* describes it, but doesn't sound very well.' (CL p. 218) A month later he writes to Mitchell Kennerley, 'I am very sorry to have caused trouble by coming in late with my revision of the play, *The Widowing of Mrs. Holroyd*. The MS. had lain with Mr. Garnett for nearly two years: he had had it typed, and I had seen nothing of it till I asked for it a week or two back. Then I saw how it needed altering—refining. Particularly I hated it in the last act, where the man and woman wrangled rather shallowly across the dead body of the husband. And it seemed nasty that they should make love where he lay drunk. I hope to heaven I have come in time to have it made decent.' (CL p. 223) This and subsequent letters anxiously refer to the worry about correcting proofs; a process which, it would appear, Lawrence was eventually content to leave in the hands of Edwin Björkman with whose 'beautiful and laudatory' remarks in the Preface he expressed himself well pleased.

In later life, however, Lawrence recalled how '. . . in a cottage by the sea in Italy, I re-wrote almost entirely that play, *The Widowing of Mrs. Holroyd* right on the proofs which Mitchell Kennerley had sent me. And he nobly forebore with me.'[1] So it

[1] In 'Introduction to *A Bibliography of D. H. Lawrence*, by Edward D. McDonald', *Phoenix*, p. 233.

seems likely that Kennerley relented and allowed Lawrence to make further major alterations before the play finally appeared in print.

What we know today then, as *The Widowing of Mrs. Holroyd*, is a very different play from the one that so much pleased Garnett in 1911, and whether the original was more or less conventionally 'stagey' than the final version, it is unfortunately impossible now to know. For all Lawrence's alterations, however, the play remains more obviously shaped towards its climax than the 'formless' and inconclusive *A Collier's Friday Night* whose unconventional shape and lack of formal resolution were so far ahead of their time that even in 1968 the critics found them *avant garde* and experimental.

Although Lawrence wrote a letter at the time of the play's first professional production in 1926 'authenticating' the life portrayed in the play by assuring his friend Rolf Gardiner that ' "Mrs. Holroyd" was an aunt of mine—she lived in a tiny cottage, just up the line from the railway-crossing at Brinsley. near Eastwood', (CL p. 953) there is nothing like the difficulty that there was in *A Collier's Friday Night* in separating what we know of Lawrence's life from the life-like impression created by *The Widowing of Mrs. Holroyd*. In a much more obvious sense then, we are able to look at the latter play as a created dramatic fiction. We may take it, for example, that Lawrence is telling the truth when he implies in his letter that Mrs. Holroyd is a character 'modelled from life', but we do not—perhaps fortunately— have to consider whether that aunt's life further resembled the life led by Mrs. Holroyd in the play. We do, however, note that her son Jack has a close biographical resemblance to the boy Lawrence in his ambivalent attitude towards a hard-drinking collier father.

There is evidence for this resemblance in Jessie Chambers' memoir in which it is often remarked that, from boyhood, Lawrence seldom spoke of his father, appearing to regard him with such habitual dislike that he assumed that Jessie's reluctance to visit his home was 'because of father'. Once though, when organising a dancing session in the Chambers' kitchen, he said, 'Father says one ought to be able to dance on a threepenny bit', and, pressed for further information about the father of whom he so rarely spoke, added briefly, 'He used to when he was a young man. He ran a dancing class at one time.'[2]

As in *Sons and Lovers*, the boyish admiration for the father's prowess at dancing—an admiration shared by Lawrence's own mother as well as by the characters Mrs. Morel and Mrs. Holroyd —is registered in *The Widowing of Mrs. Holroyd* when Jack, delivering his shocked report of the scene of his father's gallivanting in the pub, cannot prevent a note of reluctant admiration creeping into his tone when he says 'He can dance, can't he Mam?' Though she ignores the question at this point in the play, Holroyd's physical attractions, among which the skill at dancing is one, play a large part in defining for us the ambivalence of the relationship between Lizzie and Charles Holroyd, and Lizzie's consequent reluctance to leave her husband for Blackmore. To this extent then, it is perhaps fair to compare Lizzie Holroyd with a younger Mrs. Morel, and to see in Jack resemblances both to the boy Paul Morel and thence to the boy Lawrence himself.

As we saw in *A Collier's Friday Night*, where so much more of this extra-textual biographical information had to be accommodated, the real life experience incorporated in the play has very little bearing on the real life effect created by *The Widowing of Mrs. Holroyd*. We are drawn into the life of the latter play as we were into that of the former by the formal method employed in both plays of presenting a setting which is immediately established in the stage directions as a representative part of a wider whole; a synechdochic image for the life of the coal-mining community, with its conflicts between dirt and cleanliness; between the warmth of the fire-glow in the cottage grate and the icy terror of Holroyd's death, trapped in the mine from which that coal is dug; between the breathing reality of human emotion and the de-humanising, mechanical forces imposed upon it by work in the pit. In its physical relation to the pit, the Holroyd cottage is a model for that conflict.

Inside the cottage the stage directions call for a deep full red fire. A white curtained window is set beside the outer door which will be left open as Lizzie Holroyd enters in the opening scene of Act I to reveal 'the colliery rail not far from the threshold and away back the headstocks of a pit'. Into this cottage Lizzie carries

[2] *D. H. Lawrence: A Personal Record*, p. 30.

a basket 'heaped full of washing'. She sets the clothes to dry by the fire, using the very coal that makes washing a never-ending task in her life to help her in her daily work of keeping the cottage and its occupants clean.

Surprised by the arrival of Blackmore, Lizzie scolds him for appearing 'like the evil one out of the darkness'. Blackmore reminds her that he is an electrician, 'a gentleman in the mine' and therefore a cut above those who toil underground—of whom Holroyd is one. Their first flirtatious conversation is brought to a halt when Blackmore mentions the Holroyd children and Lizzie remembers her status as a married woman and mother. This pattern is repeated when she brings a clean towel for Blackmore who teases her about her housewifely pride, and their playful talk is interrupted by the arrival of Jack. That it is an interruption is brought out by Lizzie's sharp tone which surprises the boy, and it is his sister who has to remind him of the tale they both have to tell. Foreshadowing the quarrels that we will see between their mother and father, the children here squabble over who shall tell Lizzie the larger share of the details of the exploits of their father whom they have seen drinking and dancing in the New Inn with a pair of women from Nottingham.

Angered by the report Lizzie breaks the lamp glass and Blackmore appears again—this time to the children's surprise—offering to fetch a replacement from the pit. 'I shan't be a minute' he says, ignoring Lizzie's protest and stressing once again the proximity of the pit to the cottage. While he is away the children elaborate on the story about their father and Lizzie desperately plans to put a stop to the gossip that this latest of Holroyd's exploits will cause. In this respect too, the action of the play tells us that Lizzie must 'clean up' after Holroyd who repeatedly besmirches the respectable reputation she strives to maintain for her family, and we see the physical battle against dirt paralleled by the struggle at an abstract moral level.

When Blackmore returns with the lamp glass, the light that it sheds reveals the children's admiration of him and impresses us with how much they prefer him to their own father. Lizzie enlists Holroyd's help in folding the sheet which he admires for its whiteness, but she calls attention to the smuts and complains, 'I'd never have come to live here, in all the thick of the pit grime,

66

and lonely, if it hadn't been for him, so that he shouldn't call in a public house on his road home from work.' Literally and metaphorically her efforts are frustrated. The washing gets covered in smuts and Holroyd slinks past the house to the New Inn instead of coming in for his dinner.

Blackmore admires the cottage, and Lizzie, pleased at first at his flattery, sends the children out to fetch the last of the washed clothes, stilling their fears of the rats they may meet. The rats too are a manifestation of the pit grime in the dirty vine that Holroyd never has time to cut down. Lizzie yearns to get away from her constant struggle against the dirt, but Blackmore, still cajoling, tells her that he would '. . . miss it if you weren't here', transposing his wooing of the woman into terms of the firelight in the cottage and the warmth of the wall outside the chimney, as these stand for the warmth and light that he feels in Lizzie's presence.

Again their flirtation is interrupted by the children. Lizzie resumes her matronly role by offering Blackmore tea. The children's plea that he should stay with them brings to a close this first scene in which, without obvious 'exposition' Lawrence has made clear to his audience both the background to the central situation that the play will explore, and the state of affairs which currently prevails within that situation. We have been given a sense of the passage of time past, and a concern with what will happen in the future. Perhaps most important of all, we have grasped that the possibilities open to the people we will meet in this situation are limited by the constraints of the milieu in which they live and work.

We are prepared then, to weigh up the possibility of Lizzie's making a better life for herself and her children by accepting the offer that Blackmore is evidently on the brink of making, against that of her improving her lot by sticking to her duty as wife to the problematic Holroyd. Her indecision is expressed in this scene in the line in which she says of the rats (identified, we remember, with the pit grime and thence with Holroyd), 'I s'll get used to them', a prediction which she immediately contradicts by exclaiming, 'I'd give anything to be out of this place.' Can Blackmore offer Lizzie a 'real' alternative or simply a variation of the drudgery to which she is accustomed? This is the question that the play poses in terms of the two men's relation to their working life in which Blackmore is, after all, only a cut above Holroyd. A 'light bringer' and a 'gentleman' in and around the pit, working at a higher level than Holroyd, Blackmore is nevertheless bound like his rival to the pit's conditions of labour. We will see later in the play that, when Blackmore does suggest to Lizzie that they should escape together, it is to Spain—right away from the colliery context—that he proposes they should go. But the impressions made by the solidly real detail of the first scene, together perhaps with the fantasy-world connotations of 'castles in Spain', will persuade us that his proposal is unlikely to be put into effect; that it is a mere dream, incapable of realisation in contrast with the reality of the mining community of which the design of the play so powerfully convinces us.

Scene 2 extends our knowledge of the factors that Lizzie must take into account in making her decision between staying with Holroyd or 'cutting clean' away from him. She is shown, as the scene opens, dutifully continuing to toil at her washing, but, work for the moment done, she bursts into defiant tears crying, 'Why should *I* put up with it all?—He can do what he likes. But I don't care, no, I don't—' Her weeping is interrupted by the sound of Holroyd's deep guffaws and the arrival of one of the two 'brazen hussies' with whom he has been cavorting at the New Inn. Accustomed to keeping 'dirt' at bay, Lizzie attempts to refuse the revellers entry, but she fails. Clara and Laura, blowsy and over-dressed but not altogether unattractive, romp in followed by the unsteady Holroyd. The moment is dramatically decisive. Our sympathy must hold with Lizzie, driven to defend her cottage-fortress, but we must also be able to see in the big, blond figure of Holroyd, now 'rather tipsy and lawless', some vestige of an ex-planation of how she ever came to be attracted enough to marry him and bear his two children.

Lawrence's stage directions consistently provide the guidance for a performance which will enable an audience to take in the crucial ambiguity in the relation between husband and wife. Lizzie's disgust at the insolent invasion freezes her into a 'dramatic pose' which Clara regards curiously, as Holroyd blunders out to find something for his guests to drink. Lizzie's silent contempt is shattered by the rat careering out of the scullery. In the mêlée that follows Lizzie's concern is all for Holroyd who 'approaches and stoops to attack the rat'. Hateful as her husband has just been shown to seem to her, Lizzie nevertheless screams: 'Don't, he'll fly at you. . . . He will, he will—and they're poisonous. (She ends on a very high note. Leaning forward on the sofa as far as she dares, she stretches out her arms to keep back her husband, who is about to kneel and search under the sofa for the rat).'

This direction for the performance of a key incident exemplifies the way in which the naturalistic action is invested with subtextual significance. Lizzie is afraid of the rat. We see her 'bunched up on the sofa' and we know from the previous scene that rats are synonymous with danger as well as with dirt in the terminology particular to this household. To our natural horror of rats Lawrence has added the particular horror that they hold for Lizzie Holroyd. The rat has run out of the scullery into which Holroyd has just been seen to go. Its appearance has caused havoc in the kitchen, almost making Clara smash the lamp as she leaps up onto the table, and paralysing Laura in her chair. Terrorised too, Lizzie is nevertheless able to try to defend Holroyd from this 'monster'. He thrusts her away and defies her plea to open the door and let the rat go. At the climax of this frenetic episode, Lizzie overcomes her own fear, bounds down from the door and rushes back to the safety of her sofa perch. In violent action we have here a measure of her feelings for Holroyd, expressed in a great burst of dramatic energy. There can be no doubt that Lawrence's text calls for us to feel that Lizzie, at some level, still loves her husband. Trying to look cold and contemptuous after this revelation of her suppressed feelings, Lizzie stands by while Holroyd ministers to his flustered hussies, but there is no forgetting the impact of her impulse to protect him.

When the children make their appearance on this bizarre scene Lizzie becomes surer of her ground. We have already seen, in the first scene of this Act, how the children were used to show Lizzie being brought back to 'reality' from her escape into Blackmore's affectionate attentions. Here, though they disobey her order to go back to bed, they are shown restoring her sense of having a maternal role to play, and in so doing they create a fragile alliance between husband and wife. Torn between fear and fascination (as Lizzie herself was by the rat), Minnie and Jack restore too some sense of propriety to the befuddled Holroyd. When Jack lingers behind after Lizzie has comforted and carried off the frightened Minnie, it is Holroyd who orders the boy to follow his mother. Intrigued by Clara's gew-gaws the boy 'takes no notice'. We are made to see through Holroyd's eyes the ease with which the boy is captivated by the tawdry bracelet, and understand the father's recognition of his own failings in being attracted to the cheap, showy women. The play underlines this recognition for us when Holroyd repeats his order to his son to 'get off after' his mother.

Seeing his children beside the women has put Holroyd into quite a different mood from that in which he first blustered into his kitchen. Clara and Laura call attention to the change by noticing that he is 'different' and he, obviously shamed by what his children have seen, tries to persuade them to leave. In no hurry to go out again into the cold night, Clara and Laura renew their blandishments, but Holroyd roughly rejects their advances, and, on Lizzie's return, slams out of the room leaving his wife to do his dirty work and rid their home of the 'rubbish' he has brought into it. Composed and ladylike she soon succeeds, well as she knows that Holroyd is not the man to thank her for it.

Lizzie has had to listen to the sad tale of Clara's brutish husband; a tale which we may not find so very different in its essentials from the troubles that Lizzie herself has had to bear. But Lizzie refuses to see any similarity between herself and the newly widowed Clara, and sweeps the women out of her home. Once she has 'cleaned up' for him, Holroyd can again take Lizzie for granted. Sitting 'Ashamed yet defiant, withal anxious to apologise', Holroyd reasserts his authority by demanding 'Wheer's my slippers?' Lizzie takes no notice. She refuses to be touched by the anxiety to apologise, felt as an undercurrent to Holroyd's resumption of their family bond. Angered at her rejection, Holroyd stamps about in his stockinged feet and cuts his foot on the glass he has broken. But Lizzie still refuses to attend to him, and snatches out of his hand the clean white rag with which he means to bind his wound. Her withholding of attention here is seen to be in striking contrast to her brave leap to his defence against

70

the rat. Holroyd must now be made to suffer for his latest outrage; must be brought to heel by her deliberately cold and unfeeling attitude.

A quarrel flares up. Forced into a corner by Lizzie's contempt,
Holroyd taunts her with the patent untruth that Laura and Clara
are 'as good as you are'. We have seen that he does not believe
what he says in his shame that his children should have encountered the women. But Lizzie's gentility drives him to desperate
measures. Driving home the attack, he accuses her of scheming
with Blackmore to 'put him down' now that she has a little money
of her own. The outrage of bringing Clara and Laura home was
motivated, it is suggested here, by Holroyd's jealousy of Lizzie's
relationship with Blackmore; a jealousy which continually
smoulders not far beneath his apparently callous treatment of a
wife who thinks herself too good for him.

Disgusted and furiously jealous on her own part, Lizzie defies
her husband's bullying threats to reassert his mastery over her,
and declares her intention to be rid of him. Weariness succeeds
her hysterical collapse into tears and it is the 'dull, inflexible'
tone of her command to 'Go, I mean it, go out again. And if you
never come back again, I'm glad. I've had enough' that forces
him—reluctantly—to leave the house.

Without breaking the naturalistic frame, Lawrence packs this
scene with incisive dramatic points in which the highly charged
emotional conflicts are dynamically acted out. His stage directions
indicate the extent to which shifts of emotion (as with the change
in Holroyd from truculence to shame, or, in Lizzie, from hysteria
to cold despair) are to control our response to those actions in
interpreting the feelings between husband and wife that we do
not hear expressed in words. Lizzie has leapt to her husband's
defence against the rat, and the children's presence on the shameful scene of his drunken dissipation has drawn husband and wife
momentarily together. Though we see Lizzie coldly dismissing her
husband, we see too that she cannot bring herself to watch him
leave. Deep under the débris of this breaking marriage we sense
a last remaining vestige of a once strong and mutual attraction.
Beneath Lizzie's benumbed dismissal of Holroyd, we sense too
an undercurrent of ambiguity, grasped at by his act of hesitating
by the door. Only when Lizzie turns herself still further away from

71

him (as Lawrence's stage direction provides for her to do), does Holroyd despair and leave.

It is against this background of a refusal to be reconciled that the play asks us to judge of Lizzie's responsibility, first in the matter of Holroyd's drunken belligerence in Act II and later of his failure to escape death in the final act. Embittered as Lizzie is against her husband, we have, from the beginning of Act I, been given to see that the failure of the marriage may not be entirely Holroyd's fault. He is lively and extroverted; she excessively house-proud and over-protective of her family's good name. When Black-more brings home the drunken Holroyd in Act II, we are there-fore evidently meant to feel some sympathy for the husband who, after all—though with good reason—was driven out of his home by his wife.

Presented as bullish and enraged in this scene, Holroyd can nevertheless be quietened by a reminder of his children. Although she calls Holroyd a beast, we notice too that Lizzie interrupts Blackmore's comment 'He's getting fat. He must be—' with the defence 'He's big-made—he has a big frame.' As Blackmore impresses Lizzie with the care he has taken of her husband on her behalf, Holroyd wakes into a jealous rage. Ungrateful as his anger at Blackmore appears from his 'rescuer's' point of view, Holroyd is not far out in his suspicions that his wife and Blackmore are 'up to something', and he is seen to be right too in supposing that it is the electrician's 'gentlemanliness' that appeals to Lizzie.

Lawrence balances the audience's response very dexterously here. Like Lizzie we tend to favour the sober, gentlemanly Black-more who behaves so well while Holroyd conducts himself so deplorably. Yet, like Lizzie too, we feel that somewhere she has let Holroyd down; that his drunken bullying is in some way her 'fault'. Indeed we have seen her at the end of the previous scene coldly turning away from him and casting him out. What else could a man like Holroyd have done but drown his sorrows in drink? Is her coldness to him perhaps part of the reason for his preferring to slink off to the pub rather than come home for his dinner? Without referring to these possibilities in the dialogue, Lawrence directs us to infer the underlying causes for the present situation, and to consider whether praise and blame are at all applicable to either of the partners in the failed marriage. It is the pattern established by these underlying causes that we will bring to bear on our understanding of, and response to, the later and already foreshadowed circumstance of Lizzie's widowing.

In the fight that breaks out between the two men Blackmore is triumphant, proving himself a physical match for the drunken Holroyd against whom he has, throughout the play, been contrasted as more refined and intellectually superior. It is with Holroyd's collapse into a stupor that the play most pointedly prefigures the final scene of his death. All confusion, Lizzie is seen frenziedly fearing for Blackmore's safety and wishing Holroyd dead; determined, at all events, never to let her husband into her bed again. It is Blackmore who washes the unconscious Holroyd as, later, Lizzie will wash his corpse. His gentle nature restored, Blackmore is an object of wonder to Lizzie, but, when he admits, 'I wished as hard as I've ever wished anything in my life . . . that I'd killed him', she, who only a moment before had voiced the same wish that Holroyd were dead, is shocked. We see her then take over the care of Holroyd and accuse Blackmore of acting only so as 'to play on my feelings'.

Again our sympathies are divided. Like Blackmore we feel that Lizzie is fond of Holroyd 'really', and, though insisting that she no longer cares for him, Lizzie is forced to admit that she once did. 'I did care for him—now he has destroyed it' she says. Like Blackmore too we sense that in this crisis Lizzie is not being absolutely truthful. Worn into utter weariness, she insists, 'I know, tonight finished it. But it was never right between us.' We have noticed though that she has refused to answer Blackmore's question 'But was there nothing else in him but his muscles and his good looks to attract you to him?', and we register even more attentively her reluctance to accept his offer of escape that follows her challenge that she would leave her husband without caring a snap of the fingers for him. We notice too how Lawrence leaves this snap of the fingers in *action*. All the time, in fact, we see that these clues for the creation of meaning arise out of an interplay between what is said and what is done in the context of the setting which itself provides us with a glossary for interpreting the words that the characters speak.

We are reminded of the fantasy associated earlier with Blackmore's offer of escape to Spain, and we see, when this offer is repeated here, that Lizzie is questioning how possible in 'reality' such a dream might be, when she questions the reality of Blackmore's love. At twenty-seven he claims never to have known love. At thirty-two she knows enough to doubt the likelihood of a man who can give her the kind of love that she wants having reached this age without experiencing passion. On that note of doubt, the action of the play prompts us to record as significant Lizzie's readiness to slip away from her lover at the sound of the clicking latch that recalls her to her maternal duties. During her absence Holroyd wakes and staggers up to bed. Despite her determination 'never again' to allow Holroyd 'upstairs', Lizzie announces on her return that her husband is lying on the bed. She insists on making the distinction between being 'in' and 'on' the bed, and Blackmore does not question her change of heart overtly. Nevertheless we are made to feel, in his gentle insistence that Lizzie should leave with him, a fear that he may never persuade her to abandon the man she once loved.

Comforting the stricken Lizzie, Blackmore pleads with her to forget her doubts about the quality of his love and deliver him from the conflict which is tearing him in two. 'I wish either he was dead or me', he declares, able neither to face life without her, nor to go on suffering the hell of seeing Lizzie together with her husband. Still he cannot wholly win her assent. Holroyd is, after all, the children's father. Blackmore's wishing him dead will not alter that. And in this play the influence of the children is no abstract moral value, but a potent physical fact which we have seen influencing Lizzie's behaviour. Her direct denial that it is Holroyd who keeps her pitches Lizzie into Blackmore's arms, but she is still unsure of her feelings. Again a noise from above disturbs them. Driven into a corner, Lizzie excuses herself for having married Holroyd with a tale that reminds us of Clara's. Only to get away from an unbearable life did Lizzie Holroyd marry 'the first man that turned up'. At heart then, Lizzie must, we feel, have experienced a certain guilt when denying Holroyd's charge that she was no better than Clara or Laura.

Blackmore voices our doubts when he asks 'And you never cared about him?', and her answer confirms his suspicions. She did care for Holroyd but he has killed her trust: 'There's just his body and

nothing else. Nothing that keeps him, no anchor, no roots, nothing
satisfying. It's a horrible feeling there is about him, that nothing
is safe or permanent—nothing is anything—' It is the undercurrent
to this dialogue that prompts us to ask the all-important question:
what does Lizzie herself feel to have been her own part in creating the emptiness of her relationship with her husband?

Her fears about leaving her children and the 'immorality' of
leaving Holroyd remain strong, but Blackmore partly overcomes
them, and draws from her the hesitant confession 'Yes—I love you.
I do love you—', qualified immediately by 'When I look at him
and then at you—ha!' to which she adds a short laugh. Her
decision is of the moment, and is based on the comparison that
she makes in that moment between the gentlemanly Blackmore
and the bullish Holroyd. To Blackmore's final question, 'Shall you
come with me?' she replies, 'On Saturday' and the curtain falls
on Blackmore's counter-question, 'Not now?'

We understand that the delay is crucial. The moment of
decision may pass. 'I'll come on Saturday' tells us of Lizzie's deep
uncertainty. At this moment she has no doubts about her
preference for the gentle and gentlemanly Blackmore over her
coarse and 'rootless' husband. But whether she has, as Blackmore asks, cut clean of that husband for ever, is quite a different
matter.

The setting as Act III opens confirms our suspicion that the
established pattern of her familiar life will hold Lizzie to her
marriage. After the chaos of the previous night, the kitchen has
resumed its normal air. Holroyd's meal awaits him at the table
at which Lizzie is ironing the clothes that we have seen her washing and folding. 'On the hearth stand newly baked loaves of bread.'
Household chores have reasserted their pull over Lizzie, and the
scene strongly suggests that she has drawn back from thoughts of
escape into the secure—if sometimes hateful—routine of her
wifely duties. The children, playing their make-believe game of
grown-ups, firmly register the dominance of family ties. When
their game ends in a squabble, it is Minnie who says: 'I wish my
father'd come.' Irritated and petulant, the mother launches into
a familiar pattern of complaint against Holroyd, but when Jack
follows her lead with 'I hate him. I wish he'd drop down the pit
shaft', Lizzie turns on him in horror crying: 'Jack!—I never heard

such a thing in my life. You mustn't say such things, it's wicked.' Very clear in our memories is the fact that both she and Blackmore have recently uttered the same 'wicked' thought. Lizzie's guilt is manifest in her loud admonition to Jack, 'I won't have it. He's your father, remember,' Refusing to be subdued, Jack shouts back, 'Well, he's always coming home an' shouting an' banging on the table.' Here Jack speaks up for Lizzie's well-known hatred of Holroyd's boorish outward behaviour. Minnie, by contrast, voices her mother's inner doubts when she says '(wistfully) 'Appen if you said something nice to him mother, he'd happen to go to bed an' not shout.' In the children we see both sides of Lizzie's dilemma. She, however, will not face up to the truth they reveal, and diverts them with talk of going to another country. Blackmore's plan is evidently still being turned over in her mind, despite the normal appearance of the cottage kitchen.

Naturally attracted by the idea of an adventure, Minnie mirrors her mother's hesitation at the thought of leaving her father behind, and is relieved when the sound of footsteps seems to announce his home-coming. It is, however, Blackmore who appears and offers to still their concern about Holroyd's lateness by going in search of him. As the children prepare for bed we again hear Minnie pleading with her mother not to 'row' Holroyd when he returns, while Jack declares that 'It doesn't matter if we're going to leave him.'

The ambivalence of this emotional situation is dramatised again by Minnie's request for the tawdry bracelet which Clara has left behind. Reluctantly given it by her mother, Minnie gloats over the prize, admiring the rubbishy treasure as Jack had done the night before. Thus, in the living embodiment of their two children the play shows us the cross-currents of emotion that activate the relationship between Lizzie and Charles Holroyd. Each are like both mother and father in ways which Lawrence presents in terms of dramatic incident, and together they represent their parents' conflict in miniature. In a very real and concrete way they are parts of the marital situation which represent the whole.

Without breaking the naturalistic frame Lawrence draws on just those aspects of the children's behaviour which illuminate his 'strong central situation'. As the mother leads them up to bed we recognise that the scene has been invested with complex undercurrents by the way in which the dramatist has required us to look at the love-hate relationship between father and mother in terms of the children's conflicting feelings about their parents.

An elderly woman, evidently very much at home in the Holroyd kitchen, enters at this point to divert our attention from the crucial statement that has just been made about the central situation, in the sub-text of the scene between Lizzie and her children. The stage directions tell us to be aware of the new-comer's sharp inspection of the state of the place, and her *assumption* of a 'lachrymose expression' when she hears Lizzie's footsteps approaching.

Lizzie addresses her as 'mother' but we have no doubt that this woman is her mother-in-law, even before the dialogue makes the point explicitly. Taking Holroyd's side, the older Mrs. Holroyd echoes Minnie in her opinion that the trouble between Lizzie and her son is not all of the latter's making. Holroyd has reason, she maintains, for jealousy at Lizzie's relationship with Blackmore, innocent as it may be, and she hits home hard at Lizzie's pride by accusing her of being too clever and superior. 'You thought yourself above him Lizzie, and you know he's not the man to stand it.' Lizzie retaliates by accusing her mother-in-law of having concealed the truth about Holroyd from her, and it is given to the older woman sagely to reply, 'Some women could have lived with him happy enough. An' a fat lot you'd have thanked me for my telling.'

In this encounter between Holroyd's wife and mother the play seeks no easy sympathy for either woman. Both are presented as trapped in the social treadmill of a particular way of life. Old Mrs. Holroyd has learnt to bend in order to survive. Lizzie would rather have her neck broken than learn to bend in submission. Both, however, are concerned in their respective ways about what has happened to delay Holroyd, and, disguised as their anxiety is, we yet recognise in it the sense in which they both care for the man.

Again we note how naturalistically suspense is built up in this act towards the announcement of Holroyd's death. In the con-trasted family patterns of the scene between Lizzie and her children, and that between Lizzie and her mother-in-law the play has given us the necessary material to fit the last remaining pieces into the picture of Lizzie's married life. As we complete that picture, we are about to see it destroyed. Rigley comes in with his forebodings of disaster. Holroyd's mother, reminded of similar occasions in the past, fears the worst. Lizzie tries to control her own rising hysteria, and even seems calmly to be able to plan for a future in which her small inheritance may tide the family over, if Holroyd has been injured.

The surrounding world of the pit invades the kitchen as the women open the door and listen to the whirr of the colliery machines outside. Lizzie wants to rush out but her mother-in-law holds her back. In mingled hope and fear, she tries to comfort herself, '. . . perhaps while he's in bed we shall have time to change him. He'll happen to be a better man.'

It is, of course, a forlorn hope as is the mother-in-law's encouragement 'Well, you can but try. Many a woman's thought the same.' And it is here, at a moment of intense narrative suspense, that we are told how Lizzie sees her marriage, and how, for all its failure, she would still rather try to make a go of it than 'cut clean' away—if only Holroyd could be made a better man. Necessarily, in order to underline this moment of choice, it is Blackmore—looking pale—who brings the tragic news. Preparing the women as best he can, he is unable to avoid delivering the shattering blow. Lizzie takes the news in first, and collapses in horror. The mother, moaning, wails 'O Lizzie . . . if only you'd have tried to be different with him.' Blackmore makes them face the practical reality of laying out the dead body. In his cold clear tone we are to hear no regret for the accident that has befallen Holroyd. As Lizzie has suspected, he is not a man subject to passions which he cannot control.

Lizzie is reduced to witlessness and distraction by Rigley's description of the fall of coal that 'fell a back of him and shut him in as you might shut a loaf in the oven. It never touched him.' Not crushed but suffocated, Holroyd had time to know that he was going to die. Like Rigley, with his homely metaphor of the loaf which approximates the disaster in the pit to the life in the cottage, the colliers who carry in Holroyd's body are matter-of-fact in their condolences. 'Gesticulating freely', the manager mimes the unique circumstances that must have conspired to trap Holroyd, and Lizzie's horror is increased when she learns that her husband had time to struggle, scraping helplessly at the fallen coal with his bare hands, on which the nails are bleeding and broken.

Overcome by hysteria now, she must be calmed by reminders of her children and of the inquest that must routinely take place on the following day. Rigley's efforts to exonerate himself from the blame of having allowed Holroyd to lag behind counterpoint Lizzie's own feelings of guilt. Yet innocence and guilt are plainly shown to be irrelevant to the stark fact of death, manifest on the stage in the shape of Holroyd's corpse, still in its 'pit grime'.

Here the full effect of the interaction between clean cottage and black pit; that interaction which has underscored the naturalism of the play as a whole, is felt, as the neat, cosy cleanness of the cottage is ravaged by the human wreckage cast into it from the pit. Emotional and physical 'reality', constantly inter-related by the imagery of the play, here come powerfully together in a climax that affects the spectator with cumulative force.

For all her care in keeping the cottage clean, Lizzie is found wanting in this hour of most desperate necessity. She has worked and struggled to keep up a respectable 'front'; to silence the tongues that gossiped about Holroyd and his 'beastly' ways. But there has been more talk about Lizzie herself than about Holroyd. By the standards of this community she has been spending her efforts in the wrong direction. Again this mis-spent energy is revealed to us in the play by means of a naturalistic detail. All through the play we have seen Lizzie drudging at her washing and ironing: now, with her irons still hot from her most recent toil, it is discovered that she has not 'put by' the traditional white garments for the dressing of a corpse; not a pair of clean white stockings, nor a white shirt. All she can offer is Holroyd's white cricketing shirt which her mother-in-law dismisses as 'a cold, canvas thing wi' a turn down collar'. No matter that the dead man will not feel its stiffness; the cricketing shirt is not the 'thing' for this occasion, and Charles Holroyd must got to his grave in his father's 'gear'. Unlike Lizzie, the mother-in-law knows all too well what is required on occasions like this, and it is a measure of her superior knowledge in such circumstances that she considers it 'right' to leave Lizzie alone in Blackmore's company while she is away fetching the clothes.

It is in this 'natural' absence of the mother-in-law that the encounter between Lizzie and Blackmore takes place. Their wishes have been fulfilled and Holroyd lies dead before them. As we watch the play it does not occur to us that the scene has been arranged or selected by dramatic connivance. Nor do we question the inner meaning which we read into the wife's failure to have put by the necessary grave clothes. It all, as has often been observed by spectators to the play 'falls perfectly naturally'. What else could be expected of a woman like Lizzie who has failed to bend to the constraints of her circumstances, but that she would be found wanting in matters that would be habitual to a woman who 'knew her place'? In the face of disaster too, old Mrs. Holroyd knows that there is no need to fear wagging tongues by leaving Blackmore to keep Lizzie company by the side of the dead body.

Though he is presented as shocked by the disaster, it is nevertheless made quite clear that Blackmore is able to see it as a release, while Lizzie, faced with the unequivocal fact of death, sees it as a judgement. Holroyd has been 'murdered' by their wishing him dead: 'He'd have come up with the others, if he hadn't felt—felt me murdering him', she maintains. Blackmore tries to assuage her guilt, but she cannot accept his comfort. In their turn Lizzie and Blackmore reach deadlock over an issue which they are unable to see in the same terms. Adamant Lizzie insists, 'I've killed him that's all.' Blackmore contradicts, 'No you haven't.' Lizzie repeats, 'Yes, I have.' Blackmore consoles 'We couldn't help it.' It is a pattern of dialogue that is child-like—recalling, as it does, the rhythm of the squabbles between Minnie and Jack—and it is this child-like quality which we are given to understand would underlie any future relationship between these two. Here the dead body of Holroyd lies before them as they, in Lawrence's own words, 'wrangle over it', but, even when Holroyd is in his grave, the terms of their fundamental disagreement must, we are made to feel, persist, undermining any mutuality that they may have hoped to find.

Unable to face the thought of being left alone with the corpse, Lizzie inclines to let Blackmore stay with her, but it is not as a lover that she wants him by her. It is to herself that she speaks when she admits, 'I don't love him. Now he's dead. I don't love him. He lies like he did yesterday.' But when Blackmore begins to take up the implications of Holroyd's death, Lizzie overcomes her fears and sends him away, to return—perhaps—tomorrow. In the ambiguity of this parting there can be no certainty about what will happen between these two, except that whatever does happen will inevitably be shaped by Lizzie's sense of responsibility for Holroyd's death. The parallels between this parting and the parting at the end of Act II are made inescapable by the form of the play. The day of Lizzie's departure with Blackmore is once again indefinitely postponed.

Left alone on the stage with the body Lizzie stoops down to sponge the dead man's face, overcoming her fear and guilt as she performs this last office for the man whom she now bitterly and impotently regrets never having been able to love enough in life. Lizzie's soliloquy is at once the emotional climax to this deeply moving play and a perfect example of Lawrence's mastery of naturalism. Unquestionably this 'keening' over the body is accepted by an audience as what would 'actually happen' in such a situation in life. The newly bereaved widow talks quite naturally to the husband to whom she could not voice her deepest feelings when he was alive and able to respond to them. Yet, in this natural outpouring of grief we are also given the dramatic crux of the play. The sub-text comes to the surface and binds together the reading between the lines that we have been making all along:

> I never loved you enough—I never did. What a shame for you! It was a shame. But you didn't—you didn't try. I *would* have loved you—I tried hard. What a shame for you! It was so cruel for you. You couldn't help it—my dear, my dear. You couldn't help it. And I can't do anything for you, and it hurt you so!

There is an absolution for Lizzie as her tears fall on the face of the dead man, and 'suddenly she kisses him'. Holroyd was the children's father; Lizzie too late regrets that she wasn't good to him. But 'things aren't fair'; almost inevitably they 'went wrong'. Lizzie understands that there is no one to blame for what has happened. Her guilt leaves her and she is unafraid.

When Holroyd's mother returns, there is a sympathy between

the two women that there had not been before. Together they complete the 'laying out' of the body, remembering as mother and wife those things about Holroyd that had endeared him to them; his 'rare smile', his white skin. Only when they come to the broken, bloody hands does Lizzie quail back in horror. The mark of his suffering at the very last is almost too much to be borne, but, bending her once proud neck to the inevitable, she continues with her last, ritual duty as a wife.

At peace with her inner strife, Lizzie finds the strength to join with Holroyd's mother in the deep and touching grief of the play's final moments which, in their dreadful submission to the reality of death, have a genuinely tragic stature. Here too we notice how firmly the play remains within the naturalistic frame. The ending of the play has been compared to a '*pietà*', and its ritual, emblematic quality is indeed striking. But, for all its dramatic power, we feel that neither of the women says or does anything that might not have been said or done on such an occasion in life, and we are made to forget for the moment that we are accepting the reality of this life on trust. Few members of an audience to this play are likely to have experience of an occasion just like the one presented, but this does not at all disturb spectators' conviction that it is 'authentic'. Even the practical concern shown by the women for the preparation of the body before it stiffens is subsumed in this 'authentic' atmosphere of human sorrow.

It is not, of course, by accident that this impression is created. Here again we can plainly see that Lawrence has not merely recorded an episode from life as a passive 'observer', but has actively and positively selected just those details from such an episode that will create the desired dramatic effect. The references to Holroyd's physical attractions; the last shock of guilt administered to Lizzie at the sight of Holroyd's torn hands; her weeping resignation as she pulls off the dead man's boots, are among the small touches that contribute to the overall effect of this dramatic design. In them, we are inescapably reminded of Lizzie's admission to Blackmore that she once cared for Holroyd; of her bravery in defending her husband from the rat; and of her reluctance to fetch Holroyd's slippers at a time when she might more rewardingly have submitted to serving him. It is not life as we ourselves know it, to which we respond as real as we feel the authenticity of this play, but life as Lawrence's whole shaping of the play has convinced us it actually is, in a self-contained world which conditions even the innermost feelings of the people within it. Only by examining that whole shape are we able to see that the apparently inevitable 'facts of life'—and death—contained within it, are deliberately and carefully chosen out of all the possible details that could, in the light of such a situation, have been seen as equally appropriate to an 'actual' situation in life.

As a result of this skilfully achieved natural effect, we accept that there is no requirement to allot praise or blame; to identify heroes or villains. We have, quite simply, to accept that this is how it actually was for Lizzie and Charles Holroyd. And we do so willingly, not just because (as is obviously true) such accidents are still a part of life in mining communities, but because we have been made to see the relationship between milieu and character as interdependent throughout the play. The question of whether Lizzie can escape with Blackmore, which has appeared to engage our attention, is shown, at the end, to be irrelevant. What we have been directed all along to examine is the deeper conflict in Lizzie Holroyd's heart between her loathing of the surface of the life she has chosen and her knowledge that, having chosen it, she must see it through.

It is at this level that we recognise the futility of abstract values or moral judgements. As Lawrence wrote in his essay on 'Morality and the Novel', 'Everything is true in its own time, place and circumstance, and untrue out of its own place, time, circumstance. If you try to nail anything down, in the novel, either it kills the novel, or the novel gets up and walks away with the nail.'[3] That essay was written in 1925. Much earlier in his career, Lawrence was able to achieve in his naturalistic plays what he later stated as an ideal for the novel. By creating a context, powerfully convincing in its reality of time, place and circumstance, he convinces us, in the 'colliery' plays too, of the truth to life of the characters whom he portrays within it.

It has been said that the naturalist mode of drama was a limitation upon Lawrence, and that he was more fully able to exercise his creative imagination in narrative fiction. The short

[3] 'Morality and the Novel', *Phoenix*, p. 528.

story *Odour of Chrysanthemums* is pointed to as evidence of this comparative constraint.[4] Yet it seems that such a comparison, weighted in favour of the short story, does less than justice to Lawrence's gift for exploiting the full potential of dramatic form. What is *described* so accurately and sensitively in the short story is, as we have seen, replaced in the play by an equally accurate and sensitive account, given in the form of stage action. The incident with the rat and the intrusions of the children in Act I; the fight between Blackmore and Holroyd in Act II; and the reverent washing of the body in Act III are among the major elements of this dramatic form which enact for us the underlying stresses of a complex situation. We lose nothing in the telling in either form.

Powerfully repudiating the myth that 'nothing happens'[5] in Lawrence's naturalist plays, *The Widowing of Mrs. Holroyd* provides us with a dynamic account of a breaking marriage, savagely shattered by a death which provides no solutions. Above all this play demonstrates beyond a shadow of doubt Lawrence's gift for *creating* a dramatic form that actualises emotion in the context of a life which strikes us as 'bitingly true'. So subtle and unobtrusive is this form that, in performance, we notice only the natural flow of life. Lizzie's drudging toil; the children's 'natural' curiosity; even Blackmore's attentions to Lizzie and Holroyd's drunken exploits, seem to us simply a record of how these people actually lived. Only when we come to look closely at the text, do we see how the more inward and underlying emotional and psychological pattern is integrally woven into the surface texture of life. It is a triumph of naturalism, surely, to

[4] Of the ending of *The Widowing of Mrs. Holroyd*, Raymond Williams, for example, writes: 'It is an experience that the play can represent only obliquely: by the silent product of the action. The story is so much stronger, in this last crisis, that there is hardly a comparison; it moves into a different world.' (*Drama from Ibsen to Brecht*, Pelican Edition, p. 295). Though Dr. Williams feels, in certain clearly defined respects, that *Odour of Chrysanthemums* is 'so much stronger' than the play, he is not, however, at all dismissive of Lawrence's strengths as a dramatist, to which he does persuasive justice in his chapter on Lawrence in *Drama from Ibsen to Brecht*, pp. 292–296, and in his introduction to *Three Plays by D. H. Lawrence* (Penguin: Harmondsworth, 1969) pp. 7–14.

[5] Critics of Lawrence's drama in production—whether they like the plays or not—frequently comment that 'nothing happens' in them.

have persuaded generations of critics of the play on the page, and at least one generation of spectators in the theatre, to feel that this play (in which most of what happens is, in fact, potentially so melodramatic) is characterised by the way in which it seems not to have been dramatised at all.

4

The Daughter-in-Law

So far as time of writing goes *The Daughter-in-Law* remains the most mysterious of Lawrence's plays. There is no record of his ever having mentioned it by name, and there is therefore no way of being certain whether it was among the first three 'colliery' plays, written by the summer of 1911, or whether it was the play about which Lawrence wrote to Garnett in the January of 1913. In that letter Lawrence wrote, 'I am going to send you a new play I have written. It is neither a comedy nor a tragedy—just ordinary. It is quite objective, as far as that term goes, and though no doubt, like most of my stuff, it wants weeding out a bit, yet I think the whole thing is there, laid out properly planned and progressive. If you don't think so I am disappointed.' (CL p. 175) The letter continues with the expression of delight in writing the plays that 'come so quick and exciting from the pen,' already quoted in support of Lawrence's enjoyment of dramatic form, and continues, with a plea to Garnett '. . . you mustn't growl at me, if you think them waste of time. At any rate they'll be stuff for shaping later on, when I'm more of a workman.' No more is heard of the play that Lawrence here says he is 'going to send' to Garnett. In view of the latter's dismissive rejection of *The Merry-go-Round*, *The Married Man* and *The Fight for Barbara*, all of which plays he returned to Lawrence in the February of 1913, it is possible that Lawrence decided, after all, not to send the play. His own description of it as 'neither a comedy nor a tragedy—just ordinary' has, however, been felt to be appropriate to *The Daughter-in-Law* since the rediscovery and first publication of the play in *The Complete Plays of D. H. Lawrence* in 1965.[1]

[1] See Keith Sagar, 'D. H. Lawrence: Dramatist', *The D. H. Lawrence Review*, Vol. 4, No. 2, Summer 1971, p. 173.

It has also been suggested that the writing of this play belongs to a much later stage in Lawrence's career,[2] evidence for this supposition being based, among other things, on the similarity between its subject matter and that of the short story *Fanny and Annie*. First published in *Hutchinson's Magazine* in 1921, and subsequently included in the following year in the collection of stories *England My England*, the story (which, in any case could well have been a re-casting of an earlier version) treats the theme of hypergamous marriage in a very different tone from that of the 'high' naturalism of *The Daughter-in-Law*.

A version of the play, adapted for production by Walter Greenwood[3] was presented in London in 1936 under the title of *My Son's My Son*, but the first record of a typescript of the play as we now know it occurs in F. Warren Roberts' *Bibliography of D. H. Lawrence* (1963), and it is from this typescript of 106 pages, now in the possession of the library of the University of California, that the version in the *Complete Plays* was made.

In the present state of our knowledge about this play, the actual

---

[2] By, for example, James G. Hepburn in the *Book Collector*, Vol. 14, Spring 1965, pp. 78–81. Mr. Hepburn's suggestion is based on the fact that the TS. in the library of the university of California is stamped 'Curtis Brown'. Concluding that 'this apparently indicates that it comes from a much later date than the presumed date of original composition, Brown succeeding James B. Pinker as Lawrence's literary agent only late in Lawrence's career', Mr. Hepburn overlooks the fact that Curtis Brown was also the agent for Walter Greenwood, whose version of the play was produced in 1936.

[3] In a note to his essay, 'D. H. Lawrence: Dramatist', Keith Sagar records: 'After Lawrence's death someone found in a box in an attic in Vienna or Berlin the typescript of two complete acts and the draft of a third act of a play of his called *My Son's My Son*. This is, in fact, the play we now know as *The Daughter-in-Law*. The typescript came into the hands of a theatrical manager Mr. Leon M. Lion who invited Walter Greenwood to complete the third act, which he did.' (p. 181) If this had indeed been the case, one might wonder about the origins of the complete typescript, now known as Lawrence's, from which the version of *The Daughter-in-Law* in *The Complete Plays of D. H. Lawrence* (1965) was taken. In fact, however, Walter Greenwood's version of the play was an adaptation of the complete typescript, not a completion of some other typescript, as is suggested by Dr. Sagar's note. The unpublished Prompt Copy of *My Son's My Son* (as produced in London in 1936) is now among the papers of Walter Greenwood in the library of the University of Salford.

date of composition can therefore only be a matter of conjecture. What is most important about it from the point of view of a study of Lawrence's drama is its particularly powerful exploitation of the naturalist mode that we have seen in operation in *A Collier's Friday Night* and *The Widowing of Mrs. Holroyd*, and it was no doubt by virtue of its affinity with those plays that Peter Gill chose it as the first to receive full-scale production in his revival of Lawrence's drama.

Although Gill had reached a small and appreciative audience with his Sunday night production of *A Collier's Friday Night* two years earlier, it was with this production of *The Daughter-in-Law* (again at the Royal Court Theatre, London) in March 1967 that the Lawrence revival can really be said to have begun. Some critics saw in it a treatment of the sex war theme reminiscent of Strindberg's; others, a statement about the conditions of work that led to the first national coal strike in England in 1912. All, however, agreed that the most impressive feature of the production was its fidelity to life; its almost uncannily 'realistic' recreation of a time and place and circumstance, far removed from the everyday life of a theatre audience in the late 1960s, yet close enough to their instinctive feelings about what life is actually like to impress them with the way in which the play authentically represented issues of life, not only as it was in its own time and place, but as it 'actually is' here and now.

It was not for its documentary accuracy that the play was recognised as a 'masterpiece of naturalism', but for its rendering of a truth about life that was felt to be much deeper and more universal than the particularities with which it so convincingly dealt. Again we may notice the tribute to what has been called Lawrence's poetic realism; a term coined by Desmond MacCarthy in connection with *The Widowing of Mrs. Holroyd*, and one that well expresses Lawrence's way of conveying, by means of dramatic form and action, an undercurrent of emotional and psychological truth beneath the meticulously depicted minutiae of surface reality.

In *A Collier's Friday Night* and *The Widowing of Mrs. Holroyd* we have noticed the way in which an everyday domestic activity has been used to give the play a structural unity; a firm dramatic shape securely binding form and content to the realities of our common experience of life. The baking of bread and the washing of clothes have been seen not merely to enlist our superficial belief in the reality of the people we see baking and washing but, in a poetic sense, as dynamic images of their real inner lives; of the family bond between Mrs. Lambert and her son, and of the conflicts in the marriage of Lizzie and Charles Holroyd. In *The Daughter-in-Law* the everyday concern which functions in a similar way to the baking and the washing is the use—and misuse—of money, and the play is structured against a pattern of earning and spending. In a sense this is a less obvious (though equally material) everyday concern which does not appear at first sight to offer the rhythm of process so admirably supplied by the cycles of the baking bread or the drying clothes; a rhythm which so well accompanies and underlines the emotional patterns of *A Collier's Friday Night* and *The Widowing of Mrs. Holroyd*.

Yet we will see that Lawrence has found a way of integrating the spending and earning of money into a compelling ground bass for this play which has so much to do with material survival; with the conflict between master and man, and with the parallel struggle for possession that goes on between mother and son, mother and daughter-in-law and husband and wife.

In the long opening scene of Act I, we find that this concern about money threads its way through a range of human relationships with the examination of which the play as a whole is concerned. Joe Gascoigne has suffered an accident at work. His mother is anxious that he should receive compensation for his injury. Joe, however, believes that he will not get paid out because the injury occurred while he was 'playing about' in the pit. Though, strictly speaking, he was 'at work' at the time, he was not actually working, but playing. Here, at the very beginning of the play a crucial distinction is made between what is measurable in terms of money and what is not.

A further measure according to this scale is made by Mrs. Purdy, whose daughter Bertha has casually been made pregnant by Luther, Joe's newly married brother. Luther's 'sin' can, however, be redeemed at a price of £40—the going rate for such matters in this community where everything has its price, as has already been illustrated by the fact that compensation for Joe's broken arm depends on whether he was working or playing at the time when he broke it.

Negotiating for her daughter's 'compensation', Mrs. Purdy calculates that 'we're poor an' she's poor—an' if she had a bit of money of 'er own—for we should niver touch it—it might be a inducement to some other young feller—' A bridegroom, we gather, could be bought, even for the 'fallen' Bertha with her bastard child.

Mrs. Gascoigne calculates too when she reckons that Luther's new bride should pay up on his behalf. 'She's paid for nothing but the wedding. She's got money enough if he's none. Let *her* find it. She's made the bargain and she maun stick by it.' We know by this time that Mrs. Gascoigne bitterly resents her daughter-in-law's 'superior airs' and feels that she should be taken down a peg or two. Here is the perfect opportunity; perfect because it will cost Minnie some of the money with which Mrs. Gascoigne feels that her son has been 'bought' away from her into marriage.

Joe objects. He sees things as bad enough already between his brother and sister-in-law. He thinks at once of emotional conflicts that cannot simply be settled by cash bargaining. But he has no 'right' to an opinion because he has failed to win compensation for his broken arm, and is, like a baby, dependent on his mother's ten shillings a week club money and on her decision not to allow him to pay his brother's debt with money that he himself has earned and given to her to save for him. As Mrs. Gascoigne presents it, the case is clear-cut and simple: Mrs. Purdy and her daughter have a right to compensation, and it is Luther and his wife who must settle the debt. Joe's money will not 'do', since it is not his child that Bertha is carrying.

Behind all these personal transactions we feel the consistent pressure of the impending strike. Aligned as they are on the side of their men against the 'mesters', both Mrs. Gascoigne and Luther's wife, Minnie see nothing to be gained by the strike. Both, in fact, are seen to regard it as an excuse for slacking, as the older Mrs. Gascoigne does in this first scene when she mutters, 'Strikes a' they're fit for—a pack o' slutherers'. Later we will hear Minnie use the same dialect word for hasty, careless workmen, and, in her mouth the word will take on an even more insulting connotation since she is usually so much more refined in her speech. And it will be by linking connections such as this that we will build up a picture of the life lived by these people in their relations with each other.

By comparing the issues which divide mother and son and husband and wife, we see the closeness of the interaction between working life and personal relationships, as it is presented by the form of the play. We see in action human bonds, potentially loving and caring, being severed by external considerations. Masculinity becomes equated with a capacity to work and do the job well. Wages are seen by wives and mothers as the share of the owners' profits that their men are *fit* to earn. To strike is to opt out of this system, not only causing hardship in the family, but also by un-manning the men, by separating them from the toil which is the outward sign of their manliness.

In this opening scene we see the ground plan for the emotional conflict which will provide the play with its strong, central situation; the challenge to the marriage of Minnie and Luther, set up by the antagonism of old Mrs. Gascoigne. To this situation the strike is, of course, not central, but peripheral; a context in which human effort is measured in terms of hard cash. Controlling the Gascoignes and determining the ways in which they think and feel—as well as, in material terms, determining their way of life—the relation between the pit and its workers; between masters and men, represents a world in which human values are measured against a material scale. Suffering has a set price and so does 'happiness'. A pound a week should pay for a pit injury; forty pounds of Minnie's inheritance should buy her the marital harmony that she 'bargained' for.

The play then is evidently not merely a statistical document of the relation between capital and labour. We do not abstract these material circumstances from the human pattern to make of them some socio-political 'theme'. It is presented simply as a fact of life that the colliers must work; that their work is hard and dangerous; and that they must contend with their employers in order to earn a decent living. The play persuades us very firmly of this over-riding necessity by showing its repercussions at the level of the relationships between men and women. It does not persuade us of this reality, however, in order to concentrate our attention on the Capital v. Labour issue, but to direct our interest to the way in which the system conditions modes of thought and feeling in the personal and emotional lives of people confined within it.

91

Because the play persuades us of the reality of the system, we refer to the values it represents when we interpret the behaviour of individual characters. In the pit the men barter life and limb for a wage on which to survive. In the home of the Gascoignes, love between mother and son, and between husband and wife, is measured out in pounds, shilling and pence. It is against this background that we, as audience to the play, measure and understand character in our turn.

For this reason we attach a great deal of importance to the strikingly different appearance of the kitchen furnished by young Minnie Gascoigne from that of her mother-in-law. Presented in the opening scene of the play, old Mrs. Gascoigne's kitchen establishes a standard for the audience of what a collier's kitchen should 'actually' look like. It is not poor, but it is plain: 'Windsor chairs, deal tables, dresser of painted wood, sofa covered with red cotton stuff.' As Scene 1 unfolds the kitchen becomes even more deeply impressed upon our perceptions as the normal and proper home setting for people like these; people whose lives are seen to be so intimately bound up with the material concerns of the community that encircles them.

We have been told that Minnie is superior and 'different' and that she has spent her money on 'nowt b'r old-fashioned stuff' which her mother-in-law condemns as unserviceable. When we see her kitchen, we actually experience the material quality of her 'difference'. Sharply contrasted with that of her mother-in-law, Minnie's kitchen identifies her as a misfit in the neighbourhood. The way in which she has tried to fit the environment to herself, rather than adapting herself to it, is manifest in the stage directions for Scene 2 which tell us that her kitchen is 'pretty— in "cottage" style; rush-bottomed chairs, black oak bureau, brass candlesticks, delft etc.' It will be noted that Lawrence had confidently selected here just those details which will define the precise kind of Minnie's 'good taste' in contrast to the conformity to the prevailing local mode of her mother-in-law's. Evidently the set designer must play an important part in making the distinction clear by following the directions to the letter, but we will also see—in Minnie's reactions to the pit-dirt in which Luther was accustomed to sit down to dinner at home, in her distress when Joe breaks one of her new dinner plates, and in Mrs. Purdy's comments when she visits the newly-weds—that the distinction is integrally 'written in' to the text, and would show up even if the play were produced, as *A Collier's Friday Night* originally was, without décor. We notice that Minnie is anxious for her husband's return, and, as she almost collides with him on the doorstep, we register—particularly in a full-dress production—how incongruous a figure he appears in this attractive setting, dressed in his working gear and begrimed with pit dirt.

In haste as she is to serve the meal, Minnie objects to Luther's sitting down without first washing, though he protests that 'there's scarce a collier in a thousand washes hissen afore he has his dinner. We niver did a' whoam'. Even without visual direction then, we would be made aware of the contrast between Luther's old home and his new, and would make the same interpretations of its importance to the relationship of the newly-weds. We would notice here too that this contrast in styles is not necessarily specific to colliers, but is a common source of disagreement between mothers and daughters-in-law in all times and places. By so doing we are making just those generalisations from the particular life that we are shown in the play that the mode of presentation is designed to direct us to make, and we continue to read these interpretations into the interplay that follows between the specific couple on stage. Protesting that it doesn't 'look nice' Minnie nevertheless makes a concession to Luther's habitual practice and he concedes in turn to his pretty wife's feelings by spreading newspaper on the green-cushioned armchair before sitting down in it.

Like Lizzie Holroyd in the remembered early days of her marriage, Minnie is seen here to be passionately attracted to her husband; to the bright red mouth in his black face and to the manliness that arouses her and overcomes her crossness at the mess he makes of her tidy kitchen and neatly laid table. Luther 'doesn't look nearly such a tame rabbit' in his pit dirt. Like this he is a man who works for a wife and home, not a 'mother's boy'. Like the mother-in-law whose company she avoids, Minnie, however, also disapproves of the threatened strike. In her view the men have 'no need' to complain. It is the fault of thin seams, not of the company that wages are falling. Again we are told that to these women striking seems synonymous with slacking. They see manhood in terms of good workmanship, and Luther's failure to rise to the rank of butty man in the pit hierarchy is equated by his wife with his failure to get free of his mother's apron strings rather than with any mis-management on the part of the owners of the pit.

Luther has said that the men are striking for a 'proper scale'. Here the play tells us that the womenfolk have their own scale by which a man is measured and, in Luther's case, found wanting. The differences between husband and wife which had at first seemed capable of being overcome by mutual attraction, loom large when the subject of the strike is raised, and we see that Minnie assesses Luther's manhood in terms both of his inadequacy at work and of his dependence on his mother.

It seems that it cannot be long in this household before the marriage founders, as Minnie's 'unsuitable' high standards clash with Luther Gascoigne's ingrained habits—as was the case with the Holroyds. After Holroyd's death, we saw Lizzie regretting her failure to adapt to her milieu, and realising that it is impossible to keep up the fight against hopelessly superior odds. In this play, Minnie will learn to make a kind of compromise, though not—as we shall see—without a re-alignment of her and her mother-in-law's allegiance on the side of their menfolk against their conditions at work.

Minnie's resentment of her mother-in-law's domination of Luther is at this point, however, as bitter as Mrs. Gascoigne's against her newly acquired daughter-in-law. In the pretty kitchen we must see this as the central problem of the play. Act I Scene 2 has shown us the sexual passion that *could* unite Minnie and Luther, and has gone on to set this passion in the perspective of the contrary pull of older loyalties. The cosy atmosphere has become tense as husband and wife approach, by way of their opposition over the strike, the heart of their dispute, and Joe's entry finds them at the height of a furious argument, in which Minnie has flung out as her crowning insult, 'You aren't *fit* for a woman to have married, you're not', and added that she has only married Luther 'Because I could get nobody better'.

Adopting the role of peace-maker (as he had wanted to do by settling Luther's 'debt of honour'), Joe nevertheless teases Minnie cruelly where he knows it will hurt most by deliberately dropping and smashing one of her new plates. Luther takes over the peace-making role, but, when Joe—accidentally this time—smashes another plate, Minnie's frayed temper gets the better of her and she begins to sob. Both brothers remind her that the breakages are not serious; the plates can be replaced, but she will not be comforted, and, when Joe begs a kiss, she strikes out at his injured arm.

In this incident we learn how much Minnie's possessions mean to her. They are all that she has to bolster her pride, and she will not admit that she has married 'beneath' her, *not* for the sake of being married (as she protests she has), but in the hope of achieving a sexual harmony which her small inheritance does not appear to have been able to purchase. Sympathy for her high standards and impatience with Luther's attachment to his mother is here tempered by a glimpse of Minnie's own wilfulness and incomplete honesty to her own deepest desires.

Prejudiced as we have seen old Mrs. Gascoigne to be, perhaps she is not as far out as we had supposed in disapproving of the match. Where Mrs. Gascoigne was prepared to spoon-feed the injured Joe, we see Minnie lash out at him in anger because his clumsiness smashes her plates, and we understand why the men here look upon her rage as unfeeling and disproportionate to the occasion.

In the light of what the play goes on to tell us about the immorality of possessiveness in loving relationships, we are also disturbed by this revelation of frustrations deep at the roots of the antagonism between Minnie and Luther, and of the profound disappointment of sexual expectations that prompts Minnie's angry attack on the harmless Joe. Believing that she wants to own her man as she owns her plates and as her mother-in-law owns her sons, Minnie refuses to acknowledge her real need to give freely of herself to the husband with whom she has chosen to live her life. Luther's recognition of her failure will be shown later in the scene when he expresses a preference for the liberality with which Bertha Purdy surrendered to him, and the ambiguous resolution of the final scene of the play will itself depend on the degree to which we have been made to feel that both husband and wife will be able to succeed in giving themselves freely to each other without thought of domination or possession.

95

While the episode of the smashing of the plates has this dramatic effect in making us aware of these undercurrents, it is also strictly 'in character'. If we examine what we mean by this, we find that Joe's reality as a person consists in the way in which we come to understand the apparently 'natural' psychological motivation of his fictionalised personality because of the way in which we interpret his behaviour in relation to the setting in which we 'meet' him. If we had not been made to believe in the reality of that setting, and thence in the reality of the life dramatised in the play as a *whole*, Joe would not be as convincingly 'human' as we, in fact, find him to be. There is nothing therefore intrinsically 'real' about Joe, except as that reality relates to the world chosen for us to believe in in *The Daughter-in-Law*. Those features about the dramatic character of Joe that we take as constituting his reality are tied in to the world of material values which we see as conditioning the pattern of life in the play. Joe is 'human' because he is generous with money; because he cares less about material possessions than his sister-in-law or his mother; because he is the victim of the kind of justice which compensates for human suffering only when it is sustained at work, and not when it is sustained at play. Out of the total range of possible 'human' attributes we see therefore that the dramatist here selects precisely those which inter-relate with the fabric of his dramatic design. Joe does not seem real to us because we might expect to meet someone just like him in the course of our everyday lives, but because the patterning of the play persuades us to make our judgements of him in the same way as we make our judgements of people encountered in everyday life; that is to say by assessing his outward behaviour in relation to the objective reality around him. Joe's 'reality' therefore must be seen in terms of a relation—not as an absolute, and it is in this respect that his character is representative of the way in which *dramatis personae* are endowed with 'humanity' in plays which we can describe as being in the naturalist mode.

The effect of this kind of development of character in relation to the context in which it is set, can be felt in the response we make to the continuation of the Scene as a result of our identification with the 'human' strengths and weaknesses that it seems to reveal in relationships between people. Although Joe's trick has its cruel aspect, we understand that he is trying to lighten the atmosphere of the quarrel which he interrupted, and we are aware too that Minnie will fail to see the 'funny side' of his joke because we know how she, for her part, relates to the objective reality of her surroundings. It therefore appears perfectly natural and 'expected' that she should slam out of the house leaving the brothers alone together so that Joe can reveal to Luther the true purpose of his visit.

Discussing Luther and Minnie's marriage, Joe confidently asserts, 'By the Lord she'd cop it if I had 'er'. Like his ironically liturgical diction (as, for example, in 'dearly beloved let us weep; these our dear departed dinner plates', in which he calls attention to the difference between the mishap of a broken plate and the human tragedy of a broken marriage), Joe's threat of what he would do to Minnie if he were her husband is 'taken' as a mark of his youthful ability to see the brighter side of life and to try to make others look on their problems more objectively. At a deeper level it reflects his comparative freedom as a younger son from the dominance of the possessive mother that so crucially cripples Luther's manhood. At the plot level here, this contrast works in reminding us that Joe has, after all, come round to warn Luther of the trouble that is brewing for him, and that the dinner plate 'disaster' has, among other things, succeeded in getting Minnie out of the house before this trouble appears on the doorstep in the shape of Mrs. Purdy.

By that time too, Luther has heard the news and wishes himself dead: 'I wish a ton o' rock 'ud fa' on me to-morrer', he exclaims, but Joe has no time for such hyperbole, and sketches his plan for saving the situation by secretly lending Luther the necessary forty pounds. In contrast with the absolute seriousness of the death-wish in *Mrs. Holroyd*, a similar situation here is seen to be undercut by juxtaposition with the immediate practical exigencies of the situation. Significantly too Luther agrees that the details of the story can be kept from Minnie, but fears that the fact of his having 'been with' Bertha will come between his wife and himself, whether she finds out or not. So precariously adjusted is their sexual relationship that he recognises even an unacknowledged slip as a dangerous threat.

Mrs. Purdy is seen to be as relieved as Joe that she does not

have to break her news to Minnie. We see her react politely to the
'natty' kitchen, but note her reservation, 'It's uncommon, very
uncommon, Mester Gaskin—and looks well too for them as likes
it. But it hardly goes with my fancy.' She is more concerned with
the question of who might have sat before her on the second-
hand chairs than with the half naked Luther who dries himself at
the fireside and allows her to tidy up his pit gear as if she were
his own mother. These two are clearly familiar with the same way
of life, to which Minnie is—so conspicuously—a stranger. During
the talk that they have alone, Luther admits that he might well
have been happier married to Bertha; a girl of his own kind who
thought a lot of him and 'wor better to me than iver my wife's
been'; a girl, moreover, who has proved the manhood that Minnie
doubts in becoming pregnant by him. Comparing the docile,
admiring Bertha to the haughty fault-finding Minnie, Luther
bitterly regrets having married the latter as she returns with Joe.

Her business done, Mrs. Purdy leaves, politely declining Minnie's
offer of hospitality. Minnie appears to have recovered from her
tantrum and is in a lively mood. We are directed to assume that
Joe has told her some lie about Mrs. Purdy's visit, and take it
that she suspects nothing. Comparing her behaviour to that which
we have seen earlier, we feel that she is unnaturally elated as she
flirts with Joe, lighting a cigarette for him and admiring his dark
eyes. Confused and jealous, Luther flings out, whereupon Minnie's
bright façade cracks and she sobs to Joe, 'You don't know how
hard it is with a man as—as leaves you alone all the time.' Her
heart and spirit are being broken by Luther's failure to trust her;
to give himself to her in love as she longs for him to do. But her
pride will not allow her to give him the sign that he too longs
to receive, and, putting a bright face on the matter, she sets off
with Joe for the cinematograph.

That her cheerfulness at the end of the previous Scene was only
assumed is confirmed for an audience as the curtain rises on
Act II with Minnie 'alone weeping'. Luther returns 'rather tipsy'.
Further apart in understanding than ever, husband and wife
antagonise each other into sleeping apart. As Minnie throws down
Luther's blankets and pillows onto the sofa, we feel the distance
between spoken and unspoken words in the defiant challenge of
her action. Luther wants Minnie to be as 'good' to him as Bertha

was; to yield herself to him physically with equal readiness. She, in turn, longs for him to be a man; to demonstrate that he has not married her merely for her money. We recall here the pleasure that she showed in the earlier scene when Luther admired her looks. But they are unable to give themselves freely to each other. He escapes into drink, and she demonstrates her disapproval by casting him out of her bed; the traditional tactic of the unsatisfied wife.

Coldly polite to each other, they go through their domestic chores each waiting for a sign of submission from the other. But the signs that are given are always the 'wrong' ones. Luther's offer to prepare his own food for the following day sparks off the quarrel that has been smouldering. Thinking that she has found out about Bertha, Luther misinterprets Minnie when she complains 'You do a woman wrong but you're never man enough to say you're sorry for it.' We know that the woman of whom she speaks is herself, but Luther's guilty conscience leads him to retort, 'Er wor nice wi' me, which is a thing tha's niver bin.' In turn Minnie misunderstands, believing that Luther is talking about his mother, and contemptuously harangues him with 'Pah! — you're not fit to have a wife. You only want your mother to rock you to sleep.'

Infuriated by this insult to his virility and inspired by his 'Dutch' courage, Luther speaks out to his wife, openly confessing—indeed boasting—of the mark of the manhood that Minnie accuses him of lacking as it is proved by the child that Bertha carries. 'I'm glad 'er's wi' my childt. I'm glad I did it. I'm glad! For tha's wiped tha feet on me enough,' he exults. The true reason for Luther's earlier sulks dawns on Minnie, and, in the interrogation, punctuated by silences, that follows, she draws the whole story from him. In those silences we read the adjustments that both have to make to a changed situation. Now that Luther has proved himself a man he does not have to feel so beholden to his 'superior' wife. In turn Minnie, who thought she had only her mother-in-law to contend with—realises that Luther can find sexual satisfaction in another woman. The fault for his failure with her may then be in herself, and she is forced to express her recognition of this failure in her intention to go back to her 'old place'. Totally misunderstanding this intention as a rejection of himself as a 'fitting' husband, Luther is driven even deeper into an attitude of hostility.

As observers of the play, we piece together these interpretations, while husband and wife piece together their versions of the story of Luther and Bertha from their opposed points of view. Luther is truculent—even triumphant. By his lights he has behaved 'decently' in making a clean breast of the matter as well as in being prepared to 'pay up' for his pleasure. Moreover, he refuses to accept his wife's money to pay off the debt and feels that he has been generous in trying to keep the whole matter from her. In her eyes the sin is not thus easily expiated. When he wrote saying that he was willing to marry her, Luther did so knowing that he had 'been with' Bertha. Pressing him for a further account of his sexual experience, Minnie retreats further into her habitual reserve. As they speak out more and more frankly to each other, we feel, in the undercurrents of their quarrel, that a great barrier of misunderstandings—which may well prove to be insurmountable—is being built up between them.

Luther deeply resents Minnie's doubts about his manhood. The unborn child proves to him that he is not the molly-coddled mother's boy she accuses him of being. He will show his wife that he is man enough for her by refusing her money and accepting her decision to leave him. She is just as concerned as he to keep pride intact. While she remains in the house, she will pay her own way—the ultimate insult to his manly responsibility in this world where men risk life and limb to provide the family income.

Minnie will not openly admit the jealousy and hurt that she is suffering as a result of Luther's having preferred Bertha Purdy to herself. Determined to hurt him as she has been hurt, she claws down Luther's precarious self-confidence by casting doubt on his paternity of Bertha's child. To her accusation that he is 'not a man' Luther retorts that there are 'plenty of women who would say I am' which she silences with the suspicion that these women must then be 'lying to get something out of you'.

At the point where the quarrel reaches its apparently most probing depths, we notice that neither Minnie nor Luther has spoken from the heart. From our point of view, that is to say, neither has voiced the thoughts which we have been made to feel are most relevant to their feelings. Despairing of a solution,

Luther reminds Minnie that, if she intends to leave, she had 'better go afore the strike begins', rousing in her the response that a strike would just suit his lazy, ineffectual nature. At this impasse in the situation Minnie raises her hand against Luther for accusing her of having already meted out to him the punishment he deserves. Impotently she rages, 'How *dare* you say so—oh how *dare* you! I'm too good for you!' to which he sullenly responds, 'I know.'

The apparently irreparable division between them is marked, as the Scene closes, by Minnie's lighting the candle that shows her the way alone to bed, while Luther flings himself down to sleep on the hearth-rug.

What we must visualise, in a reading of this crucial second Act of the play, is the way in which the text is designed so as to reveal in performance on the stage the contrast between Minnie and Luther's spoken and unspoken feelings for each other. On the surface they are being honest, and even brutally frank. But the dialogue and action are so intimately intertwined with each other, and with the truth to life of the setting, that we feel that we know even better than the participants themselves that the open hostility is only a mask for their hidden mutual desires.

Act III opens with Minnie *returning* to her house to find her mother-in-law alone in the kitchen. Though she suspects that something is 'amiss' between Minnie and Luther—who has not been to see her for two weeks—Mrs. Gascoigne is not aware that there has been an absolute breakdown in the marriage. The commotion of the strike, with its repercussions on the routine of daily life, together with the neighbours' word for it that Minnie has been away in Manchester 'on business', have combined to prevent her from enquiring very closely into the state of affairs in her son's home.

Serving the play's narrative consistency, this Scene provides an audience with the information that Minnie has been away for two weeks. During this time old Mrs. Gascoigne 'niver clapt eyes' on Luther, and, though her curiosity has been aroused sufficiently to question Joe about Luther's whereabouts, she had not thought to call on his wife. Unable to get a word out of Joe 'for love nor money' (a cliché which takes on a ring of new significance in this context!), Mrs. Gascoigne has eventually heard of Minnie's absence from neighbours, but still believes that her daughter-in-law has been away for only four days. Her first impulse, as we see, has been to take over the care of her married son.

Curiosity about the nature of Minnie's business in Manchester leads the mother-in-law straight to the topic of money, as she hints at the sum of forty pounds in an effort to discover whether her daughter-in-law's departure and return have anything to do with the Bertha Purdy affair. Minnie side-tracks the questioning, but comes up against further opposition when she reveals that she has stayed in Manchester with her former employer; a procedure disapproved of by the mother-in-law who feels that it is not becoming to the young bride to pour out her marital woes to a widower.

Minnie appears calm. The calm is baffling, within the play, to the mother-in-law, and even more so to the audience who have witnessed the scene of Minnie's marriage break-up and are eager to know why, having kept her word to Luther about leaving him, she has decided after all to return. Minnie's encounter, at the beginning of this Act, with old Mrs. Gascoigne serves the purpose of building up narrative suspense. In addition to this function, it works, as we have seen, to supply a limited amount of 'exposition' —just enough, in fact, to whet further curiosity—and also to underline the lack of communication between the two Mrs. Gascoignes.

With the arrival of Luther and Joe we again expect the answer to our question: why has Minnie returned? Indeed it is this question that Joe asks as soon as he sees her. 'Has thee come? . . . We thought tha'd gone for good,' he comments, but the following exchange of question and counter-question between Minnie and Joe enlightens only the mother-in-law about what has been 'amiss' between her son and his wife. It does not at all explain to us why, after all we have heard her say to Luther, Minnie has in fact returned.

Our curiosity about, and interest in, the nature of Minnie's business in Manchester, and the reason for her return, remains unsatisfied as the talk turns to the strike, and we again notice three levels at which this dramatic retardation functions. In the first place we learn—as do Minnie and her mother-in-law—what the men have 'actually' been doing. Naturalistically, this satisfies the women's curiosity, while confirming the audience's sense of a real world encompassing the lives of the characters in whom we are being asked to take a particular interest. Secondly, the 'real' issue of the strike serves, in the characters' view, to reflect the issues at stake between husband and wife. Thirdly, the digression obliquely reveals the underlying alliance between Minnie and her mother-in-law which we had noticed earlier in their reactions to talk of the strike in Act I Scenes 1 and 2. Far apart as these two women are in so many ways, they are of one mind in regarding the strike as a foolish 'game'. Moreover we see that, when Luther identifies the strike situation at work with Minnie's strike against her obligations at home, Mrs. Gascoigne refuses to take over the running of her son's marital home, and insists 'if ter wants owt tha mun come to *me*'. Since the women are adamant and, for once, united, Joe threatens to bring in a local girl to look after Luther; a girl who will function as 'blackleg' in the home strike situation.

Left together with her son and daughter-in-law, Mrs. Gascoigne takes up again the line of questioning that most interests both her and us. What is the extent of the trouble between Minnie and Luther? What did Minnie do in Manchester? Why has she come back? Here Mrs. Gascoigne re-aligns herself with her son. Luther demands to know why Minnie has come back to live with him after saying that she no longer could, and he implies that, even before her departure, she had not been 'living with' him as a wife.

Mrs. Gascoigne accuses Minnie of having brought the problem on her own head by her delay in agreeing to marry Luther, and this provokes her daughter-in-law's counter-accusation that Luther has been made incapable of being a 'proper' husband by his mother's having 'kept him like a child'. When the mother retorts 'If you made as good a wife to him as I made a mother, you'd do', we are brought to the crux of the antagonism between the two women. Their views of the man-woman relation are fundamentally opposed, just as we have seen their views on such externals as the furnishing of their homes to be. Mrs. Gascoigne's standpoint represents the traditional view of a woman in this particular community; Minnie's the view of an 'outsider'.

Between these two extremes Luther 'naturally' allies himself with the familiar point of view of his mother, agreeing with her when she claims never to have 'mollycoddled and marded' him. Minnie maintains that, though she may not appear to have spoilt her son in obvious ways, Mrs. Gascoigne has nevertheless 'told him what to do and he did it'. Striking out furiously against the possessive mother, the daughter-in-law rejects the namby-pamby who 'waits on' her 'hand and foot' and gives her 'a free hand in everything' declaring that she would rather have a 'husband who knocked me about than a husband who was good to me because he belonged to his mother'. 'He doesn't and can't *really* care for me,' she concludes. 'You stand before him. His *real* caring goes to you. Me he only wants sometimes.'

Minnie's need for Luther's 'real caring' is underscored by her threat to leave 'for good' if the girl Joe brings to care for the house crosses the threshold, and Luther's obedience to his mother's command to go and stop the girl enacts the truth of Minnie's claim that 'His mother's word is law to him.' Enlisting Joe's bachelorhood and his willingness to flirt with married women as further evidence in her case against the cripplingly possessive mothering of Mrs. Gascoigne, Minnie wins Joe's support. 'Nay mother, tha knows it's right,' he agrees. 'Tha knows tha's got me—an'll hae me till ter dies—an' after that—yi.'

Hearing Joe speak out to his mother in this way is a victory for Minnie, as is Luther's dismissal of the 'blackleg' house-keeper, and she more generously persuades her mother-in-law to change her mind and stay when the latter, crestfallen, turns to go.

In the heat of the emotional storm the characters in the play have been diverted (as, consequently, have we the audience), from the question of what Minnie did in Manchester. With the return of talk of the strike, and of the hardship it will cause, Minnie delivers her bombshell news. She has spent the hundred and twenty pounds that had represented her superiority over Luther. 'I was sick of having it between us. It was but a hundred and twenty. So I went to Manchester and spent it.'

The placing of this announcement effectively surprises us—as it does Mrs. Gascoigne, Luther and Joe—by having been held back throughout the scene. Delivered here, when the matter appears to have been 'forgotten' under pressure of more central issues, it forcefully re-directs attention to the central dramatic situation; the *value* to Minnie and Luther of the relationship that might develop between them.

Reducing herself financially to his level, Minnie dramatically demonstrates her willingness to enter that relationship on equal terms. We notice here that her action is 'dramatic' both within the real-life frame of the play *and* in its theatrical effect upon the audience. It is the combined force of these two senses of the dramatic which renders Minnie's action in spending her money, and her announcement of having done so, so powerfully influential in our response to the play. So powerful is it, that we are held back from realising at once that her gesture is incomplete. The ring and the prints are tasteful and beautiful—as well as having intrinsic value. They are then, as much a mark of Minnie's superiority as ever her money was. True, Minnie has been high-handed in ignoring the practical considerations of which her mother-in-law makes matters of such moment. But it is Luther's action in ramming the prints into the fire that emphatically rejects Minnie's bravado as a half measure.

As the prints blaze, and Minnie cries 'Ah! that's my ninety pounds gone,' she is indeed reduced to an equal footing with her husband who, in this fierce destructive action, shows himself at last capable of being the 'man' she had always wanted. Passionately throwing the ring at Luther to destroy with the prints, Minnie reveals also the extent of her attachment to the things that had kept her beyond Luther's reach. Impotent at this spectacle of 'wicked waste'—token moreover of her son's escape from her domination—Mrs. Gascoigne hastens away, bidding Luther, in a hollow echo of her former mastery over him, to do 'nowt as thee'd repent of', and reminding him that 'It's thy mother as axes thee', as she retreats with her one remaining son from the scene of her defeat.

Seen to be deposed here from the authority that she had exerted over her married son, Mrs. Gascoigne withdraws, leaving the couple to face the consequence of Luther's action in destroying the valuable prints, which physically embodied the material values according to which he had hitherto been conditioned to live. That there will be no easy path from this assertion of full independence to a loving relation between Minnie and Luther is expressed, as the Act closes, upon the silence between them and on Luther's evasion of the need to break that silence by going out of the room, and leaving Minnie, silent and alone, as the curtain falls.

Like Act II, Act IV opens with Minnie weeping. There has evidently been no reconciliation between husband and wife. There has, however, as we are told in the opening moments of this final Act, been a great change in the relation between mother-in-law and daughter-in-law since the climactic events of the preceding evening. Concern about Luther now brings Mrs. Gascoigne straight to Minnie—in sharp contrast with her having stayed away during the two weeks when, earlier, she had 'niver clapt eyes on him'. The conversation between the women tells us too that Minnie suspected Luther of following his mother home after his uncharacteristically manly outburst in burning the prints.

The women are drawn closer together as they realise that their men are serving a loyalty to the strike which both wife and mother oppose. In their fears for Luther's and Joe's safety, Minnie and Mrs. Gascoigne admit the underlying reasons for that opposition in the physical threat that it represents to their menfolk's safety. It is not entirely, as has formerly appeared to be the case, a matter of economic expediency that makes the women hostile to the strike, but a matter of life and death. Nor is it a question purely of loyalty to a cause outside their homes that attracts men to the dangers of striking but, in Mrs. Gascoigne's view at least, a question of the opportunity of deliberately running risks in order to spite their womenfolk.

The theme here, as in *The Widowing of Mrs. Holroyd* is the mastery of women by men; the necessity of such a relationship in the natural order of things. So vital is the dominance to a man, that he will go to the lengths of getting himself killed in order to assert his superiority over the woman. From her experience of a husband and six sons, Mrs. Gascoigne can assure Minnie that men are 'masters of us women when their dander's up, an' they pay us back double and treble'. Yet, for all the pain and suffering men cause, Mrs. Gascoigne would not have things otherwise: 'Th' world is made up of men for me, lass—there's only men for me. An' tha'rt similar.'

Young, and hopeful of a more equal partnership—even perhaps of retaining some measure of her 'superiority', Minnie protests,

'I'm sure it depends what you make of them.' But Mrs. Gascóigne doubts the possibility of bringing about any change. She has always tried to do her best for her lads, despite what Minnie has accused her of, earlier in the day. Moved by her mother-in-law's frankness, Minnie admits, 'I didn't mean it. I was in a rage,' and tries to comfort the older woman by pointing to her sons' affection for her; by praising the very devotion that she had earlier condemned.

In her turn Mrs. Gascoigne comforts Minnie. 'Tha' can hae Luther,' she concedes. 'Tha'lt get him and tha' can hae him.' Avowing her eagerness to her mother-in-law Minnie asks, 'Do you think I shall?' and is assured, 'He'll come to thee—an' think no more o' me as is his mother than 'e will o' that poker.' Minnie protests, but she is overruled by Mrs. Gascoigne's insistence, 'Yi—I know well—an' then that other.' Joe too will be lost to his mother when he takes a wife.

The centrality of this drawing-close in sympathy between the two women is set in focus here by the crisis of the strike which concurrently gathers outside. It is a time of danger in the 'real life' of the world invoked by the play, and, in the tension generated by the danger, the truth can 'naturally' be told.

We have therefore seen, in the heightened atmosphere of the crisis, an expression of the truth that the women believe to underlie a successful relationship between man and woman; one in which, by all means at his disposal—including the ultimate strategy of getting himself killed—a man will, and must, assert his mastery over a woman. Minnie will give assent to her mother-in-law's judgement in the matter, since, in the world in which she has chosen to live, it is the judgement which comes closest to the facts. Minnie has always wanted Luther 'at any price'. Her inheritance could not buy him, nor could the precious things on which she squandered her money. Now, even though she knows that it must mean submission to a life of 'trouble, pure and simple', she will learn to bend, as her mother-in-law has done, to the inflexible necessity of allowing Luther mastery over herself.

With Luther's return from the strike, we see the couple beginning to falter towards what the play has led us to feel is the only possible way in which they can achieve any kind of harmony.

There is no question of a moral choice. Merely an acceptance of what *must* be in life 'as it actually is' for this man and this woman. Slightly stunned, Luther ignores his mother and the incidents of the strike in his concern to assure Minnie that it 'worn't because I—I wor mad wi' thee that I didna come whoam.' In the final moments of the play, we see Mrs. Gascoigne's view of marriage beginning to be fulfilled, as Luther, child-like in his dependance on Minnie, begs her to 'Ma'e what tha can o' me.' They admit their mutual misunderstandings, and he hands himself over to her care, as she pleads, 'trust me—trust yourself to me. Let me have you now for my own', and he cries in release like a child, as the wife-mother, over whom he has won his victory, takes him in her arms.

If this was indeed the play that Lawrence referred to in the letter to Garnett, then he was perfectly right in claiming that, 'it is neither a tragedy nor a comedy—just ordinary. It is quite objective as far as that term goes. . . .' We are not asked to respond to the resolution of the play—inconclusive as it is—as a tragic submission to the inexorable force of circumstance, nor yet as a happy ending in which, as in the comedy genre, lovers are seen to be united. We are not even asked to give our approval to anything as binding as a unifying 'theme', since we are specifically *not* told that this way of life is absolutely right for all times, places and circumstances, but simply that it is the way in which these lives *may* find fulfilment.

Desmond MacCarthy wrote of *The Widowing of Mrs. Holroyd* that it was 'an early work of Mr. Lawrence's. Since then he has attempted to formulate directly his philosophy of sex relations, often to the detriment of his art for he has taken to preaching and obscure exposition.'[4] Whether or not one would want to agree with the criticism implied here of Lawrence's later 'preaching' style, or whether indeed one can be sure that *The Daughter-in-Law* is an 'early work', it can certainly be seen that both plays embody and enact their underlying themes with a conviction that arises out of their evocation of a concrete and substantial real world. At the end of *The Daughter-in-Law* we are moved neither by 'tragic' nor by 'comic' considerations, but by the

[4] *The New Statesman*, 18 December 1926, p. 310. See also Chapter II, note 13, above.

certainty that what we have encountered in the play is an experience of 'life as it actually is'.

In connection with all three of Lawrence's most purely naturalistic plays, but particularly in connection with *The Daughter-in-Law*, we notice that the dialogue is crucial among the dramatic devices upon which this impression, or effect, of real life can be shown to depend. Always oblique, this dialogue directs us to make connections between what is being said and the context in which it is spoken, in order to piece together a sub-textual meaning which we then take to be the 'real' meaning of the play. As he was later to do—notably in *Lady Chatterley's Lover*—Lawrence has, in *The Daughter-in-Law*, enlisted the linguistic barrier of dialect as a stylistic device in order to emphasise this direction. The 'unintelligibility' of the dialect makes us look elsewhere than to the spoken words for meaning. Its very obscurity and difficulty indicates to us that the words people use are less significant than the thoughts those words mask. We are required therefore, to enter fully into the world of the play, in order to interpret the words—as the characters do—in relation to their setting, and we have already seen, in connection with *A Collier's Friday Night*, how that setting is itself designed to make us see the world it represents from the point of view of the characters within it. The linguistic device of dialect is *also* used in *The Daughter-in-Law*, at a naturalising level in the play, to call attention to the surface difference between the more refined Minnie and her new family. Authenticating detail such as this, in the delineation of character, goes hand in hand with the purely linguistic tactic of using dialect to suggest that meaning is not necessarily inherent in what the characters say.

Considering the play empirically, we find that the naturalising technique works very well. While some of the lines in *The Daughter-in-Law* may appear to be 'in a foreign language', we find that there is no difficulty in understanding them if we read, as we are meant to, between dialogue and context in order to 'take' the characters' meaning. So we see that, as was the case with the objective reality of the baking in *A Collier's Friday Night* and the washing in *The Widowing of Mrs. Holroyd*, the 'realism' of the dialect in *The Daughter-in-Law* is not merely a naïve way of persuading us that this is how life really was in the homes of colliers back in the early years of this century, but an artistic and literary strategy for persuading us to enter into the life of the play; for making us work, along with the characters, in deriving meaning from all that we know about that life. Even more than Minnie, we are strangers to that life, and, like her, we must make a special effort to understand it on its own terms.

The more we examine the characters and their situation in these three plays, the more we realise that their powerful appearance of substantial human reality is an effect produced by a combination of such artistic techniques and devices, *not* a measure of the accuracy with which they have been 'observed from life'.

Before moving on to another aspect of Lawrence's drama, it is interesting to note the thematic consistency of these three naturalist 'colliery' plays. However uncertain the dates of composition of two of them may be, there is good reason in this consistency for producing them—as Peter Gill did—as a trilogy. Centrally they are all concerned with hypergamy; with the relation between a man and a woman in which the latter feels herself to be superior, and has to learn, in one way or another, to submit to the mastery of a man.

Although the arrangement may be contrary to the order in which the plays were written, it is nevertheless revealing to look first at *The Daughter-in-Law*, then at *The Widowing of Mrs. Holroyd* and finally at *A Collier's Friday Night*. In the first we see Luther and Minnie as the representative man and woman battling for supremacy over each other, and enabled by the external agency of the strike to come to a stage in their relationship where trust can be founded on the man's mastery of the wife-as-mother. From what we have been shown in this play of the fiery spirit of the woman, this can, however, be felt only as a first and tentative stage. Indeed one might feel that Minnie has been endowed with this very fieriness for the purpose of suggesting that she will not easily and immediately submit to her dominated role.

We meet Lizzie and Charles Holroyd at a further stage along the line; indeed, theirs is a line which comes to a tragic full stop. Charles Holroyd's accident certainly comes into the category of spiteful male strategies to achieve domination of the woman, of which Mrs. Gascoigne speaks in *The Daughter-in-Law*. Even without cross reference between the two plays we see, in *The Widowing of Mrs. Holroyd*, (the very title of which confirms this emphasis) that in dying Holroyd wins a victory over his wife, forcing her to ask where she went wrong, as he was unable to do in life. If, as Lizzie Holroyd had done, Minnie Gascoigne goes on trying to make a 'better man' of Luther, she will certainly antagonise his trust, and the child that Luther suggests they might have will then become the object of the love and aspiration formerly projected onto the husband.

This, at all events, is the situation we find in *A Collier's Friday Night*, where a Minnie Gascoigne or a Lizzie Holroyd has aged into a Mrs. Lambert; a woman who has never given up those ideas 'above her station' that prevent her from allowing her husband to be master in his own home. To an extent she has compromised, but we see very well that her life would be unbearable if it were not for the outlet for her hopes and her love that she finds in Ernest. And we see too how, like old Mrs. Gascoigne, she clings to this relationship in her inability to let Ernest love Maggie.

It would, of course, be all too easy to connect this theme with the facts of Lawrence's own life and with the problems of his own sexuality which he attributed to the over-close relationship with his mother. In so many other of his fictions, as well as in these three plays, Lawrence was concerned with the working out of this very problem. Indeed it has often enough been said that, in his life, Lawrence solved the problem by tackling it head-on and marrying the superior woman who, in his plays and novels, issues such a challenge to be overcome. While this line of comparison is undeniably interesting, it does not, as I have tried to show, have any real bearing on the way in which we respond to the naturalist plays as life-like—as if they were indeed documentary records of real life.

The life that we respond to as real in the plays is, as has been demonstrated, an effect wrought strictly out of a combination of several literary and dramatic strategies, devised, perhaps, as a response to difficulties encountered in the dramatist's own life, but having no further connection with that life from the point of view of *our* response, as audiences, to the plays.

Singly, or as a group, these plays are very much more than

accurately observed 'slices of life'. True as we find them to be to what we imagine—as a result of having seen or read them—to have been the actual reality of their own time, place and circumstance, we admire them most for the perfection with which they represent the naturalist mode, as it submerges the techniques of artistry in what appears to be a spontaneous rendering of 'life as it actually is'.

5

The Merry-go-Round

Of *The Merry-go-Round* there are few traces in Lawrence's letters, or in the memoirs of those who knew him between 1910 and 1913, during which period the play seems most likely to have been written. Disappointed with Garnett's indifference to *The Fight for Barbara*, which he had submitted with high hopes of approval in the October of 1912, Lawrence rather deferentially asks for the return of that play together with Garnett's reasons for disliking it. In the same letter he says also that he would like to have back '*The Merry-go-Round* and the other' which, in the light of Garnett's opinion of his plays, Lawrence dismisses as 'candidly impromptus', (CL p. 161) though whether he felt as modest about them as this term suggests is hard to tell. We may, however, be quite certain that the 'other' referred to in this letter is *The Married Man* which Lawrence thanks Garnett for returning, together with *The Merry-go-Round* and *The Fight for Barbara* in the February of 1913. (CL p. 181)

There is no evidence that Lawrence ever got around to re-casting and re-working these plays as he had said he would like to do when he asked Garnett to send them back to him. For the remainder of 1913 his dramatic concerns were confined to the re-vising of *Mrs. Holroyd*, on which he worked concurrently with the earliest versions of novels that were to become *The Rainbow*, *Women in Love* and *The Lost Girl*. Back in England where he and Frieda spent the war years, Lawrence made repeated attempts to recover the manuscript of the last named novel which, according to Richard Aldington, he had left 'with his wife's relations in Germany'[1] and was unable to retrieve until 1919. It seems more

[1] In his introduction to *The Lost Girl*, (Penguin Edition) p. 8.

than mere coincidence that the manuscripts of *The Fight for Barbara*, *The Married Man* and *The Merry-go-Round* were, according to Lawrence's bibliographer L. C. Powell, discovered together, complete and unpublished after Lawrence's death, in the attic of his sister-in-law Else in Heidelberg.[2] Unless the novel was left with some other German relative, it is difficult to understand why Lawrence went to so much trouble to retrieve that MS. while neglecting the plays, particularly as, in 1919, he was again interested in drama and was writing *Touch and Go*. The traditional view of Lawrence as being comparatively uninterested in drama must be credited with support by this omission, though we must also bear in mind that the plays had already been summarily dismissed as unsuitable for the stage by Lawrence's influential friend and adviser, Edward Garnett.

While external evidence is so scanty in regard to *The Merry-go-Round* and *The Married Man*, they have much in common with each other and with *The Fight for Barbara* in their ironically comic view of sexual relationships. Though *The Fight for Barbara* is based on what must have been an emotionally traumatic phase in the turbulent early life together of Frieda and Lawrence, it is nevertheless—as Lawrence himself describes it—a 'comedy', as indeed are *The Merry-go-Round* and *The Married Man*. Just as the 'colliery' plays can be seen to be linked in tone and theme, so too are these three satirical comedies on the theme of love and marriage.

It may seem scarcely credible that Lawrence could deal as dispassionately—even cynically—as he does with the final illness and death of Mrs. Hemstock in *The Merry-go-Round* while almost concurrently writing the harrowing account of his own mother's death as we find it in the sufferings of Paul and Mrs. Morel in *Sons and Lovers*. The nature and depth of Lawrence's relationship with his mother is so well documented that it hardly needs further comment here, yet, if a version of *The Merry-go-Round* was indeed completed before the summer of 1911, it would have to have been written between the December of 1910, when Lawrence's mother died, and the July of the following year. The question that has to be asked is whether he could have achieved the ironic

[2] L. C. Powell, *The Manuscripts of D. H. Lawrence: A Descriptive Catalogue* (Los Angeles, 1937), p. 43.

detachment from the recent personal tragedy necessary for the portrayal of Mrs. Hemstock in the play. When we see Harry Hemstock's confusion and grief; the poignancy of his feelings close by the graveyard, and the fierceness of his anger when the will is wrenched from the bed-post of his newly dead mother, we feel that the achievement of the apparent detachment is not only possible but likely. The ambivalence in the play; its swift changes of mood and tone, could indeed be accounted for by the very ambivalence of the dramatist's feelings at the time of writing—though, as always, one would want to qualify any too easy assumptions of a connection between art and life.

Bearing such qualifications in mind, it does, however, seem characteristic of this group of Lawrence's plays that they portray situations, that we feel to have been experienced in life, in a particularly cool and formal manner. The experience appears to be held at arm's length, captured, as it is, in a pattern which imposes ordered clarity upon the chaos of the real-life situations out of which we suppose the works of dramatic literature to have arisen. This, as we will see, is certainly the case with *The Fight for Barbara*, written in the October of 1912 in the very midst of those events which many of Lawrence's biographers value it only for portraying.[3] Lawrence, the writer, could evidently stand back from his own personal involvement in events of great moment and render them deftly into art—especially, it would appear, into dramatic art of a particular tragi-comic genre.

It is also relevant to remember that, deeply affected as he was by his mother's death, Lawrence in a sense felt liberated by it from an influence that was almost too overpowering. In the 'colliery' plays this feeling that the relationship with an idolised mother overpowered him is transmuted, as we have seen, into portrayals of domineering and inordinately possessive mothers who wreck their sons' sex lives. Lawrence's ambivalent feelings towards his father have also been seen to have received a fairer showing in those naturalistic plays, in which the father figure is

[3] In his biography of Frieda Lawrence, Robert Lucas, for example, writes, 'As a form of relaxation (from the writing of *The Rainbow* and *Women in Love*) he scribbled down a four-act comedy, *Fight for Barbara*, in the space of three days. The play has no literary value, but it has some interest for the biographer.' *Frieda Lawrence* (1973), p. 93.

credited with at least some of the qualities for which the young Lawrence furtively admired his own father, than he gets in, for example, *Sons and Lovers*.

We have also to take into account the fervour with which, in real life, Lawrence threw himself into the business of *living* as the bond with his mother came closer to being finally severed in the last phase of her illness. Only six days before she died, he proposed to Louie Burrows—on impulse, in a train—and she accepted him. The letters in which he describes this proposal most movingly convey the confused state of his emotions; the fierce conflict between his devotion to his dying mother and his urgent desire to love and live.

On the very day of that proposal (December 3rd, 1910) he writes to Rachel Annand Taylor, 'My mother is very near the end. Today I have been to Leicester. I did not get home till half past nine. Then I ran upstairs. Oh she was very bad. The pains had been again.' So great was his mother's agony and weariness that the son could only 'wish she could die tonight'. It is in that intensity of agonised despair that Lawrence goes on in the letter to examine the nature of his relationship with his mother and its effect on his capacity for love. Of the 'kind of bond between me and my mother' he writes, 'We have loved each other, almost with a husband and wife love, as well as filial and maternal. . . . I think this peculiar fusion of soul (don't think me high-falutin) never comes twice in a life-time—it doesn't seem natural. . . . Now my mother is nearly dead, and I don't quite know how I am.' (CL pp. 69–71)

Without a break Lawrence plunges in the following paragraph of the letter into the story of his proposal to Louie. 'I have been to Leicester today. I have met a girl who has always been warm for me—like a sunny happy day—and I've gone and asked her to marry me: in the train, quite unpremeditated. . . .' Thinking of Louie makes him feel happy 'with a sort of warm radiation'; thinking of his mother makes him feel like a champagne glass, crushed between someone's fingers. Yet, 'There is no hostility between the warm happiness and the crush of misery: but one is concentrated in my chest, and one is diffuse—a suffusion, vague.' It is this ambivalence—this conflict without hostility—that one feels underlying the treatment of illness and death in *The Merry-*

go-Round, supporting the conjecture that the play could well have been written—almost, perhaps, as a gesture of cathartic defiance —in the months immediately following his personal loss.

One other piece of circumstantial evidence that appears to pinpoint the first writing of the play during those months is the description of a classroom reading of *As You Like It*, about which Lawrence writes to Louie Burrows on March 29th, 1911. 'We have just finished As You Like It. It's very jolly and the boys enjoy it: only they do want to caper round in a dance while Rosalind delivers the epilogue, and there's not enough room.'[4] The letter goes on to describe Lawrence's lively involvement in other dramatic activities in the school; activities which he quotes as they are recorded in the boys' compositions where he reports finding the 'jewel' of a comment: '*A Pot of Broth*, an Irish play, was perfectly performed under the direction of Mr. McLeod, before gorgeous scenery, exquisitely painted by Mr. Lawrence.' Returning at the end of the letter to the recent classroom reading, still fresh in his mind, Lawrence concludes, 'Goodbye, my dear, I wish things happened like As You Like It. I reckon you're a lot like Rosalind. I always think of you.'

The Merry-go-Round is avowedly a Nottinghamshire *As You Like It*. In it a bereaved son becomes engaged to a girl, full of spirit and passion, only days after his mother's death. It does not therefore seem to be stretching the available facts too far to suppose that the genesis of the play belongs to the experiences of that spring of 1911, even though we do not hear mention of it by name until the latter part of 1912, when Lawrence writes to Garnett of his eagerness to re-cast and re-work the play.

As the text stands, *The Merry-go-Round* presents certain problems in staging that Peter Gill overcame, when he produced the play in 1973, by making adaptations along the lines that he felt Lawrence would have agreed to had he still been alive. Like his earlier Lawrence revivals, Gill's *Merry-go-Round* was a great success, much admired for its movingly human mix of comedy and seriousness. The effect of the adaptations shifted this play closer to the naturalist mode of the three plays already revived, and made it appear an entirely appropriate companion piece to *A Collier's Friday Night*, *The Widowing of Mrs. Holroyd* and

[4] *Lawrence in Love*, pp. 86–88.

The Daughter-in-Law. Praiseworthy as the adapted text undoubtedly was, and faithful in every way to the spirit of Lawrence's naturalist drama, it did, however, evade the challenge posed by the play as Lawrence wrote it; as a combination not only of laughter and tears, but of realism and fantasy.

Turning to that text we notice at once a major structural difference between it and the plays examined in previous chapters. Where the naturalist plays kept to the close intimacy of the miners' kitchens, around which the life of a community was felt to circulate, *The Merry-go-Round* goes out into the life of the village itself, visiting the nurse's room, the countryside between cottage and village, the dining-room and garden of the vicarage, and the porch of the parish church. True to its title this play does not depict the still centre of a life, around which other lives revolve, but itself spins and gyrates as the couples within it change partners to the hurdy-gurdy rhythm of a spritely country dance.

With the naturalist plays we felt ourselves to be present at an experience of life, so convincingly authentic that we found ourselves drawn in to participate as silent characters in the action. In *The Merry-go-Round* we find ourselves by contrast spun off to a distance from the action, and feel that we are placed on the periphery of a 'life' which we watch from the outside. As the characters whirl around, we see each successive episode as a separate section of the turning merry-go-round, steadied into slow motion as it passes before our eyes.

If we come to the play with responses conditioned by our experience of the 'colliery' plays, the very first scene of *The Merry-go-Round* will, from the point of view of setting at least, immediately suggest to us that we are about to encounter a play in the same mode. Mrs. Hemstock lies in her bed; a pitiful invalid surrounded by 'medicine bottles and sickroom paraphernalia'. The stage directions indicate that this is not a bedroom, but the 'downstairs front room of a moderate-sized cottage'; the 'parlour', normally used only for special occasions—weddings, christenings, funerals and the like. Here it is 'realistically' used as a sickroom for the practical benefit of both the invalid and her family, so that she can be accessible to them and they to her. In dramatic terms the special function of the room—that which distinguishes its use as a sickroom from its normal function as the setting for notable family occasions—serves to characterise Mrs. Hemstock. Even as death approaches, her shrivelling figure still dominates the household. There is no question, we feel, that such an invalid could be banished to a remote upstairs room, far from the activity of family life.

But the naturalistic surface of the play is immediately broken in the first words of dialogue between Nurse Broadbanks and her patient, and we learn at once that something quite other than 'life as it actually is' must be in store. Mrs. Hemstock talks very strangely. Very well, we may say, she is an invalid and her curious way of talking; her morbid imagery, is a naturalistic rendering of her wandering mind. But it soon becomes apparent that Mrs. Hemstock, ill as she is, has a perfectly clear head. She imagines the little fat chap in the mirror as vividly as she does the 'gallivanting' of her husband, or the likelihood of her son's committing suicide. Her own illness is like 'a fish flopping around' in her inside; her son Harry has a leech on his heart that he bred as 'a mackerel's head breeds maggots'. These fearsome images make a striking contrast to the naturalistic action as the well-built nurse methodically washes and tidies the fretful invalid.

What kind of impression are we being directed to form of Mrs. Hemstock? Not, it is clear, an altogether sympathetic one. She confesses that her son's strangeness is the result of her rejection of him: 'I got sick of him stormin' about like a cat lookin' for her kittens, so I hustled him out', she almost boasts to the busy nurse. Mrs. Hemstock has no high opinion of Rachel Wilcox, the girl to whom Harry turned when his mother withdrew her affection, but, although she disapproves of Rachel's passionate eagerness for her son, Mrs. Hemstock has encouraged the relationship, believing that 'he wor such a soft 'un at 'is age—a man o' thirty'. Rachel, it seems, has 'cured him of women', and we are directed to ask whether this is why Mrs. Hemstock has pushed her son in Rachel's direction—precisely, that is to say, in order to 'cure' him of women, while protesting to want the opposite for him.

At the realistic level of the play Mrs. Hemstock is a natural source of exposition. A sick woman, neglected—or so she would have us believe—by her family, she pours out all her troubles to the nurse. It is the history itself which is, by contrast, unnatural. Mr. Hemstock is a womaniser and Harry is surly and suicidal;

'harsh' like his father in caring more for his pet animals than he does for his mother, at whom he once threw a hammer for daring to criticise his treatment of a pet rabbit.

But, when we meet Mr. Hemstock, he is a white-haired, clean-shaven old man with a 'certain courtliness and quiet bearing' who 'bows by instinct' to the nurse. In reply to his wife's accusation of hours of neglect, he explains to the nurse that he has only been away for ten minutes and, in any case, has been doing errands for his wife. The 'monstrous' Harry is innocently digging in the garden, and Mr. Hemstock is out of breath from running, not, as his wife maintains, after women, but after his daughter's children who have been teasing the fowls.

More and more we feel that Mrs. Hemstock maligns her menfolk. Thirteen months 'bedfast', she still has the strength to order her husband around, even though she has shrunk from a 'staunch fourteen stone woman' to 'nowt but noggins o' bone, like iron bars in a paper bag'. Neglected she may be, but it is at least partly her own fault. She refuses, for example, to let her daughter Susy come near her, even though the young widow is her only close neighbour. Clearly there must be a motive for all this malignity, and that motive is shown when Mrs. Hemstock entrusts Nurse Broadbanks with the secret of her will's hiding-place.

Refusing to tell the nurse—or us—to whom she has left her fortune of over £500, Mrs. Hemstock implies that the legacy will not benefit Mr. Hemstock or Harry or Susy, even though the hardship resulting from a strike will reduce them to living on their own small savings. Nurse Broadbanks reflects our impressions by finding Mrs. Hemstock's behaviour 'queer', but the sick old lady claims to be no more queer than the Almighty, whose ways, like her own, are mysterious.

Called to help with the bed making, Harry Hemstock comes in for his share of his mother's nagging. He is pale and withdrawn; 'A certain furious shrinking from contact makes him seem young in spite of a heavy hangdog slouch.' While he prepares to help the nurse with lifting the invalid, Mrs. Hemstock heaps scorn on her son for neglecting her, for having no 'gumption', and for being 'so scared to death of a wench that he goes about with a goose'.

Here the play poses a very real production problem. Patty, the pet goose 'comes padding into the room and goes up to Harry'. At this point, as later in the play, the goose symbolises a bond between Harry and the Nurse. Unlike Mrs. Hemstock, nurse is fond of Patty and thinks her 'a dear old thing'. On that evidence Mrs. Hemstock concludes that nurse will like Harry for 'He's just the same; soft, canna say a word for himself, an' scared to death o' nowt.' In a naturalistic production it is hard to imagine how even the most resourceful producer could manage Patty on stage, though the difficulty can be overcome well enough by leaving her out altogether and allowing the points for which she stands to be made in the dialogue. Alternatively though, it might be very interesting to see Lawrence's fantasy extended here to the portrayal of Patty as a pantomime goose; an effect which would tie in well with the scenes in which the Baron and Baroness von Ruge lend themselves equally well to presentation as larger-than-life figures of pantomime. Later in the scene too we see how well this could work when nurse strokes and later stumbles over Patty. A larger-than-life size bird would exaggeratedly draw attention to Harry's fantasy in choosing a pet fowl as the object of his rejected affections and would also contribute the surreal touch which Lawrence's text calls for here and on many subsequent occasions in the play. It would, of course, be a bold stroke, but one that would work very potently in directing an audience away from the error of looking upon *The Merry-go-Round* as simply a further slice of Midland mining life.

As we have also seen though, this difficulty could be overcome by dispensing altogether with Patty's appearances and allowing the dialogue to convey the significance of Harry's rejected love being lavished on a pet goose, who becomes almost completely identified with her owner. When, for example, Harry leaves the sickroom to fetch clean bedding, Mrs. Hemstock asks 'Isna 'e like that there goose, now?' Nurse Broadbanks restricts the reference of her answer to Patty: 'Well, I'm sure Patty's a very lovable creature.' Making no distinction between man and goose, Mrs. Hemstock sails on to interpret this answer as meaning that Nurse Broadbanks finds Harry lovable. Towards the end of the scene, the identification is made even more closely when Mrs. Hemstock instructs the nurse to transfer her fondness for Patty to Harry and, 'Stroke him Nurse—and say "Poor old Harry".' The com-

121

parison between the man and his pet goose points not only towards Mrs. Hemstock's scorn for her son, but also towards a relationship that she hopes will develop between Harry and the woman who is fond of his pet.

The invalid's bitter denunciation of marriage and family life in this first scene is dramatised in terms of her withered, shrunken helplessness. Against that we have to set the contrast of the nurse's warm, healthy capability; her desire for a home of her own and for someone to take care of her in it. We also see Harry, maligned by his mother, producing the sheets that he has taken the trouble to air, and helping the radiantly glowing nurse to make the sick woman's bed. Like Mrs. Hemstock we interpret Nurse Broadbank's affection for Patty as a sign of her affection for Harry, and we feel the possibility of a developing relationship between this superficially ill-assorted pair.

Mrs. Hemstock probes to find out whether the possibility of such a relationship has occurred to the nurse whom she has entrusted with the secret of her will's hiding place, and again we sense the placing of a narrative clue in the play's plot. At the very end of the scene, however, Mrs. Hemstock's questioning reveals the surprising information (surprising, that is, in the light of the way that the plot *appeared* to be developing) that Nurse Broadbanks once had a doctor sweetheart, and that, by some extraordinary coincidence, he is none other than the new assistant whom Mrs. Hemstock so much prefers to the old doctor. The likelihood of Nurse Broadbanks being unaware of this until Mrs. Hemstock tells her about it is, to say the least, remote, in anything resembling naturalistic terms. Once again then, we are directed *away* from responding to the play as if it were life-like.

Quite obviously the whole of this scene has a dimension foreign to the naturalism that, at some levels, it seems to aim for. What we notice, in fact, is that the naturalistic elements serve a tragi-comedy of symbols. The 'real' here is indeed felt to be 'queer' or 'strange', and it is this quality which makes us respond with a curious sense of disturbance to a scene superficially realistic in its everyday authenticity. There is fairy-tale or nursery-rhyme fantasy in the role played by Patty, the goose, whether or not she appears on stage; the intrigue of melodrama in the secret of the will; and near farcical 'romance' in the unexpected arrival on the scene of Nurse Broadbanks' former sweetheart. Clearly we cannot 'believe in' the reality of this life as we were so well able to do in the lives of the 'colliery' plays.

Instead of attending to unspoken undercurrents, we are here directed to interpret heightened overtones, loaded with erotic double meanings. Rachel Wilcox is 'a pussy cat always rubbin' 'erself agen a man's legs'. In Mrs. Hemstock's vivid terms Rachel 'melts herself into a man like butter in a hot tater. She ma'es him feel like a pearl button swimmin' away in hot vinegar.' Harry is a goose to be stroked, and Nurse Broadbanks, herself alive with blooming vitality, radiates an inviting, if unfulfilled, sexuality in striking contract with the frail invalid who 'canna abide to feel a man's arms shiver agen me. It makes me feel like a tallywag post hummin'.' It is these currents of sexuality that we feel as driving forces in this curiously unreal 'slice of life', and these that we will follow as they vibrate between the various pairs of potential lovers who will appear before us as the play continues.

Scene 2 takes us away from the sickroom into the Hemstocks' kitchen, where Harry and his father are engaged in domestic tasks. Harry has just administered rough justice to one of his widowed sister's children who has been setting the dog on the fowls. Into this scene (again superficially naturalistic) a figure of pure fantasy intrudes in the shape of the Baron von Ruge; an exiled Polish aristocrat who speaks with 'a very strong German accent' and, for no clearly explained reason, has come to be vicar of this remote English mining community. The Baron calls to see the sick woman, but Mrs. Hemstock does not want to see him, and her son, aided by his faithful goose, protects her from the unwanted caller. The summary dismissal of the Baron will, we are told, have dire consequences. Harry has angered the Baron who has influence with the mine owners. Now that the strike is over and the men are returning to work (on the same terms, it is emphasised as those against which they had protested by striking), Harry will be unable to find a job because he has offended the Baron. Again we feel fairy-tale colliding with realism, although Patty—far from laying golden eggs—has probably depressed the family fortunes even further by helping Harry to drive off the Baron.

Nurse Broadbanks defends the Baron as a brave man and a good gentleman, but the Hemstocks cannot agree with her. Job

Arthur the baker takes their side. He is a rough plain-spoken man with a habit of comparing women to the wares he sells. Rachel Wilcox is 'a cream horn o' plenty' too 'rich' for Harry; Susy Smalley a 'brown crusty loaf'. Crusty she certainly appears as she storms into berate her brother for chastising her son. Susy is a widow with no time for niceties. She considers Harry and the nurse to be a 'pair of mealy-mouthed creeps, deep as they make 'em', and her father not much better. In her view Nurse Broadbanks 'only comes carneyin' round for what she can get.' Harry, however, feels that it is Susy who is only after her mother's money. Nurse Broadbanks exclaims, 'How dreadful! You are a strange family.' Strange they are certainly presented as being, but we are aware here that only Nurse Broadbanks knows the location of Mrs. Hemstock's hidden will. No one, it seems, can be taken entirely at their word.

The mystery of the will looms very large at this point in the play. We see Nurse Broadbanks clearing the sickroom, as Harry and his father return to their chores in this 'motherless' household, and we are reminded that nurse has warned of Mrs. Hemstock's critical condition by suggesting that a minister should be allowed to call. Any solution to the mystery is, however, retarded as Mr. Hemstock goes off to the shops leaving Nurse Broadbanks to watch over the invalid—and to face the arrival of Dr. Foules, her sweetheart from the past.

As in the scene of the bed-making, the encounter between the nurse and the doctor is suffused with an atmosphere of suppressed sexuality. Emotions are masked under their polite exchange of Latin tags which suggests to us that this pair are better 'matched' than are Harry and the nurse. Yet it is Harry who cleans Nurse's galoshes, and she in turn insists on caring for the wounded goose when it is attacked at the end of the scene by the Smalleys' vicious dog.

More concerned with Nurse Broadbank's safety than with Patty's, Harry reveals his admiration for the unattainable woman who, exercising her professional skills on the damaged bird, is the centre of attention as the scene closes. Both Harry and Dr. Foules appear here equally reduced to the role of impotent bystanders.

At the end of Act I then, we are left with a tangle of plot

threads and no indication of the way in which they will be un-ravelled; no clue as to which of the signs and portents arrayed before us will prove the most satisfactory guides to any con-ceivable outcome. Above all, we have been deprived of the com-fortable proposition that the situation is life-like, and can therefore be predicted in realistic terms.

Although it will ultimately prove to be a false trail, Mrs. Hem-stock's will seems crucial among the plot threads at this stage of the play. Hitherto at least it has provided a consistent narrative line, and we are therefore alerted to picking it up again at the be-ginning of Act II in the baker's reference to another inheritance that Rachel Wilcox may expect from her father. Here we discover too that Nurse Broadbanks has yet another admirer in old Mr. Wilcox. Although he protests that he 'heaves' at the sight of her, Harry clearly desires Rachel, with or without her fortune, and is jealous of the other men whom she entertains in the vicarage where she is a servant of the von Ruges. Job Arthur avows a preference for Susy, whose eligibility in turn hangs on the money she may or may not inherit from her mother. Susy herself bursts in upon the discussion and matches Job Arthur in plain speaking as she haughtily dismisses the baker's offer of himself in marriage to her at the bargain price of £200. Susy is unimpressed by Job Arthur's declaration that his price to Rachel would be £250, and her attitude is more fully explained when we learn that he had missed an earlier chance of marrying her.

Rachel Wilcox is the next figure to appear in view as the merry-go-round gathers momentum. The stage directions describe her as having 'a consumed look as if her quiet pallor smothered a fire' and we recall the smothered fires masked by the smoke-screen of cultivated conversation in the scene between Nurse Broadbanks and Dr. Foules. Job Arthur offers himself again as a husband; this time to Rachel for the 'full price' of £250. Harry returns asking for Nurse Broadbanks before Rachel can give her answer, but the baker repeats his offer which is turned down by both Susy and Rachel with cynical contempt. Refusing Rachel's request to visit her at the vicarage, Job Arthur leaves. Rachel declares, 'I hate him' and Susy announces, 'I'm going home'.

The play now focuses on a pairing about which much has already been heard: Rachel and Harry. It is Harry evidently whom

Rachel has come to see. But she finds it hard to get any response from him. Only when she bursts into tears does he return more than monosyllables, and then it is to heap abuse on her for her promiscuity. Provoked into accusing him of being 'full of saw-dust', Rachel arouses Harry's suppressed passion. He binds her to a chair and forces her to confess that she has told another man intimate secrets of their courtship. The scene is a violent parody of the encounter between Nurse Broadbanks and Dr. Foules. Where the passions of the more cultured pair had been hidden beneath polite words, the feelings of Harry and Rachel are pre-sented beneath a cloak of cries and blows. Threatening to 'brain' the terrorised girl if she says a word to him, Harry forbids Rachel to touch him, then releases her from her bonds and shakes her off as she at once ignores his threats and 'lays her hand on his sleeve'. Reduced again to weeping Rachel leaves, though not before obey-ing Harry's more gentle command to wrap herself in her shawl against the raw night. His fury spent Harry, left alone, goes to the cupboard where the wounded Patty receives his caress and the triumphant challenge, 'We'll settle her Pat—eh? We'll stop her gallop. Hey Pat!'

By now the pattern of pairing has begun to take a firmer shape. Under all the disguises, we see that Nurse Broadbanks is destined for Dr. Foules; Susy for Job Arthur, and Rachel for Harry. But they clearly have a long way to go before the merry-go-round slows down sufficiently for them to arrive safely at their several destinations. Clearly too, it is money that makes the merry-go-round spin, confusing issues that cannot be cleared until its motive power runs out and the couples' choices can be freely made.

The scene moves from the kitchen to the road outside the Hemstocks' cottage. Rachel, drying her tears, mistakes Susy for Harry. A hasty alliance, struck up between them to secure Nurse Broadbanks for Mr. Wilcox, Harry for Rachel and Job Arthur for Susy, founders in mutual hostility, but the two are drawn to-gether again by the appearance of the Baron and Baroness von Ruge who are out on their regular Monday night hunt for lovers. In an extraordinary conversation between the vicar and his wife, we are offered a grotesque caricature of puritanical prurience. Gloating over the 'sins' they have encountered in their night's work, the pair turn to vilification of the Hemstocks, and the von Ruge concept of 'virtue' is crystallised when the baron declares of Mrs. Hemstock, 'I will not bury her, heathen and blasphemous woman. She shall not soil my graveyard of good dead.'

Mistaking Susy and Rachel for yet another pair of courting 'sinners', the Baron and his wife draw upon themselves a violent attack from Susy who is enraged by a blow from the Baron's stick. Rachel rushes to Susy's aid, reducing the spluttering Baron to 'a foreign fizzle'. Nurse Broadbanks stumbles into the mêlée rapidly followed by Harry who quickly recognises his sister and attempts to rescue the Baron from her clutches. Ungratefully the Baron whacks his saviour who trips up and allows the Baron and his wife to escape. Nurse Broadbanks pleads for an end to the shameful affair. The von Ruges, minus a hat, a lantern and a 'galosher', make for home, pursued by Harry's muttered insults and Susy's ungracious comment to her brother that 'It serves thee right.'

This scene is, of course, pure pantomime with all 'normal' values turned upside down. Susy is mistaken for a man; defenders for attackers, and allies for enemies. But its hysterical atmosphere symbolises the perverse view of sex as sin which bedevils the love-lives of each of the courting pairs, and it is the vicar and his wife who here paradoxically represent the Demon King and his Consort in their prurient pursuit of 'animal' lovers. Naturalistically the scene is unstageable. At a surreal level, however, it is crucial to the play; illuminating as it does the false values against which the lovers must contend if they are to arrive at their predestined happy ends.

Back in the Hemstocks' kitchen, the following scene brings Harry home wounded to the gentle ministrations of Nurse Broadbanks. Just as she tended the goose at the end of Act I, the nurse here binds the wounds of the man who has been so closely identified with his feathered pet. Confessing how much he needs her loving care, and coming close to making an open declaration of love, Harry, in his confusion, discloses to the nurse the secret of his dependence on his mother; his fear of losing the woman whom he has 'lived by', though he can no longer bear the thought of her continuing to suffer. It is mothering that Harry begs for from Nurse Broadbanks, and she, we observe, is willing enough to give

127

it to him—at least while he is wounded and in need. We might make much of this, as an audience in search of clues as to how to interpret the curious chaos of events with which the play presents us, were it not for the fact that Mr. Hemstock's comment on the condition of the invalid, directs our attention elsewhere.

Supporting our train of thought, Mr. Hemstock has gently reproved the nurse for spoiling Harry. She protests, 'It is what will do him good—to be spoiled a while.' Mr. Hemstock remains doubtful, having seen what has become of Harry as a result of his mother's care. 'Spoilin' is spoilin', Nurse, especially for a man,' he chides enigmatically. Making light of this reproof, she enquires after Mrs. Hemstock, and is answered by Mr. Hemstock's, 'Funny. I canna ma'e heads or tails of her.' As the curtain falls on this ominous observation, we are therefore left with a doubt as to the relative importance of what will happen next in the relationship between Harry and his nurse-mother-figure; a development which is overshadowed by our expectation of a death that will work great changes in the life of the Hemstock family.

With Act II closing on this reminder that Mrs. Hemstock's life is nearing its close, we are directed to re-examine the questions of inheritance and marriage that have integrated the various episodes so far encountered. Mrs. Hemstock, the 'devoted' wife and mother, has now been seen to have alienated her husband and her children, and to have shrivelled away in her efforts to possess and dominate them. His virility repressed by maternal constraints, Harry lavishes affection on his goose, worships the mother-substitute nurse, and is cruelly vindictive to the girl who arouses the sexual energy, about which he has been made to feel so much guilt. Susy, a vengeful virago, is similarly damaged by her mother's domination. Even now, when she is dying, Mrs. Hemstock retains a hold over her family in her refusal to disclose the secrets of her will.

Further parodying the moral values upon which such lives are built, the Baron and Baroness von Ruge are the absurd figures of fun who stand for spiritual guidance. Their time, they feel, is better spent hunting down lovers with sticks than guiding them by example into more 'God-fearing' ways. As foreigners, the von Ruges are emblematic outsiders, imposing an alien order on lives from which they are far removed.

This distance between church establishment and alienated parishioners is caricatured in the Ruritanian intrigue of Act III Scene 1, in which the 'martial looking' Baron plans his campaign of revenge on his godless attackers. The terms of religion are here mocked by the Baroness' belief that the return of her lost possessions will be 'salvation' and a 'miracle'. The incident of the previous night is enlarged into an ambush inspired by the 'power of evil'. While Nurse Broadbanks attempts to calm the outraged 'commander' of the church militant, the Baroness catches the baker kissing Rachel in the kitchen. Interrogating the couple, the Baron is driven to admit failure in the 'three campaigns which are my life', and to comfort his hurt pride, Job Arthur—who finds nothing surprising—proposes to Rachel who accepts him.

Having by threats, cajolery and moral blackmail forced Rachel and Job Arthur to submit to his false 'foreign' standards by plighting a troth which the terms of the play have told us cannot be honoured, the Baron next tackles Harry who comes to return the lost lantern. Harry insists on speaking the truth and is not to be brow-beaten into accepting the Baron's code. It was two women who attack the Baron and Baroness, and it was Harry who hauled off the attackers. Anxious to protect Susy and Rachel, Nurse Broadbanks insists that the attackers were men; a story much better calculated to feed the Baron's pride. Called in to bear witness, Rachel confirms the nurse's lie that Harry had defended the von Ruges from two male attackers. Accused of lying by his idol Nurse Broadbanks, Harry departs, leaving her to make up for the wrong she has done him by persuading the Baron to reward his modest rescuer by using his influence with the mine owners to get Harry a job.

In this Scene we see two wrongs perpetrated in the name of morality and the church militant. Honest Harry is dishonoured in the interests of expediency; manipulated by the well-intentioned schemes of the nurse who believes that she knows—mother-like—better what is good for him than he does himself. Concurrently we see the 'moral leader' Baron, declaring himself a soldier and claiming that 'It is not good for the enemies of God to prosper', nevertheless writing to his nephew commanding him to be the instrument of relieving him of his debt to Harry, which he describes contemptuously as 'this burden of gratitude contracted to one of such order'.

The merry-go-round is now spinning at full speed. From the vicarage we are whirled to the room in the miner's cottage, in which we see Nurse Broadbanks receiving three successive gentleman callers who tread hard upon each other's heels. First comes old Mr. Wilcox who asks—with ludicrous circumlocution—for a wife, but clearly *wants* a housekeeper. Disturbing the pompous old gentleman in his choral courtship, Dr. Foules arrives. It is as a wife that *he* wants Nurse Broadbanks, but he finds it difficult to disentangle himself from the maternal bonds that have for so long kept him from attaining his goal. His dilemma is manifest in the difficulty he finds in unbending from his stiff pose of professional detachment for long enough to ask the vital question. Teetering on the verge of it, he in turn is disturbed by the arrival of Harry, and leaves believing that Harry is a third suitor for the nurse's hand. To some extent he is right, though Harry's suit is very different from that of his two predecessors. He has called to ask nurse to visit his mother, but he stays to assert his determination to resist the efforts that have been made to brand him as a liar and a swine.

Pleased to be back at work, but ignorant of Nurse Broadbanks' role in getting him his new job, Harry still smarts under the injury of having been made to look a liar and a fool 'in front of other folks' by a woman who is 'reckoned to be pinin'' for him, and by the conniving which prevented him from telling the Baron the shaming truth that his 'dangerous attackers' were a pair of women. Any designs Harry may have had upon Nurse Broadbanks are frustrated here by his aggressive honesty which is summed up by her as a 'state of chronic bad temper'.

Earlier in the scene, Mr. Wilcox had fared little better. His representation of himself as a steady, careful man, with four good houses and a tidy bit in the bank, is politely received, as is his mournful serenade. But he has to hasten away on the appearance of his younger and better qualified rival. His departure, we see, is well advised, for it is Dr. Foules whom Nurse Broadbanks obviously loves, even though she greets his declaration with plain speaking: 'Look here Arthur,' she reminds him, 'you have lived like a smug little candle in a corner, with your mother to shelter you from every draught. Now you can get blown a bit. I do not feel inclined to shelter you for the rest of your life.' Arthur must learn to love her for herself, not, as Harry has been seen to do, as a nurse, before she will accept him. To show that he has done so he must 'come down from his high horse' and there is no doubt, in the play's terms, that he will learn to do that too. Harry's arrival, which precipitates the doctor's departure, therefore presents no threat to the eventual happy outcome for the nurse and her doctor suitor. The episodic merry-go-round technique assures us of this succession of events. Suspense and interest are not generated towards the way in which things will finally turn out. The continual frustration of our interest in the several plot threads makes this very clear. What we *are* to be concerned with is the immediate present; the relationship to a value system of the present event in the series.

Having established this pattern of response, the play next focuses on the grim tableau in the Hemstock kitchen. Mrs. Hemstock has died, 'a fair skeleton', and Nurse Broadbanks has stayed to keep Susy company until the menfolk return. When Harry comes home in his pit dirt, it is his sister who washes him—symbolising her return to the family fold in her assumption of its womanly duties—while the nurse looks on, considering the pros and cons of marrying a collier. She washes the sick in the course of her duties. Here, that aspect of professional care is contrasted with the everyday familiarity and the intimate physical involvement of the task in the life of a miner's wife.

It is Susy who brings up the question of the will, returning our attention from reflection on suitable pairings between the various couples to the pursuit of the play's narrative line. Nurse Broadbanks readily reveals the secret that has been entrusted to her, and leaves to minister to the needs of the Baron and Baroness and Mr. Wilcox from whom Rachel has brought messages. Left alone with Harry, Rachel gently wins his confidence in the sincerity of her love for him. Confessing that she has behaved badly, she protests that it was done out of jealousy. Now that Harry's mother is dead, Rachel can accept that he will never love a wife as much. The two confirm their vows by going to look at the body and return red-eyed to find Susy anxiously looking for them. Overcome by emotion, Harry goes out, leaving Susy and

Rachel together. Superstitiously terrorised by the presence of the corpse, the two young women nevertheless overcome their fears sufficiently to seek out the will. It is Patty—not a ghost!—who moves in the sickroom, toppling Rachel from her perch as she retrieves the will from its bedpost hiding-place, but the fright that both women get registers the power that Mrs. Hemstock continues to wield from beyond the grave.

This is re-emphasised in Harry's disapproval of their unseemly haste. Opening the will he reveals that five hundred and fifty pounds have been left to nurse and himself if they marry. If not, the money is to be divided between Harry and Susy. There are then, no unreasonable conditions to satisfy. Despite the fairy-tale trappings of the play, the will itself is down-to-earth and human. Bitterly Harry reproaches Susy and Rachel for thinking no more of the dead woman than 'if she wor a dead fish wi' the money in her mouth'. They in turn berate him for plotting with Nurse Broadbanks to cheat them out of their inheritance. On her return, Nurse Broadbanks refuses to discuss the matter—out of respect for the dead. Harry declares that 'she's a lady an' she makes you two look small.' Rachel defends herself hotly. She only retrieved the will to help Susy, and she asserts her independence fiercely as the scene ends on a wild outburst of mocking cries of 'Cuckoo! Cuckoo! Cuckoo!'

Mrs. Hemstock's influence is penetratingly felt throughout this wildly macabre scene which spins between the extremes of naturalism (as in the conversation between Rachel and Harry) and the high-pitched *guignol* of Rachel and Susy's venture into the chamber of death. Satisfying the expectation that Mrs. Hemstock's ghost will make an appearance, the stage directions call for Patty to represent such a manifestation. At all events, an audience here can be seen to be effectively played upon by the disconcerting mixture of styles which prevents them from identifying in sympathy with any one of the merry-go-round figures, and it is at this point that we receive the full impact of the roundabout technique of the play.

For the final Act, the spinning movement which, in the previous scene, has flashed all the issues so rapidly before our eyes that we have been made to see each superimposed on the other in a chaotic blur, slows down in transporting us to the porch of the

village church. It is Sunday and the Hemstocks have just attended
a post-funeral service. Conversation among the mourners issuing
from the church is not about the recently departed Mrs. Hemstock, but about news of forthcoming marriages. The threads of
the plot, which had been so intricately enmeshed, now begin to
separate out. Two sets of banns have been put up on this funeral
Sunday. The mourners feel that it is 'not decent'. We feel, when we
hear of the couples concerned in the banns, that it cannot be
likely. Job Arthur and Rachel could be a *possible* couple, though
we have seen that their consent to marry was made under duress.
Nurse Broadbanks and Mr. Wilcox, however, cannot be a match
under any of the circumstances with which we have been presented. In considerable confusion, we may feel here that the whirling pace of the plot and its constant shifts of direction may have
been mere sleight-of-hand devices to soften us up for a surprise
ending.

Only Mr. Hemstock recalls the wife he has so recently lost, and
even his bereavement is ignored as the marital muddle begins to
clear. Dr. Foules takes his place in the queue waiting for Nurse
Broadbanks to explain herself. It is the pompous Baron, however,
who suffers the worst outrage. Job Arthur backs down from his
commitment to marry Rachel; she has 'given him the sack'. Nurse
Broadbanks denounces Mr. Wilcox as a wicked old man who has
insulted her.

All the masks are dropped as the Baron expostulates against the
indignities heaped upon his church, and he too is 'unveiled'—as
a villain—when Job Arthur's bargaining with the women is explained by the fact that the baker owes the vicar £180. Rachel
is called for, but does not appear until the following scene which
takes place outside the vicarage garden as the merry-go-round
winds to a halt.

Harry learns from Rachel, who is posted Humpty-Dumpty-like
atop the garden wall, that she has indeed rejected Job Arthur.
Their reconciliation is intruded upon by the bereaved Mr. Hemstock who again objects at the unseemly haste of Harry's decision
to marry so soon after his mother's death. We feel Mrs. Hemstock's power ebbing away here, represented as it is only by the
protests of the husband whom, in life, she despised. Harry is truly
escaping from her thrall. Even the temptation of sharing his

mother's entire fortune with Nurse Broadbanks fails to persuade Harry to follow his mother's posthumous wishes.

Boldly he challenges his father's objections with 'It ma'es no difference to her do it', and Mr. Hemstock is reduced to carrying out his mission of bringing Rachel before the Baron. Back in the church porch the final scene sees the merry-go-round reaching a standstill. All the passing figures are gathered together. Against a background of the outraged Baron—still spluttering his accusations of blasphemy—the 'Eastwood "As You Lump It"' draws to a close, as the pairs of lovers, cleared of misunderstandings and freed from the bondage of false values, declare their true affections. True too to his literary pretensions, it is Dr. Foules who calls upon the Baron to 'play Duke to our "As You Like It"' as, in turn, the couples plight their troths.

Dr. Foules seals his vow to Nurse Broadbanks with a kiss on the hand; Job Arthur, his to Susy with a kiss on the cheek; Rachel and Harry wordlessly seal theirs with a kiss on the mouth. The old men are confounded. Life asserts itself in despite of 'decency', and the play ends by binding its three pairs of true lovers in a triple happy ending.

Good faith triumphs over bad, and the spectre of Mrs. Hemstock is eclipsed by the dawn of love, freely offered and accepted. False morality in the shape of the Baron von Ruge is seen to be overthrown. Susy escapes from the enslavement of widowhood; Dr. Foules from that of his demanding mother. Job Arthur and Rachel gain their hearts' desires, and Harry learns to be the man his mother would never allow him to be.

Following their feelings the couples spare no thought for the cold care of money which has stood throughout for the conventional values stifling their happiness. With its delightfully arbitrary ending, this play is plainly cast in the fairy-tale mode and, like all good fairy-tales (as well as like the mature Shakespearian comedy on which its finale is modelled) it has had its darker side, against which the life-loving moral of the ending glows all the more brightly.

Although the play has been generally felt to need the revision that Lawrence never got around to giving it, it is possible to look upon it, not as a flawed piece of naturalism, but as an achievement of quite another kind. In all its swift changes of mood and mode *The Merry-go-Round* can be seen to have its own mode of unity in a design that flouts naturalism, but could lend itself very well to styles of production far removed from the straightforwardly realistic; styles that could imaginatively display the succession of allegorical tableaux which Lawrence chooses to group around the central organising symbol of his merry-go-round, foiling as he does so our desire to follow up narrative threads, and rewarding us instead with a magical resolution of all problems which joyfully confounds the calculating deliberations of cold reason and logical consequence.

6

The Married Man

One of the last remaining plays still awaiting production, *The Married Man* has, at first sight, an unpolished look that seems to justify its author's description of it as 'candidly an impromptu'. Act I is suspiciously short in relation to the other Acts, and there is a possible explanation for this brevity in the bibliographical information relating to the manuscripts of the plays. As it is important to our assessment of the kind of dramatic form towards which Lawrence was moving, after the perfected naturalism of *A Collier's Friday Night* and *The Widowing of Mrs. Holroyd*, it is well worth assembling this information, in order to get a clear picture of what is actually being dealt with in the shape of *The Married Man* as we now have it.

In 1937, L. C. Powell described *The Merry-go-Round*, *The Fight for Barbara* and *The Married Man* as 'three full-length plays, complete and unpublished',[1] but some reason to doubt the absolute accuracy of this description is introduced by the subsequent note on *The Married Man* which records that this play was produced in England in the summer of 1936 from this manuscript. The play produced was, in fact, Walter Greenwood's adaptation of *The Daughter-in-Law*, which was presented at the Playhouse Theatre, London, under the title of *My Son's My Son*. In 1948, E. W. Tedlock Junior's revised bibliography of these manuscripts was able to call on the publication in *The Virginia Quarterly Review* (Autumn 1940) as a further means of identifying *The Married Man* which, in Tedlock's catalogue, is described as being untitled, incomplete, and lacking its first five pages.[2]

[1] L. C. Powell, *The Manuscripts of D. H. Lawrence*, p. 43.
[2] E. W. Tedlock Jr., *The Frieda Lawrence Collection of D. H. Lawrence Manuscripts* (Albuquerque, 1948), p. 118.

The version in *The Complete Plays of D. H. Lawrence* conforms to that published in *The Virginia Quarterly Review*, and begins rather abruptly in what appears to be the middle of a scene between Grainger and Brentnall in the bedroom of Mrs. Plum's cottage.

When examining *The Married Man* and considering its stage-worthiness, we must therefore bear in mind the fact that the version with which we are dealing may well be incomplete, and we must be careful not to confuse this aspect of it with Lawrence's description of the play as an impromptu.

Though it would be very satisfying if further research were to restore to us the missing pages of the opening of the first scene, we can still feel with confidence that what we have of the play clearly demonstrates a formal movement away from the close realism of the 'colliery' plays. In place of the compellingly life-like realism that we found in those plays, we have, in *The Married Man*, a formal pattern of shifting relationships within a setting which makes no attempt to reproduce the forms of 'actual' life. Against a very generalised background the constantly changing partnerships in *The Married Man* are presented as kinetic elements in a design in which each of the several couples can be seen as possible permutations. The shape of the play is very much like that of the dances that take place within it, and it is in this sense that we can perhaps most usefully think of it as an impromptu.

The married man, George Grainger, ends up with his wife whom he describes as 'the only girl I could have married', but we have to ask whether the play persuades us that what he says is true, or whether that partnership at the end of the play is simply the result of the impromptu having come to a temporary halt. If, we might put it, the music of the dance were to start up again, might there not be further changes in the pairings with which we are left at the end of the play?

Before looking into the play itself for the answer to that question, it is interesting to speculate on the nature of the relationship between the events in Lawrence's life which find a place in this play and the kaleidoscopic view of love and marriage reflected in its form. We have already seen the dramatist at work transmuting intensely personal concerns with growing up, and with the relation of a dominant mother to her grown-up sons, framed into the dramatic modes of *A Collier's Friday Night, The Widowing of Mrs. Holroyd* and *The Daughter-in-Law*. With each, the aesthetic space between life and art has been seen to widen. With *The Married Man*, as we have seen in *The Merry-go-Round* and will notice again in *The Fight for Barbara*, the dramatist's preoccupation with ways of creating that space direct us even further away from regarding the plays as records of events that actually took place in Lawrence's life. In these plays indeed, the characters are so far distanced from what we may want to think of as Lawrence's personal experience that we tend to view them as experiments in the creation of purely fictive personae. Deployed as they are in a form designed to illustrate the making and breaking of relationships, they move as in some elaborately choreographed dance, in which each movement is predetermined by clearly defined rules.

The connections between what happens in the plays and the experiences on which we might very tenuously feel those happenings might be based become very complex. We know, for example, that Lawrence himself was involved in a succession of relationships of varying degrees of seriousness during his years in Croydon. Among these, his engagement to Louie Burrows, his infatuation with a school teacher colleague, and his intellectual attachment to Helen Corke are the most fully documented. At the same time he was still under the influence of his youthful passion for Jessie Chambers, the complexities of which are minutely described from Lawrence's point of view in *Sons and Lovers* and from Jessie's in her 'Personal Record'.

It is from the latter account that we learn of the young Lawrence's horror in the spring of 1906 at hearing that an acquaintance had 'got a girl into trouble', and of his relief expressed in a heartfelt 'thank God . . . I've been saved from that . . . so far'.[3] It was a rather more sophisticated Lawrence who wrote in April 1912 of a visit to his friend George Neville who 'is married—did you know?—last November, on the q-t. His baby was born in January. He had to leave Amblecoats. They gave him a tiny temporary place in the country near Leek, where I stayed with him. His wife is with her parents in Stourbridge,

---

[3] *D. H. Lawrence: A Personal Record*, pp. 125–126.

some 50 miles away. He lives "en bachelier". Which is quite a story!'⁴

A month earlier, Lawrence had written about this story to Garnett, telling him also that his 'Don Juanish' friend already had an illegitimate child, born five years before the marriage to another girl who had since married a collier. Lawrence recounts to Garnett how, before her wedding, this girl went to the parents of her baby's father and showed them the child. They agreed that the likeness between the baby and their son was sufficient to confirm her story. 'Whereupon Lizzie went away satisfied, got married to a collier, and lives in Cordy Lane. She, with one or two others, will rejoice over George's final nabbing. Isn't it awful?' Lawrence ends by asking, and, as if he himself could hardly believe the tale, adds 'All this, by the way, is quite verbal truth.' (CL p. 103)

There is no evidence that the incident which so much upset Lawrence in 1906 had any connection with the later story. In all likelihood there were many such unwanted pregnancies in and around Eastwood, where, as the first Act of *The Daughter-in-Law* demonstrates, such goings-on, though morally reprehensible, were sufficiently commonplace to command a set price (of £40) from the 'sinner'. Nevertheless, the concern Lawrence felt, and according to Jessie, expressed in 1906 was for a friend who had been involved in just such an unfortunate situation, and the time-lapse of five years between that incident and the story of 1912 seems to suggest that there could very well have been a link; that, in fact, the later and overtly more worldly Lawrence was merely affecting to make light of a matter which five years earlier had shocked him to the core.

All this, of course, suggests that the worldly wisdom of 1912 was more than likely a cover for the shock that Lawrence still felt. That he was indeed ambivalent is reflected both in his letter to Garnett, in which he admits 'This has upset me—you never know what will happen' and in *The Married Man* in which there is evidently an element of satisfaction in the conclusion that brings the erring Dr. Grainger 'safe home to port' in the arms of his wife and baby. We see in the play too how Grainger's friend Billy Brentnall successfully breaks up the philandering Doctor's amours with Annie Calladine and Sally Magneer. The

⁴ *Lawrence in Love*, p. 167.

play indeed glorifies Billy for his part in bringing Grainger to heel; a part that Lawrence may have felt that he himself played during his stay with his 'Don Juanish' friend in the latter's cottage lodgings in the little village of Bradnop near Leek.

As with all Lawrence's work, the element of biography is simply a starting point, interesting for us in this particular case because it helps to date the time of writing of *The Married Man* between April and October 1912—months during which Lawrence's own life was so complicated that it might otherwise seem unlikely that he could engage himself in the composition of a play which treats affairs of the heart in the blithe spirit of farce.

At the point where the play as we have it begins, Grainger and Brentnall are discussing the possible courses of action that the former might take in response to a piece of news which has obviously just been sprung on them, and which has so much impressed Grainger's landlady Mrs. Plum that she 'can't get it out of my head, that there what you've just told me'. The conversation that follows Mrs. Plum's exit clears up the details of the story that has so confused the good landlady that she has forgotten to bring up her favourite lodger's collars.

Billy puts the facts squarely before Grainger: 'The girl is gone on you, the kid is yours. You are a married man, and you mean to abide by your family.' Grainger concedes, 'What the devil else is there to do?', and Billy pursues him with practical questions about his intentions of finding a job to go to 'on Saturday when you've finished here'. Billy's pressing questions elucidate the admission from Grainger that he has been over to see his wife only once since he was married—and that was when the baby was first born. Since then he has been living the life of a 'gay bachelor', and it is to this life that he is about to introduce the apparently disapproving Billy.

George Grainger shows little affection for his wife or for his child. Indeed he professes that he cares for the latter less than for, 'that younster at my digs in Wolverhampton'. Billy is critical, but George's farmer friend, the 'fine fellow' Jack Magneer arrives to save the erring husband from further scolding.

Jack is presented as a good-hearted chap. A bluff thirty-three year old bachelor, he has a sister Sally whom Billy admires, though it is in pursuit of the three orphaned Calladine sisters

140

that the three men are preparing themselves to spend the evening. Jack insists that the sisters are 'nice girls' and that Billy makes a welcome addition to the party by evening up the numbers. There is a suggestion that two of the girls are 'spoken for' so that Billy must content himself with the one 'left over', but Jack with his characteristic generosity wants everyone to have a good time, and is willing to 'step aside' if the newcomer should prefer the sister who normally keeps company with him. The scene ends on Grainger's emphatic insistence that there is no need for Billy to don his dinner jacket, further implying that the sisters—'nice' as they may be—do not set a great deal of store by formal propriety. There is indeed more than a hint, under the cloak of respectable geniality in this scene, that none of the men have intentions which could remotely be described as honourable, and that the sisters, though similarly genteel in appearance, are unlikely to offer much resistance to any proposals that may be made.

Truncated as this opening Act may be, it sets the scene adequately for subsequent developments and prepares well for the highly respectable setting of the following Act, in which we have been led to expect highly indecorous behaviour. The dining-room belonging to the Misses Annie, Ada and Emily Calladine is tastefully furnished, and in it we first meet the oldest of the sisters alone. The stage directions call for her to be 'aged 32, tall, slim, pale, dressed in black, wearing Parma violets'. She 'looks ladylike but rather yearning' and 'walks about restlessly'. The 'yearning' look is evidently associated with Annie's feelings for Dr. Grainger which are not, as we are shown in their first encounter, fully requited. The kiss she receives from him is hasty, furtive and unwilling. Yet it is she who expresses concern lest their relationship should cause malicious gossip. Grainger quiets her fears by announcing his imminent departure for some unknown but distant destination in 'Scotland or London', though the announcement distresses rather than calms her. It is clear that George Grainger is toying with Annie Calladine; playing on her passion for him in a cruel and calculating way. On her side too there is clearly calculation, since her fears of gossip are evidently intended to draw from him a declaration of *his* intention to make a respectable woman of her.

George clearly demonstrates his unwillingness to make any such commitment by crushing her in an embrace which effectively creates an embarrassing moment for Annie as her sisters make their appearance. They have disposed of an unwanted visitor[5] by saying that Annie is engaged, and are delighted by the discomfiture that their double meaning causes George to suffer. Caught in rather a tight spot, he reveals his character by making off to rally the friends who are to provide him with masculine support, and leaving the sisters alone to discuss the situation in which Annie's failure to pin down George Grainger has placed them.

Here we learn that the sisters, so apparently 'free' in their behaviour, nevertheless conform to conventional standards. Annie has only encouraged George because she 'thought he was a gentleman'. Jack Magneer's assurance to Billy in Act I that the Misses Calladine are 'nice girls' and that 'the oldest of them will happen to be Mrs. Grainger' account for the cordiality with which George has been received. Indeed it is only because Grainger was introduced by the honest and well-meaning Jack that Annie had ever consented to receive him. Although they do not yet know that George is a married man, the sisters realise that his intentions are far from honourable, and we see, from their several reactions to the truth of the matter, a model for their likely behaviour in the circumstances that are to follow.

Annie is flustered and angry, but determined to prove herself a lady. Emily (described in the stage directions as '27, quiet, self-possessed, dressed all in black') is prepared to sail through whatever storms may arise by despising Dr. Grainger. And Ada, who is 'aged 23, rather slim, handsome, charmingly young and wicked looking, dressed in black and purple, with a crimson flower', is determined to regard the whole matter as 'ripping fun'. In the various ways in which the orphaned sisters adopt the conventions of mourning, we have indeed a particularly good example of Lawrence's dramatic sense of the possibilities inherent in the visual presentation of character. Like her yearning

[5] It is interesting that this visitor is called 'Mrs. Wesson', a surname that Lawrence was to use again in *The Fight for Barbara*, thus suggesting a proximity in time of writing between the two plays. A similar instance, of a common name occurs in *The Lost Girl*, completed in 1919, and the play, *Touch and Go*, written in the same year, in both of which the surname, 'Houghton' is given to a major character.

look, Annie's Parma violets give us a first clue as to how we are to 'take' her. Emily, by contrast, is the totally serious sister in unrelieved black, while Ada who enlivens her mourning most vividly can be expected to offer a 'wicked' commentary on the proceedings.

While the younger sisters go off to receive their callers, Annie is seen very carefully to *assume* an air of composure. Apparent in this opportunity for the audience to observe a character assuming a role is the farcical structure on which the play is based. There will be no actual falling of trousers or hiding in wardrobes, but the events of the play will provide substitutes for these trappings of farce in the losing of assumed attitudes and the discovery of hidden secrets.

In the sexual cat-and-mouse game there are rules which some of the characters will observe, while others—equally predictably—will endeavour to break them. As we shall see, only Elsa Smith proves to be altogether free of these rules, as will be indicated by her arrival in a motor car, like a modern goddess out of the machine, to unravel the tangled web that the others have woven. At this earlier point in the play, Annie Calladine is shown establishing *her* role as a keeper of the rules in the most conventional sense. Grainger, who also acknowledges the existence of the rules in his very flouting of them, may be toying with her affections. Annie, however, will preserve her lady-*like* manner. It will be evident to all (on stage) that she is available only to an honourable suitor. As privileged spectators we know full well that Grainger is very far from being that, and we also know that Billy Brentnall is primed to rid Annie of her illusions.

Decisively then the play at this point focuses on the encounter between Annie and Billy. It is he, the newcomer, who holds the centre of the stage and must appear to be—paradoxically—most 'at home'. Admiring the flowers, he expresses surprise that Farmer Jack should have thought to bring them. His arch literary reference to the properties of couches and prompt acceptance of Annie's invitation to sit beside her (equally promptly evaded as Jack hints that Billy should choose elsewhere among the sisters) prepare for his introduction of the dangerous topic of marriage—to which state it is he who proposes a toast. George becomes more and more uncomfortable as the atmosphere warms up, with Jack first putting his arm around Emily's waist and Billy racing ahead to win a kiss from the boldly forthcoming Ada. Concealed behind spread newspapers the two couples still considerably embarrass George who is thus—designedly—'left out in the cold' with Annie.

The butt of Billy's teasing, Grainger crossly throws cushions through the paper screens and becomes even angrier when Billy broaches the subject of 'Dr. Grainger's secret'. This turn of the plot serves to provide an opportunity for us to observe Billy and Annie alone together in a situation that is essential to the presentation of the theme of the play. Billy's advice to Annie to 'Know men and have men if you must, but keep your soul virgin, wait and believe in the *good* man you may never have,' stands out as almost completely serious in the absurd context. It may well be agreed that this is one of the crucial instances of the play's need for the re-casting that it never received. Somewhere along the line, of course, Lawrence has to get across this contrast between the pretences and evasions of the more or less conventional lovers and the essential passions that are being concealed. Billy's straight talking is, however, uncomfortably at odds with the situation. One can clearly see that Lawrence has devised the mechanism for the mediation of that statement. Billy is shown up as almost as devious as George. Annie is shown to have asked for all she got from Grainger, and the *relative* honesty of that 'devil, Billy Brentnall' is plainly indicated here, both by the immediate transference of Annie's affections to him, and by the well-timed entry of down-to-earth Sally Magneer who puts a stop to further preaching by Billy. In order to make the point without radically altering the text, one would hope here to provide Billy with a mannered and affected way of delivering his speeches that would throw into relief the contrast between their homiletic tone and its inappropriateness to the occasion.

As self-appointed truth teller, Billy warns Annie of the danger to herself of seeking to identify every man who arouses her with the man she *could* love. What is evidently required, in order to recuperate this conversation into the overall style of the play, is therefore, some mode of stylisation that could encompass the whole as a comedy of manners in something of the Restoration tradition. Taking such an approach the characters could effectively be rendered as 'types' rather than as the rounded 'human beings' of the naturalist convention. In this way we could receive Annie quite satisfactorily in her sharply defined role as a despairing spinster; Emily as the cynical prude, and Ada as the tomboyish coquette. Jack Magneer could then be presented as the clod-hopping would-be gallant, with the confirmed misogynist George Grainger and the 'honest' Billy Brentnall as his perfect counter-types. With Sally Magneer as a latter day 'Hoyden', and George's unfortunate wife as the perennially deceived married woman, the role call would be almost complete.

It is clear that some such design underlies the form of the play as we can see, for example, in such structural devices as Sally's cutting in on the *tête-à-tête* between Annie and Billy, and the shattering effect this intrusion has upon the degree of serious-ness with which we receive Billy's advice. Even before this we have had Annie's impulsive confession to Billy, 'I could love you', as a guide to the kind of credence which we are being asked to give to any of the characters' pretensions. It is the gentility of Annie's pretence that is being mocked here, just as it is the incongruity with his own behaviour of Billy's high-sounding principles that will be mocked when he is revealed as the liar that he is.

At one level we note that the portrayal of Annie Calladine protests against the obvious social constraints of her particular context in time and place, challenging these constraints by ask-ing (in Billy's terms) why she should not enjoy the sexual free-dom available to men. But, at the same time, George Grainger's plight as a married man, trapped by a wife and baby, declares that idea of masculine freedom to be meaningless. Like Annie's genteel yearning, George's pose of gay bachelorhood is a hollow sham. Everyone in the play—with the ambivalent exception of Elsa Smith—is held in the thrall of just such a hollow sham, imposed on sexual relationships by social convention. No one is free, but, at least until Elsa intervenes, each must play the role allotted to them by the rules of the game.

Sally Magneer's bluntness is no less subject to these rules than Annie Calladine's assumed modesty. Despite her show of dis-approval at the philandering licensed by the the Calladine sisters, Sally is immediately recognised as a man-hunter by Billy who observes 'She's made a dead set at Grainger. If he weren't married, she'd get him.' 'Honest' Jack Magneer also plays according to the rules. His sister and Grainger may have been up to 'some little game', but he refuses to stand by and see any man stampeded into marriage. Brother or not, it is his part to stand by a fellow bachelor (as he still believes Grainger to be) and he does so by warning Sally bluntly that 'Charlie Greenhalgh is your man: you stick to him, and leave other young fellows alone' when his sister brazenly calls Grainger to task for carrying on with Ada Calladine. Jack's 'honesty' here is in turn called into question as Sally ripostes with a showing up of her brother's duplicity: 'Oh you *are* good Jack! And what about the girl *you* took to Blackpool?'

Innocence is more often assumed than genuine, Billy reminds Annie when they are once more left alone together. Even in comforting her, however, the audience is directed to note that Billy too becomes drawn into the game as he belies the good advice '. . . *do* be honest' with the kiss that he bestows upon Annie 'rather sorrowfully as he departs' having promised to return if he can. Heeding the part of Billy's counsel that it suits her to heed, Annie confides in her sisters that 'Dr. Grainger is only married and got a child', but panics when Ada (the 'wicked' one) threatens to write to Mrs. Grainger 'to come and look after' her husband. The cat is out of one particular bag here, and Annie's plea to Ada not to let it stray any further is effectively stifled by the fall of the curtain.

Moving from the genteel setting of the Calladine dining-room, Act III broadens the comedy in the cheerful and relaxed atmosphere of the Magneer farmhouse kitchen. Old Mr. Magneer is 'rather maudlin'; Jack, a sporting figure in riding breeches and leggings, is matched by George and Billy in their tennis flannels. Giving the lie most manifestly to his sympathetic honesty in the previous Act, Billy is now seen to be flirting outrageously with Ada Calladine.

As the punch is liberally served and the girls giggle more and more uncontrollably, we are shown at a closer and less flattering range the motivating appetites that were thinly veiled by gentility in the Calladine ménage. Slightly tipsy, Sally makes overt advances to Grainger who gingerly edges away. Billy leaves off flirting with Ada to comfort Sally who readily responds to his suggestion that she would as leave have him as Dr. Grainger. In the polka, pranced to the strains of old Mr. Magneer's comb band, the couples parody the ritualised motions of the love-and-courtship measure that they have been treading throughout the play. Like the musician 'all the men are affected by drink', and their true natures begin to emerge as the couples cast aside propriety in the wild dance. Paired with Grainger, Sally begs a meeting for the following day, and the philandering doctor grants her request. Emily draws a proposal from the hesitant Jack, and Ada reveals to Billy that she has written to Grainger's wife. Instead of praising her for her honesty, Billy, we note, rewards this extension of his own truth-telling by calling his disciple a vixen and an imp.

For the waltz-valeta that follows, there is a change of partners. Paired this time with Billy, Sally learns that Grainger is married, and is restored from tears by the solicitous kisses of her new partner. Emily and Jack are absorbed in confirming their engagement, while Ada and George are, like the others, engrossed in conversation. It is at this critical moment, just as we feel that the masks are about to be dropped, that the real 'truth-teller' appears on the scene. 'A LADY in motor cloak and wrap appears in the doorway. . . . No one notices the newcomer.' Indeed, she stands silently observing the scene until Ada and George Grainger see her and are surprised into guiltily 'breaking apart'. It is Ada who has written to George's wife and George who seems most surprised to see the lady, so we are at once tricked into supposing that she must be the married man's wife. But it is Billy whom the Lady has called to see. Before going to meet his visitor, Billy gallantly escorts the stumbling Sally to a seat and bestows a gentle caress on her cheek. Then he proceeds 'reeling slightly' towards the door to make his rather unconvincing excuses to the Lady who requires none of them. She is 'not in the least' cross with Billy for kissing and cuddling Sally and indeed suggests that he should return to kiss her again. 'Poor Sally,' Billy sheepishly laments. 'I don't want to kiss her now.'

Introduced to the others as 'My betrothed, my fiancée, my girl' Elsa Smith is unconstrained by the need to appear lady-like. Indeed, in contrast to Annie Calladine who must struggle to keep up appearances, Billy's fiancée *is* a lady. It may of course be coincidence that 'LADY' is capitalised in the stage directions, but there can be no doubt that Elsa Smith is designed to be seen as belonging to a different class from the women we have met so far in the play. Defined as belonging to a superior order by her imposing costume, her arrival in a motor car (with friends who turn out to be similarly elegant), and by her attitude to the kitchen frolics. Elsa is most especially characterised as being a LADY by her cool and generous acceptance of Billy's involvement in whatever it is that may be going on.

Hitherto we recall that only Annie Calladine and ourselves had been privy to Billy's secret, and even we have been duped into believing that the new arrival had more to do with Grainger's private life than with Billy's. The tables can therefore most effectively be turned to present Billy Brentnall as every bit as much the deceiving villain of the piece as Grainger himself. When Elsa goes off to bring her two friends to join the party, leaving Billy to face the shocked amazement of the assembled company, it is appropriately George Grainger—the one who has suffered most from Billy's 'honesty'—who explodes 'Well, you devil Billy Brentnall', and we are inclined to agree with him. Privy as we have been to Billy's secret through all his protestations of candour, we are directed here to feel that he will have to learn his lessons more thoroughly if he is to satisfy the high standards of honesty and freedom maintained by his superior (and undeniably patronising) fiancée.

We find a hint that Lawrence means Elsa Smith to appear altogether *too* patronising when she returns with her elegant friends Tom and Gladys. Tom is made cynically to observe 'I suppose these are adventures', which Elsa is allowed to criticise with her assertion: 'This is fun.' Again we feel the need for re-working. There is clearly a problem here in the ambiguity of the superior outsiders who come to 'slum it' in the Magneer kitchen. Elsa at least is evidently meant to be admirable if the play is to work, and the resentment of the note of patronage is tentatively re-directed towards Tom. Somehow or other, if the play as written is to be realised, the audience's sympathies must be engaged by Elsa Smith, and, if she is presented as the stunning good-looker called for by the stage directions, that goal might well be achieved.

On paper certainly her remarks are irritating and affected, but, spoken on stage by a very beautiful actress, poised, self-assured and genuinely delighted with the revels into which she has intruded, one can see how the irritation might be counteracted. If the play is to be considered viable in production, this would be a most necessary part of its scheme. There is a mixture of resentment and admiration inherent in the way in which the character of Elsa Smith is portrayed for us, but the admiration must predominate. We will see though, at the very end of the play, that the suppressed resentment gets expression in Grainger's final words.

Here, on her first appearance, Elsa must win approval for her radiant freedom, as a glowing guardian angel come to confer her good wishes on the revellers. As the dance re-forms for the final waltz measure, we see how she is designed to liberate the participants from false constraints in the comic finale of Lawrence's potentially riotous third Act. And we see too how the Restoration style could lend polish and point to the conscious typology that the mode of this particular play requires.

The showing up of Billy Brentnall in Act III is, of course, only a structural and narrative prelude to the climactic showing up of George Grainger, the eponymous married man. By the opening of Act IV which brings us back to where the action began in the bedroom of Mrs. Plum's cottage, most of the characters already know George's erstwhile secret. Expectations—diverted by the arrival of Elsa Smith—have also been aroused as to the part that Grainger's wife will play in the final working out of the comedy.

Tousled with sleep, 'Beau' Grainger and 'Beau' Brentnall open the scene by reviewing the chaos of the previous night. Accusing Billy of being 'a better sleeper even than a liar', George sees trouble ahead from Sally who won't, he feels, be fobbed off as easily as Billy had planned. Their scheming is interrupted by the arrival of Jack who has come for a settling of affairs between his friends and the women they have dazzled. George is in a tight spot, but Billy still has a trick or two up his sleeve.

Faced by Jack's statement of the facts of the matter, George can only confess sheepishly that he is indeed married and the father of a child, whereupon Billy leaps in to demand, 'Well, Jack, say he has your sympathy', thereby turning the tables on the accuser. Pressing for a further advantage, Billy takes the words out of Jack's mouth. 'Don't, Jack,' he remonstrates, 'Don't you see, I could give the whole of that recitation. "We've been good friends, George, and you'd no need to keep me in the dark like that. It's a false position for me, as well as for you etc., etc,".' Leaving Jack no time to reply, Billy proceeds with his apologia for George which puts the bald facts of the case in a light that is more than just to the married man.

Robbed of *his* best case, Jack nevertheless persists: 'There's our Sally, and there's Annie. . . . He's courted 'em both—they're both up to their eyes in love with him.' Billy can trump that trick too. As far as Annie goes, Billy is able to maintain, 'On the quiet she's rather gone on *me*. I showed George up in his true light to her.' Over-riding George's objection 'Rotter—rotter!' and Jack's remonstrance 'You're a devil Billy', the skilful trouble-shooter goes on to make use of the facts he has just learned from George about Sally to persuade Jack to sort out the problems of the re-jected Charlie Greenhalgh, and make a match between him and the girl who has thrown him over in favour of George.

Bewildered by Billy's quick talking, Jack makes his peace with George and goes off feeling—incorrectly in our view—that justice has been done. Billy breathes a sigh of relief, but George remains troubled. He has indeed been saved from the consequences of his most recent philanderings, but at the cost of being made to look a cad. He fumes as Billy blandly informs him that, in order to save him from Annie, his friend has had to represent him as being 'quite manly and couldn't help yourself; all the virtues of good nature and so on, but a bit of a libidinous goat.' 'Thank you— very nice of you,' George snaps back sarcastically. But that is not all as Billy blithely continues, 'Add to this that you won't face a situation, but always funk it, and you understand why Annie suddenly transferred her affections to me. For I showed my-self, by contrast, a paragon of all virtues.' Here our sympathy and agreement are with George for his verdict on Billy: 'You would.'

Billy has shown himself to be a dab hand at appearing to be a 'paragon', but, as he freely admits here, his virtue is just as much of a 'show' as George's vice. Refusing any longer to be beholden to such a friend, George makes to rise, but is prevented from getting very far by the arrival of none other than his long-suffering wife Ethel.

It will be remembered, of course, that throughout the scene so far Billy and George have remained in bed, and the 'seriousness' of the discussions that have been held have consequently been consistently undermined by the jaded and debauched appearance of the beleaguered young men. Now the situation is exploited still further as Ethel launches into a heart to heart talk with her erring husband without even noticing that he has a bedfellow.

Ethel begins by trying to maintain a calm and sensible exterior, for all the world as though she were simply a polite morning caller, but her agitation becomes more and more uncontrollable as she approaches the true motive for her unexpected visit; confirmation —or denial—of the infidelity hinted at in Ada Calladine's letter. The possibilities for hilarious by-play in this scene, though not indicated in the authorial stage directions, are nevertheless implicit in the situation in which George and Ethel strive unsuccessfully to keep calm in their marital crisis, while Billy lies waiting his opportunity to imitate the 'deus ex machina' appearance so effectively accomplished by Elsa Smith in the previous Act.

'I love you George, I love you,' Ethel weeps, to be comforted by George's fond reply, 'Poor old Ethel—and I love you. And whoever says I don't, is a liar.' Bearing in mind the proximity of Billy and the two friends' opinions of each other's honesty, it is easy enough to see the rich opportunities for comic business allowed for, if not in fact commanded, by Lawrence's text at this point. Unsuspecting Ethel is, however, heartened by her husband's affirmation of love sufficiently to ask, 'You've been true to me, George?' Again we may imagine the outraged signs emitted by the more or less concealed Billy beside George in the bed, especially when the latter evades his wife's question with 'What do you mean?' 'Have you been true to me?' Ethel plaintively repeats, whereupon Billy, unable any longer to control his feelings, pops up characteristically to declare 'No, he hasn't,' and to present his credentials for appearing and intervening at this intimate moment. 'I am your husband's old friend Brentnall, and *your* friend, Mrs. Grainger' announces the incorrigible Billy, accompanying his statement by getting out of bed and shaking hands with Ethel.

THE PLAYS OF D. H. LAWRENCE

Apart from the immediate comedy of this ridiculous moment, we recognise in it a parody of Elsa's appearance on the previous night. Tousled with sleep, and evidently improperly clad for an introduction of this formal nature, Billy must present a striking contrast with the poised and elegant Elsa. Inherent in this contrast is a satire of the ideals of freedom that Elsa has waved like a magic wand over the intrigues of the several couples in the Magneer kitchen. Imperfectly performing the principles laid down by his fiancée's 'advanced' philosophy, Billy implicitly holds those principles up for criticism if not for ridicule.

The cool absurdity of the confrontation between Billy and the startled Ethel emphasises here the absurdity to which the potential tragedy of deserted wife and baby is reduced. Billy the 'liar' and the 'devil' has once more taken it upon himself to represent 'honesty'. Here indeed is the stuff of farce, undercutting, as we see, the homiletic tone of the play's overt 'message' about honesty in sex relations.

In terms of plot we are asked to question whether Billy Brentnall, the self-appointed arbiter of justice between man and wife, will bring reconciliation with his suspect honesty. It seems likely that he will, as he stands by to referee the final rounds of the contest between George and Ethel, the present bout of which ends in victory for the wife as George, driven into his corner, explodes, 'You can do what the hell you like', to which Ethel victoriously replies, 'Then I shall live with you, from this minute onwards.'

Again one sees how the fun could be kept fast and furious by a stylised production which would bring out the sparring element inherent in the text. Brentnall confers victory on Ethel with his verdict, 'Knocked out George', while the loser impotently rages, 'Curse you Brentnall', and the victorious Ethel departs to answer the call of her crying baby.

But before George can resign himself to the fate of living in the 'cursed rotten hole' that he has dug for himself, he has more work to do in clearing up the confusions that his deceptions have created. Ethel returns to usher in an irate Sally Magneer whose *amour propre* is severely dented by the wife's accusation that 'the fact that Dr. Grainger chose to keep his marriage a secret wouldn't have hurt *you*, unless you'd rushed in to be hurt'. Sally bounces back with her assertion that Grainger invited pursuit, and calls in an ally in Annie Calladine who is also hovering in the wings waiting to state *her* case. Annie speaks up plainly: 'I don't wish to say everything I can against you, Dr. Grainger. But I do wish to say this, that you are a danger to every unmarried girl when you go about as you *have* gone, here. And Mrs. Grainger had better look after you very closely, if she means to keep you.'

Despite Billy's attempt to soothe her, Ethel sees these revelations as insuperable obstacles to her future happiness, and cannot accept her caddish husband as 'all right really'. In this conviction she is ably supported by both Annie and Sally.

Onto this scene of near disaster—rendered ridiculous by its being played in the bedroom, with the two men at a distinct disadvantage!—Elsa Smith appears to restore peace one again. There can, of course, be little doubt that Elsa (earlier described as 'a handsome woman, large, blonde, about 30' in the stage directions to Act III) is modelled on Frieda Lawrence, idealised here as the wise 'fairy godmother' whose liberated view of sex brings the comedy of intrigue to its highly contrived, and deliberately fantasied, conclusion. Billy, we are directed to understand, could never solve his friend's problems alone. He is, as Elsa calls him, 'a dear, but a dreadful liar', and almost as bad as George in having what Elsa also describes as 'one philosophy when you are with men, in your smoke-room, and another when you are with me, in the drawing-room', It is this duplicity that Billy must learn to give up, if he is to be a satisfactory partner for the woman who declares: 'I want the real you, not your fiction.'

Here then is the 'lesson' of *The Married Man*. It is not having affairs with others that constitutes infidelity, but a failure to be 'decent' and 'honest' about them. Elsa expounds this philosophy as she comforts Sally with her view that 'I think a man ought to be fair. He ought to offer his love for just what it is—the love of a man married to another woman—and so on. And, if there is any strain, he ought to tell his wife—"I love this other woman".' Sally protests, 'It's worse than Mormons', but Billy— the eager disciple—counters her objection with, 'But better than subterfuge, bestiality, or starvation and sterility.'

'Very quaint and very earnest' as the stage directions call for her to be, Elsa nevertheless succeeds in soothing the outraged women, even including Ethel, who is still—understandably— suffering from shock.

Sweeping out with her dutiful apprentice in tow, Elsa leaves the married man and his lawful wife to a tearful reconciliation. The 'lesson' has been learned. With all his promiscuous 'sins' revealed, George can feel free 'decently' and 'honestly' to declare, 'You're the only girl I could have married, Ethel. I've been a rotter to you.' To which she can equally honestly—though, in all the circumstances, one should add, optimistically—reply, 'Never mind, we *shall* get on together, we shall.'

As the curtain falls, the reunion is cemented by Mrs. Plum's delivery of the baby into George Grainger's fatherly arms, the sentimental resolution being most effectively undermined by George's fierce rejection of Billy's encouraging 'That's the way George' with his angry exclamation 'Shut up fool.'

When all is said and done then; when hurt pride has been comforted and philosophies have been expounded, and when all have made the impossible vow to be more 'decent' and 'honest' in future, the rosy picture is not as complacently self-satisfied as might at first appear. It is on the note of George's dismissal of Billy as a too talkative fool that the play ends, commenting lightheartedly but critically on any facile optimism that may be generated by the stylised happy ending.

Billy has been set up as Elsa's devoted admirer, but all his fumbling attempts to spread her gospel have been shown up as foolish, ridiculous and riddled with inconsistencies. We remember the discussion between Annie and Billy and his stated convictions about honesty in sex relations which are subsequently undermined by the patent dishonesty and 'smoking-room' duplicity of his behaviour with her sister. Even more vividly we have been impressed by his buffoonish appearance, popping up out of bed to pour Elsa Smith's brand of oil on the troubled waters of the Grainger marriage. That we are meant to register these inconsistencies is underlined by the ending of the play in which Billy is bluntly dismissed as a fool by the unfortunate George who is obviously making the best of what he sees as a bad job. Elsa's peace-making may seem to be taking effect for the moment, but the play has warned us to be wary of men's tactics in the sex war, and made us feel that George is complying with Elsa's philosophy only because he sees no immediate alternative.

The ending of the play casts doubt on the seriousness with which we are to regard Elsa's doctrine, and this ambiguity is essential to the spontaneous sense of fun that animates the play. Perhaps Lawrence might have further emphasised the normative value represented by that sense of fun had he re-worked the play. As it stands, however, there are undoubtedly difficulties in ensuring in production that the immanent ambiguities are fully realised in, for example, the 'serious' discussion between Annie and Billy in Act II, and even in the glibness of Elsa's resolution of all the difficulties in the final scene. There is the possibility that the play could be presented in all seriousness as a statement of Lawrence's philosophy of sex relations, expounded with the direct and unmediated didacticism of Chapter 13 of *Aaron's Rod* (to cite only one of a legion of possible examples). Yet, where the unmediated didacticism may ruin the narrative fiction beyond repair, we see how, even in the unrevised play, that dogmatic tone is counterpoised by the sense in which ambiguities creep in to modify the 'preaching' and to confirm the impression that Lawrence himself (at least in the pre-war years) was not as wholeheartedly convinced as he might have liked to appear of the all-healing powers of sexual liberation and the independence of the individual in a love relationship.

Providing that a producer could rid himself of prejudices about Lawrence's lack of sense of humour, one can see how, in spite of the difficulties, a successful production could exploit these ambiguities in contrasting the face value of what is said with the absurdity of the context in which it is offered. In the face of such a production we might well conclude that the 'message' of the play is by no means over-simplified. On the contrary, performance, and a chance to place the philosophical content against its genuinely farcical background, could well reveal a comedy of considerable subtlety ready to escape from the constraints of the mere words of the pages of the text.

7

The Fight for Barbara

Rather better documented in Lawrence's letters than the companion pieces with which it was left abandoned in the Heidelberg attic, *The Fight for Barbara* can be very accurately dated as having been written in the October of 1912. After his initial enthusiasm for *The Widowing of Mrs. Holroyd*, Garnett, as we have seen, failed to give Lawrence much further encouragement for his plays, and made no attempt, as far as can be gathered, to publish or produce the other two 'colliery' plays that Lawrence had such difficulty in retrieving for him. Successively then, the letters, in which Lawrence writes to him of drama, become more and more deferential, though the deference is always balanced by an underlying note of confidence in his own plays that Lawrence seems to have been unable completely to suppress—perhaps in defiance of Garnett's continued indifference.

The submission of *The Fight for Barbara* is typical of such letters. In it Lawrence begins by thanking Garnett for some books, and get around to drama via the forceful criticism of Strindberg (as 'unnatural, forced, a bit indecent') already quoted in Chapter 1. Castigating Conrad too for 'being so sad and for giving in', Lawrence launches his own latest creation as a kind of afterthought: 'I've written the comedy I send you by this post in the last three days, as a sort of interlude to *Paul Morel*. I've done all but the last hundred or so pages of that great work, and those I funk. But it'll be done easily in a fortnight, then I start *Scargill Street*.[1] This comedy will amuse you fearfully—much of it is

[1] *Paul Morel* was Lawrence's original title for the novel that became *Sons and Lovers*. According to Richard Aldington, (in his introduction to

word for word true—it will interest you. I think it's good. Frieda makes me send it to you straight away. She says I have gilded myself beyond recognition, and put her in rags. I leave it to the world and to you to judge.' (CL p. 152)

It is easy to see from that letter how the impression has grown up that Lawrence regarded plays as a relaxation—or, as he says here, as an 'interlude'—from the writing of novels. But one must remember that he is writing to Garnett, whose opinion of the plays Lawrence sent him had only been favourable in the case of *The Widowing of Mrs. Holroyd*. The effort that has already been described as having been put into the revision of that play gives some indication of the amount of trouble that Lawrence might have gone to in preparing his other plays for publication, had he been given the slightest encouragement to do so. Bearing this in mind, the apparent dismissal of the play, as being less important than work on the novels, begins to look rather like strategy on Lawrence's part. Notice how he throws in the completion of *Paul Morel* and the beginning of *Scargill Street* as a kind of peace-offering to Garnett, before going on to write about the play, and notice too that, though he casually slips in his own view that the play is good, Lawrence chiefly hopes to attract Garnett's attention to it through the latter's interest in the course of his life in Italy with Frieda; in that element of the comedy which Lawrence describes as 'word for word true'.

That it is tact, rather than a genuine lack of interest in his own play that makes Lawrence so cautious in this letter, is borne out by the subsequent correspondence on the subject of *The Fight for Barbara*. While awaiting Garnett's verdict on the play, Lawrence writes a long and light-hearted letter in which he talks about everything *but* his 'comedy', reference to which he tucks in at the end of a long postscript, after a flattering comment on a play of Garnett's own. (CL p. 155) Shortly afterwards, Lawrence writes a long and complimentary letter to Garnett about the latter's play, *The Trial of Jeanne D'Arc*, in praise of which Lawrence—apparently ingenuously—offers penetrating criticism

the Penguin edition of *The Lost Girl*, p. 8) the first draft of *The Lost Girl* 'was begun in November 1912 and was apparently called *Scargill Street*.' Aldington interestingly adds, 'Lawrence was not good at titles.'

of the play's 'accomplished' dramatic techniques.[2] Garnett, however, did not swallow the bait. Nor did he return the compliment.

Lawrence's next letter to Garnett defends himself against criticism of *Paul Morel*, about which he feels sufficiently confident to insist, 'I tell you I have written a great book', while, of the apparently equally harshly criticised play, he writes only: 'As for *The Fight for Barbara*—I don't know much about plays. If ever you have time, you might tell me where you find fault with *The Fight for Barbara*.' Asking too for the return of *The Merry-go-Round* and *The Married Man*, Lawrence once again puts his priorities in the order that he seems to have felt that Garnett expected of him. (CL p. 161)

His deferential attitude is clear enough too in the suggestion he goes on to make that he would like to dedicate *Paul Morel* to Garnett, and in the comfort he offers for the hostile reception awarded to Garnett's own play. Though he tries to get on to other topics, the play clearly remains in his mind as he writes: 'When you have time, do tell me about the *Fight for Barbara*. You think it wouldn't be any use for the stage? I think the new generation is rather different from the old. I think they will read me more gratefully. But there, one can only go on.' Whilst this letter is polite and tactful, Lawrence's feelings about Garnett's dismissal of the play were not, in fact, as cool as he tried to make them appear. To Garnett's son David he writes: 'Your Dad doesn't like the play, and Frieda wants to hit him.' (CL p. 163) One suspects that Lawrence's own feelings are here being ascribed to Frieda, and to what Lawrence jokingly calls the 'warlike' tendencies of her family.

When the play was finally returned to Lawrence, apparently without any further explanation of why Garnett felt it to be un-

---

[2] Lawrence's private opinion of Garnett's plays was not always as flattering as the one conveyed in these letters. In November 1911, for example, he wrote to Louie Burrows, 'I don't care for Garnett's plays—they are not alive.' (*Lawrence in Love*, p. 148) To be fair, it must be pointed out that he was there commenting on *The Breaking Point* and *The Feud*, both earlier plays of Garnett's than *The Trial of Jeanne D'Arc*. Interestingly too, Garnett's plays succeeded (where Lawrence's failed) in being produced at Miss Horniman's Gaiety Theatre, Manchester; a fact which may have accounted for Garnett's ability to interest Iden Payne in *The Widowing of Mrs. Holroyd*.

suitable for the stage, and together with *The Married Man* and *The Merry-go-Round*, the rejection drew from Lawrence the outburst about the contemporary English theatre in which he likens himself to Chekhov in needing a producer to do him justice. The strength of that outburst, and its insight into the preoccupations of the stage of the time, are a measure, as has already been suggested, of the enthusiasm that Lawrence might have felt, had an opportunity to break in on that 'bony, bloodless theatre' with living plays of his own presented itself. Since Garnett rejected the 'comedies' and appeared to show no interest in the play that Lawrence was so hopefully 'going to send' him in the month before that rejection, any chance of achieving such a break-through must thereafter have seemed to depend entirely upon *The Widowing of Mrs. Holroyd*, into the revisions of which Lawrence consequently threw himself with such vigour.

Despite his efforts to tempt Garnett into reading *The Fight for Barbara* because 'much as it is word for word true', Lawrence was clearly aware of the distinction that has been noted in earlier plays between 'life as it actually is' and the life that appears so real in his drama. Of his early days in Germany with Frieda he wrote: 'Frieda isn't in any book, and I'm not and life hurts—and sometimes rejoices one. But—you see—in life one's own flesh and blood goes through the mill—and F's eyes are tired now.' (CL p. 125–6) For Lawrence the burning question was always to find the way to transmute experience of life into something that would bear the stamp of that experience, but yet achieve the quite separate character of art. As he writes to Ernest Collings: 'I always say my motto is "Art for my sake". If I *want* to write, I write—and if I don't want to, I won't. The difficulty is to find exactly the form one's passion—work is produced by passion with me, like kisses—is it with you?—wants to take.' (CL p. 171)

In *The Fight for Barbara*, the passion of the early days with Frieda takes the form of a play, cool, poised and distant. The personal agony is there, but it is held at arm's length in the dramatic form in which Lawrence was so pre-eminently capable of crystallising the experience of life. Almost a comedy, this play represents the culmination of a second phase in Lawrence's drama; a phase in which he forged a new stylistic mode for the rendering of life experience in the white-hot fire of his personal emotion.

Lawrence opens this play on the empty kitchen of an Italian villa, and, as with the earlier 'colliery' plays, is careful to give the details of stage setting that provide the essentials upon which a director can build the appropriate frame of real life experience. Again too the life-like impression is initially created by the relations of the setting to the world outside. Urgent attention to that world is called for by the sound of a ringing doorbell, followed by a banging on the door. In answer to this summons, Jimmy Wesson, tousled and newly roused from sleep, crosses the stage to return with a pretty girl dressed in Italian style and carrying a saucepan of milk.

The location of the play; its truth to the place in which it is set, is further authenticated for the audience by the confused conversation in which Jimmy tries to follow Francesca's attempts to communicate with him. Though dragged from his bed Jimmy is evidently not angry. He and the girl laugh as they make halting attempts to understand each other. There is an intimacy in their early morning language lesson so obvious that the girl 'blushes and turns away' before bowing herself respectfully out of the young gentleman's presence. Evidently stimulated by the encounter Jimmy whistles 'Put me among the girls' as he busies himself with his kitchen chores.

At this point Lawrence introduces Barbara as a 'rather fine young woman, holding her blue silk dressing gown about her'. She stands in the doorway holding up her finger. Her appearance is designed to strike an audience as impressive and arresting. She does not rise to answer early morning callers, nor apparently, does she tackle domestic tasks. Her first words tease Jimmy for his flirtatiousness, over which she continues provocatively to take him to task as he gets on with lighting the fire and complains of the matches which are the 'stinking devil'. Barbara agrees, having experienced the smell of the matches when lighting a cigarette. In this tiny detail Barbara is placed as the lady who smokes while her man minds the house. Her dominance also extends to the choice of names, for though Jimmy says, 'I hate to be Italianized', Barbara responds only by diminishing 'Giacomo' to 'Giacometti', and goes on criticising him for flirting with Francesca. 'Remember, you're a gentleman in her eyes', she scolds ironically. In whose eyes, the attentive spectator must ask at this point, is

Jimmy Wesson *not* a gentleman? He, significantly, does not seem to find the implication out of place, and excuses his behaviour with Francesca on the grounds that there could be no harm in his 'Oh!' of approval at the sight of the pretty girl in her mantilla.

Barbara's pursuit of the topic is interrupted by the blazing up of the fire; Jimmy's work taking effect! In its light, the relative status of Jimmy to Barbara is made clear to the audience. Though she is evidently a 'lady', she has chosen to be with a man who can only offer her a hundred and twenty pounds a year and the possibility of having to do her own housework. Refusing to be 'put down', Barbara revels in the romantic aspects of what is revealed to be her elopement to Italy with Jimmy, whose origins as the son of a coalminer are of less consequence to her than his lovely hair that 'makes waves just like the Apollo Belvedere'.

At this point Lawrence fills exposition 'naturally' into the dialogue as Barbara and Jimmy contemplate the outlook for their future, based as it is on so short an acquaintance, and threatened by Barbara's desertion of her 'good and loving husband' whom Jimmy defines as: 'Frederick Tressider, doctor of medicine. Gentleman of means. Worth a dozen of me.' Running away with this son of a coal miner, Barbara has also disappointed the hopes of her titled father, though she protests that *his* feelings are unworthy of consideration since he has kept a mistress 'all his life'.

It is against this background of retribution from her abandoned family that Barbara and Jimmy try to track down the essence of their own relationship; he resenting her reluctance to belong to him, while she claims her right to freedom in the love for which she has made such great sacrifices.

Thematic here, as in *The Married Man*, this preoccupation with a theoretical possibility of 'freedom' in a loving relationship is questioned as often as it arises. It has already been cast into doubt by Barbara's response to Jimmy's flirting with Francesca, and that incident is paralleled, at this crucial phase in the debate between the lovers, by the powerful attraction that Barbara feels towards the handsome young Italian butcher. In his turn Jimmy objects to Barbara's flirtation which, he claims, is altogether more sensuously provocative than his own encounter with Francesca had been.

With skilful economy, Lawrence has thus provided the audience with a balance upon which to weigh the love that Barbara and Jimmy so vehemently express for each other. The way is also prepared for a response to the attack which is about to be launched on that 'love' by the arrival of the postman—the 'serpent' in Jimmy's Eden—who brings letters from Barbara's mother and from Frederick.

The threat from outside the lovers' hideaway is brought dramatically closer by their readings from the letters which harrowingly describe the damage to her husband's sanity and her father's health wrought by Barbara's scandalous flight.

Though Barbara brushes away her tears and tries to baby-talk Jimmy out of his gloomy premonitions, she is seen to be severely shaken by the postal onslaught. When he continues to resist her advances, she admits her fear and the act ends upon Jimmy's accusation: 'Then you're frightened of yourself, of your own hesitating half-and-half, neither fish flesh-fowl-nor good red-herring self.' Clearly the attainment of freedom is to be no easy matter for Barbara, faced as she is with the demands of a potentially possessive lover on her escape from the tenacious grip of marriage. The play's title, as well as the alternative 'Keeping Barbara' define her as an object to be struggled for or kept, and the play, as we shall see, consistently portrays her as trapped between belonging to one man or the other.

Act II moves to the setting of the dining-room, where Barbara and Jimmy are together on a couch; physically close, but kept apart by the shadow of Frederick, whose adoration of her chin Barbara recollects when Jimmy admires it. There is a tension in this dialogue which replicates the pull between Jimmy's trust in, and Barbara's suspicion of, the binding state of marriage.

Barbara's mother is expected, but, immersed in their problems, the lovers are put into a flurry by her arrival. Acting her part of the defier of conventions, Barbara wears a peasant dress 'with bare arms and throat'. To contrast with her attractively 'free' appearance, Lawrence calls for Lady Charlcote who is 'about sixty—white hair, stout, rather handsome' to be 'uglily dressed'. Conventionally polite, she is directed to appear nervous, and enters abruptly upon the subject of her mission by taxing Wesson with the wrongness of his snatching away a married woman, daughter of a high-born and cultured gentleman, and keeping her without hope of either respectability or adequate sustenance. Cruelly she reminds Jimmy of his poverty with the thrust that the very bills for Barbara's last dresses have been left for her husband to pay.

Barbara rises bravely to the taunts, protesting that she is 'not a horse to be kept', but Jimmy is ill-equipped to stand up against the onslaught. Where Barbara wants things done openly, he is anxious to avoid 'talk', but they are both reduced to silence by Lady Charlcote's account of the state of her husband's health, and by the hint that he has come with her in a bid to make Barbara 'see sense'.

While Wesson tactfully withdraws, Barbara and her mother talk of Frederick, for whom Barbara is shown to feel genuine concern, but, with Jimmy's return, the conversation reverts to the prospect of Barbara's visiting her father.

By presenting Lady Charlcote here as a money-conscious snob, the play weights the scales in favour of Jimmy, but redresses the balance somewhat by directing us to feel that Barbara's concern for Frederick is sincere. In a sense, of course, this too is presented in such a way as to favour Jimmy, since it is the latter's un-characteristically tactful withdrawal which allows for the wife's true feelings to be shown. Yet the balance is sufficiently fairly held for it to be impossible for an audience simply to side whole-heartedly with the lovers' defiance of convention. Much more is at stake, as Barbara's attempts to smooth over the disturbance created by her mother's visit indicate. The situation cannot be laughed into resolution as easily as Barbara is seen to wish, and the issue centrally concerned is not the freedom with which con-vention can be defied, but the struggle within Barbara herself to find freedom in her love for Jimmy. This is the aspect, at all events, that the play undertakes most fully to dramatise, and it is this struggle which is resumed as Barbara laughingly scolds Jimmy for being so 'crumpled up' by her mother's onslaught. At great length she acts out Jimmy's resemblance to a frightened dog with its little tail between its legs; portraying a degree of timidity which exceeds what we have just seen of Jimmy's 'crumpling' in the presence of Lady Charlcote.

Trying to remain calm in the face of this provocation, Jimmy is driven finally to accuse Barbara of enjoying torturing him as she tortured Frederick, and, when she continues to mock, he adds deeds to words and overpowers her with a fierce embrace, reasserting the strength of the physical passion against which he has reason to believe that the outside forces are powerless. It is on this moment that Lawrence closes the second Act of the play, forcefully underlining the theme of sexuality as dominant, and, in the end decisive, in the man-woman relation—however much the issue may be complicated by social circumstance. We see too that Barbara's escape is conceived of as depending on her willingness to accept a dominated role in this relationship.

In the very directness with which form here reinforces thematic content we are, of course, made very much aware—whether Lawrence 'intended' it or not—of a further level of conflict, reflected in an implicit approval of Barbara's aristocratic highhandedness, and also in the explicit disapproval of the element of 'shamming' in upper-class good manners. Appearing consciously to satirise himself in the guise of Jimmy, who crumples up under Lady Charlcote's attack, Lawrence nevertheless gives away his covert admiration for the strong-minded women with a recognised 'place' in society.

It is, of course, these ambiguities and hesitations that make the play so interesting and so much more than either a biographical record or an eternal triangle stereotype. The emotional patterns never quite match the dramatic shape in which they are offered, and it is this disparity which allows for the stimulus of multiple meaning. It is not a simple case of Frieda being misrepresented; of being, as Lawrence reports her to have expressed it in his letter to Garnett, 'put in rags', while Lawrence has 'gilded himself beyond recognition'. We feel, for example, that the relation between life and the art of the play is particularly complex when, at the end of this act, we find that Barbara's hysterical outburst appears to be designed structurally to direct our admiration towards her and away from her lover.

Barbara's outburst develops as a climax to the contest that has been seen to take place between mother, daughter and lover. In the course of that contest the mother has behaved, as Barbara describes it, 'Like any of the women of the common people you've told me about'. Jimmy, however, feels this behaviour as 'natural' and even admires the common touch: 'At any rate she wasn't lofty', he comments. He resents Lady Charlcote's dragging in of 'the money business' not, as Barbara does, because he feels it to be 'like kicking a man when he's down', but because he feels that the question of money places him in a different class.[3] Admiring Lady Charlcote's air of not *seeming* superior, Jimmy can claim that he does not care 'what the old Mrs. Baronet says', but, as Barbara points out, his behaviour during the confrontation has plainly shown that he does care.

We have seen him leave his mistress and her mother alone together and return with 'wine, biscuits, bread and butter', and, in this inappropriate gesture of hospitality, have noted the role that Jimmy allocates to himself in the situation. He, at any rate, behaves like one of the 'common people' about whom he has told Barbara, taking upon himself the traditionally feminine role of the class from which he comes by attempting to smooth over difficulties with his offer of refreshment. When Lady Charlcote refuses, he persists, 'Could I make you a cup of tea?' and we feel very strongly the contrast between his effort at polite behaviour and the way in which Barbara would prefer him to behave.

As she demands afterwards, we are made to wonder 'Why didn't you suddenly get up and flap your arms like a cockerel and crow?' We may not, of course, see it in exactly those terms, but we have been made to feel that Jimmy should at least have made some demonstration of defiance that 'would have been so beautiful', and we are no more content than Barbara with his argument, 'But what good would it have done?' since we have been shown that what Barbara requires is a spirit as strong and expressive as her own in the lover who can help her to get away from emotional entanglements and family ties.

Jimmy's pathetic failure to rise to this occasion diminishes him in our eyes as well as in Barbara's. He has been seen to 'crumple up'; to be unable to carry off the crisis in anything approaching the grand or heroic manner that Barbara requires of him. At the same time the play has directed us to see how much Jimmy admires the grand and heroic manner in Barbara, and how large a part that aspect of her personality plays in his love for her.

[3] Similar attitudes (to class and money) to those noted here in the play can be found in the chapter entitled 'A Railway Journey' in *Aaron's Rod*.

Under the lash of her scorn he again offers food, presenting himself to his mistress as a servant, when what she demands is a master. Driven to continue her mockery until she provokes in her lover the anger that matches her own, Barbara's taunts become crueller. Prostrating herself at his feet, she parodies the servility she despises in him and at last arouses the dominant masculinity of his 'fierce embrace'. Here at last we are shown the Jimmy to whom—the play asks us to believe—Barbara has gladly surrendered herself, willingly abandoning all the material advantages that he fears might call her away from him. Despite all the evidence of conflicting loyalties which account for the insecurity voiced in Jimmy's agonised cry, 'Oh you're not faithful to me,' Barbara's affirmation '(thickly) I am,' is emphatically confirmed by the victory of passion on which the Act closes.

Jimmy's way to victory—on her terms at least—in the fight for Barbara has been clearly demonstrated in this Act. He must be assertive, dominant and 'masculine', if he is to win her entirely away from the family that threatens to re-possess her. To Jimmy himself, however, the way is shown to be neither clear nor even ultimately attainable. In the following Act, we see once again that it is his submissiveness and lack of ability to stand up against his adversaries that is the motif for strife between the lovers. In Barbara and Jimmy, we begin to see that Lawrence is setting up, once again, his 'philosophy of sex relations', and that, rather than representing Frieda and Lawrence, the central characters act out opposing aspects of that philosophy. It is a balance between the necessary relation (as Lawrence sees it) between a man and a woman, and the equally necessary measure of freedom that must be granted to each of them as individuals, that must be struck in order that an 'ideal' relationship may be created.

These oppositions are brought into play as Act III opens on Barbara's demand that Jimmy should stand up together with her and fight openly against their mutual foes. 'Why don't you say I *oughtn't* to go for a drive with Mama without you?', she asks petulantly. Jimmy refuses to give up his 'true self' in order to be the champion she requires. She must, in turn, be true to his kind of fidelity, if their love is to survive. Unable, on this occasion to lash him into action, Barbara flounces out, leaving Jimmy to a muttered and revealing soliloquy, in which he tells us of his own stubborn class pride, while purporting to 'show up' Barbara's inability to abandon herself to him. 'I should like to murder the twopence-halfpenny lot of them, with their grizzling and whining and chuffing,' he fumes, as Barbara leaves for her meeting with her mother. 'If they'd leave us alone we should be alright—damn them! Miserable bits of shouters! My mother was worth a million of 'em, for they've none of 'em the backbone of a flea. She doesn't *want* to stick to me—she doesn't *want* to love me—she won't *let* herself love me. She wants to save some rotten rag of independence—she's afraid to let herself go and to belong to me.'

Far from being a straightforward statement of Jimmy's view of the situation, this outburst is riddled with contradictions and confusions in the light of what the play has actually shown us. Barbara's family are not 'miserable bits of shouters' if what we have seen of Lady Charlcote is anything to go by. Jimmy, moreover, is thoroughly cowed in her presence, while Barbara has shown courage in defying her. In one breath Jimmy demands that Barbara come to him of her own free will and remain with him as a free individual, while in the next he rages that she will not 'belong' to him.

Aware perhaps of the ambivalence of this revelation, Lawrence builds up the element of sympathy for Jimmy by rendering Sir William ridiculous in the ensuing confrontation between father and lover. Again we see the 'hero' making frustrated attempts to be gentlemanly by offering hospitality to his unwanted guest. In Barbara's absence these efforts take on a more admirable aspect. Against the short, shout gentleman 'with a bristling moustache' who is Barbara's father, 'ill-bred' Jimmy is made to appear impressive as one of 'nature's gentlemen'. Abruptly—and indeed churlishly—dismissing Jimmy's hospitality, Sir William immediately gets down to business, taxing Jimmy with 'a crime against society' in luring Barbara away from her husband, and in keeping her with him against all the dictates of morality. Rendered absurd by his accusation that Jimmy is committing 'a criminal act against the State, against the rights of man altogether, against Dr. Tressider, and against my daughter', Sir William's tirade is interrupted by Barbara's return with her mother. Here too Lawrence undermines any sympathy we might feel for the outraged father by providing him with the melodramatic exit line (as he picks up his hat), 'I never want to see you again'. The weeping mother follows, vowing never to leave her daughter in the lurch, and Jimmy returns from politely seeing them out to face Barbara's renewed accusation of having behaved like a 'poor worm'.

Despite the buffoonish figure that Sir William has been made to cut in this parody of a Victorian rejection scene, we find ourselves again sympathising with Barbara. Jimmy has been seen to be incapable of routing the enemy alone—even though that enemy has also been set up as pretty poor stuff. Barbara has to play the man's part in the struggle and she tells us that it is this responsibility which is driving her mad: 'I have to fight for you as if you weren't a man,' she complains bitterly. 'I didn't think it would be so hard—I have to fight you, and them, and everybody. Not a soul in the world gives me the tiniest bit of help.' So far everything in the play has persuaded us of the truth of Barbara's statement and denied Jimmy's view that 'she doesn't *want* to love me—she won't *let* herself love me.' Very far then from 'gilding' Lawrence and putting Frieda 'in rags', the play here glorifies Barbara's heroism and diminishes Jimmy's stature in a way that, once again, suggests how mistaken it would be to identify either of the two leading characters in the dramatic fiction too closely with the man and woman who took part in the real life drama, on which the play is so equivocally based.

It has been made easy by the tone of the dialogue in the scene between Jimmy and Sir William for the former to score against the latter. Indeed the clichés make of Sir William a positive figure of fun, fully justifying the description of the play as a comedy. We might notice, for example, how he is systematically deprived even of that degree of dignity with which John Osborne credits his outraged father figure in the similar situation portrayed in *Look Back in Anger* (a play with which *The Fight for Barbara* has many striking affinities). Yet, even against the background of the caricatured father, Jimmy is seen to be a 'poor worm' in Barbara's eyes. Towards that father Barbara herself has felt both love and hate, the love having been overtaken by hatred of her father's cowardice in the matter of his affair with Selma. Now Jimmy, as lover, must prove himself braver than the father who 'broke' under his wife's discovery of his infidelity.

Barbara asks a great deal of Jimmy, and the sympathetic light in which she is presented is to an extent counterbalanced by the extravagance of her emotional demands. In the crisis of Act II she has been seen to be won over by Jimmy's passion. Here (in Act III Scene 1) she is once again appeased, this time by the tenderness rather than the ferocity of his love. Slowly we are made to feel that Jimmy is winning his fight for Barbara—not on his original uncompromising terms, but through an effort to see the situation from her point of view.

She can laugh with him and love him as he sets her fears in perspective by telling her that Frederick is unlikely to go mad at the sight of her. 'You're not such a magical person as all that', he teases, undermining her fantasy of playing Desdemona to Frederick's Othello. A sense of humour plays a large part here (as it will do in the resolution of the final scene) in winning Barbara over from the hold of the melodramatic and intensely serious Frederick. The degree to which laughter and tenderness are triumphant at this point is registered in Barbara's cry of 'O, I love you!' on which the scene ends, even though the curtain falls on Jimmy's still doubting 'Do you?'

As that note of doubt prompts us to suppose, Barbara's confidence in her own strength and independence still resists the complete capitulation that Jimmy requires of her. At the beginning of Act III Scene 2 she appears 'resplendent in an evening dress with an ornament in her hair'. Jimmy is to be dazzled by her unaccustomed finery, but he resists: 'You put it on for Frederick, not for me.' He does not want to be seen to be impressed by her appearance as a grand lady—though the play has already revealed to us how much this aspect of Barbara does, in fact, impress him. Mocking him for wanting to drag her down by preferring her in a kitchen pinafore, Barbara nevertheless senses the importance to Jimmy of her dress as a sign of her relationship to him, and is about to change, when she is disturbed by the arrival of Lady Charlcote with Frederick.

In the encounter with Barbara's mother, Jimmy was presented as courteous and indeed almost servile; with Sir William, less so, and with Frederick even less—to the point indeed of positive rudeness. Cumulatively therefore, the structuring of the play around these three encounters calls our attention to the increasingly dangerous threat to the lovers' happiness made by the successive intruders. At the same time, the interludes between the onslaughts have shown Jimmy progressively overcoming Barbara's fierce will to be free and independent.

Here in Act III Scene 2 Jimmy offers nothing to the visitor. To Lady Charlcote, we recall, he had brought food and wine, and even offered a homely cup of tea; to Sir William, a cigarette, albeit one from a 'threepenny packet'. To Frederick he offers nothing, and does not even acknowledge the husband's presence, as he requires Barbara to dismiss him herself before he will agree to leave her alone with the man whom she has deserted for his sake.

At this point in the play, it is Barbara who is reduced to hesitation and uncertainty, while Jimmy is decisive and stubborn. Only at Barbara's insistence does he withdraw, and then to the bedroom which she is too embarrassed to name. Imperious Barbara, we notice, falters as she orders Jimmy away 'to—one of the other rooms'. Defiantly specific, he retorts, 'I'll go to the bedroom then.'

After Jimmy's reluctant withdrawal we are presented with the crucial scene between Barbara and Frederick. However 'word for word true' we may take the play to be up to this point (with, of course, the exception of Barbara's brief conversation with her mother in Jimmy's absence), it is here that we must, in the crudest biographical terms, be aware that the dialogue is an imaginative construction. At the very least, we might concede it to be an imaginative reconstruction of Frieda's report to Lawrence of a similar occasion in life. But, on turning to the biography proper, we interestingly find that there was no such visit from Frieda's husband. Nor, of course, were Frieda's parents the outraged English aristocrats portrayed by Sir William and Lady Charlcote. As we know, Frieda's family took the elopement surprisingly well, and, in the fullness of time, Frieda's mother became extremely attached to Lawrence. It also becomes vital to recall that the cause of Frieda's deepest suffering in the real-life situation was the separation from her children that is omitted from the play.

With the encounter between Barbara and Frederick then, we are brought face to face with the radical error of confusing art with life. What we actually have in the play is an imaginative endeavour to reconstruct (to paraphrase Ibsen) the emotional crisis as it was in life, in the form of dramatic art which, while changing the 'facts', nevertheless renders the truth of an emotional experience that has been 'lived through' by the dramatist himself.[4]

As we notice in the play, the children, who were such an important part of that experience, are not mentioned.[5] Instead, the degree of Barbara's suffering is measured in terms of her struggle to free herself from the bonds that tie her to her husband so that she may enter into a quite differently based relationship with her lover. Frieda's attachment to her children might therefore be felt to have been transposed into the element of imperious independence in Barbara's character; that element of which Jimmy complains when he declares: 'She wants to save some rotten rag of independence—she's afraid to let herself go and to belong to me.' Just the same, as we have already noted several times, this is an element in Barbara's character that Jimmy greatly admires.

It is this fear that Barbara will not abandon her independence which is acted out for us in Act III Scene 2. Jimmy's reluctance to leave husband and wife together, and the depth of the relationship revealed between them when they *are* left alone, forcefully presents to us the source of Jimmy's fear that he can never win the fight for Barbara; that there will always be some part of her that belongs to her husband and the past.

Frederick is given a highly melodramatic line to take in this important scene. Indeed at one point he is made to say to Barbara: 'I've no doubt it all sounds very melodramatic—but it's the truth for me.' Just as the character of Sir William was undercut by cliché-ridden dialogue, Frederick's here is satirised by the absurdity of his hyperbolic declarations. 'I would have

[4] See, *Ibsen: Letters and Speeches*, ed. Evert Sprinchorn (New York, 1964; London, 1965), p. 222 et passim.

[5] The omission of the subject of the children is overlooked by Robert Lucas, when he writes, of *The Fight for Barbara*, 'Barbara's husband, a professor arrives unexpectedly and urges her to return with him to their children.' (*Frieda Lawrence*, p. 94) There is, however, a direct reference to Frieda's children in the title of the play, Barbara being the name of her younger daughter.

spilt my blood on every paving stone in Bromley for you, if you had wanted me to' is the kind of speech that undermines Frederick's posturing as the wronged husband. He is almost too consciously and calculatingly set up so as to appear ridiculous in our eyes. Against this, however, we must balance the fact that Barbara is shown almost to be won over by his pleas.

Frederick's stiffness and want of humour are exactly the characteristics from which Barbara is escaping. In this respect at least, she is shown to have made a better choice in Jimmy who can laugh with her and tease her. It is evidently hopeless for her to have wanted Frederick to have 'come near' to her. He has worshipped her as she never wanted to be worshipped, 'kissing my feet instead of helping me'. In Frederick's ludicrous stiffness, as manifested in this scene, we are shown the contrast between the husband who has set his wife on a pedestal and the lover who can tell her that she is not such a magical person as she imagines herself to be.

Provoked by Barbara's taunts, Frederick resorts to a physical onslaught, and here too we are presented with a sharp contrast between the husband who comes close to strangle and the lover who attacks only to kiss. Frederick's physical approach is an almost murderous attempt to re-possess her, while Jimmy has been able to use his strength as a triumphant assertion of passion. Frederick's grip on Barbara is a forceful dramatic figure for the difference between her relationship with each of the men, and, in terms of action, it succeeds only in widening the gulf between man and wife, as is illustrated in the stage direction: 'He releases her—she flings herself face down on the sofa—he sits crouching, glaring. Silence for some time.' Very reminiscent of the scene representing the breakdown of the relationship between the Holroyds, this moment obviously represents a paradigmatic Lawrentian view of the final break in a man-woman relationship.

In the metaphor that Frederick is given to express the way in which he feels that Barbara has used him and the love he has lavished upon her, we are again directed to see the husband as ridiculously inadequate to the spirit of the woman he has married. Frederick's love has been thrown away 'like a piece of dirty paper wrapping'. Over-ruling her protest he continues, 'You have thrown me away like a bit of paper off a parcel. You got all the goods out of the packet, and threw me away—' Again, after the threat of violence, Frederick reverts to his reduction of himself to a piece of 'waste-paper that has wrapped up a few years of your life'.

In the fact of such absurd comparisons, with their reductively material implications, Barbara is seen to have no difficulty in resisting the histrionic plea for her return. It could not be otherwise for a woman of the kind that Barbara has been presented as representing, taxed with a husband who compares himself to wrapping-paper and tries to reinstate himself in her affections with his declaration of having been willing to spill blood on every paving stone in Bromley in order to satisfy her desires. Yet she does feel torn between her deserted husband and her lover. 'It pulls both ways,' she cries as Frederick presses for a decision that will, one way or the other, put him out of the misery of uncertainty. Unmoved by the words that give away those aspects of her husband's character to which she is most hostile, Barbara is nevertheless shown to feel that Frederick might go out of his mind, or even kill himself, and, when he breaks down into tears, she is won over almost to tenderness.

It is in her indecision at this critical point that the play enacts the threat from the past which jeopardises the lovers' security. In turn Lady Charlcote, Sir William and Frederick have been shown up as impotent outsiders who do not understand the nature of the attachment between Jimmy and Barbara. At the close of the interview with Frederick, we are made nevertheless strongly to feel that Barbara herself is not absolutely sure, and it is in *her* insecurity that the real threat lies. Promising to give Frederick her definite answer 'tomorrow', she allows her husband to fold her in his arms, and puts her head back as he kisses her. Submitting thus to Frederick's embrace, Barbara is positively seen to be torn between the two men. Jimmy, this image tells us, has been right to fear her uncertainty.

Having won some hope Frederick 'dashes out' leaving Barbara to report the outcome of their talk to Lady Charlcote and Jimmy. Against the grain of the way in which she earlier had been characterised, Lady Charlcote is here portrayed as commendably honest. We remember, however, that she has been the least hostile of the three intruders; the one prepared to stand by her daughter at all costs, and we are aware of the contrast between *her* objections to Jimmy and Frederick's, particularly when she advises her daughter not to make 'a double mess of it'. 'You'll have to stick to one or the other now, at any rate—so you'd better stick to the one you can live with, and not to the one you can do without— for if you get the wrong one, you might as well drown two people then instead of one,' she continues, in a tone that enlists our agreement as downright common sense after Frederick's high- flown rhetoric.

Lady Charlcote's comparative detachment here places the emphasis for making a decision on the lovers themselves. It is not a question of Jimmy being opposed by an army of hostile foes, but of his ability, in single combat, to win Barbara from her former attachments.

As the scene ends we are shown the weakness of his position. In demanding of Barbara that she leave at once 'If you're going back to Frederick in the morning,' Jimmy asserts that very possessiveness from which Barbara is struggling to escape in her relationship with Frederick.

'All men are alike,' she bursts out. 'They don't care what a woman wants. They try to get hold of what they want them- selves. . . .' She will not stay with Jimmy on those terms, ex- changing slavery to one man for the same condition under the domination of another, and the scene ends with her defiant taking up of Jimmy's challenge to leave the house at once.

There are elements in the play that incline us to feel that it should end here on the note of indecision that has been con- sistently sounded. Against these we must, however, weigh the equally powerful forces in the play that justify Lawrence's des- cription of it as a comedy. We have, as has been noted, been made aware throughout that there is a joy in the love between Barbara and Jimmy that has never existed between Barbara and Frederick. Manifested in the humour of the way in which the relationship between the lovers is presented, as well as in the absurdity of those hostile to them, this joy has also been shown to spring from the mutuality of their physical passion—an element conspicuously missing from the husband-wife relation.

The final scene in which all is resolved is therefore less arbitrary than might at first appear. It is not merely a 'happy ending', tacked on for the sake of biographical accuracy, or even—in a formal sense—for the sake of fidelity to the comic genre. On the contrary, it grows organically from the pattern set up by the structure of the play; a pattern in which the joy of the lovers' mutual passion has been seen to triumph successively over progressively more dangerous attacks.

In Act I the skirmishes over Francesca and the butcher had threatened the security, born of that mutual joy, in a light-hearted way. In Act II Lady Charlcote provided a more serious threat, increased in intensity through the two scenes of Act III by the intrusions of Sir William and Frederick. After each attack, Jimmy and Barbara's ability to reassert their love has been more severely tested until, at the end of Act III, it appears finally to have been defeated. Yet, in keeping with the pattern, the brief final Act shows the power of passion to be sufficiently strong, indeed perhaps even more resilient than it had formerly been, in its capacity to unite the lovers. The crux is reached when Barbara, dressed for immediate departure, provokes Jimmy to a display of physical strength almost as melodramatic as Frederick's. Even up to this point, there has been a sharp humour enlivening the crisis of the imminent break. Barbara—characteristically—has forgotten her hankies; she has no money, and the impoverished Jimmy has only ten lira to give her. The fight between them is indeed a 'Fool's idiotic theatrical game' as Jimmy describes it. But it is a game that has to be played out before the lovers can recover their composure, and return to tenderness.

As it happens the play does end on a note of indecision, but it is an indecision that points hopefully forward to a possible future for Jimmy and Barbara. The ghost of Frederick *will* be exorcised, even though Barbara threatens that, 'if he dies, I shall torment the life out of you'. 'You'll do that anyway,' Jimmy cheerfully retorts.

For both of them, it is the recognition that their love is a joy which provides security and hope for the future. 'Say I am a joy to you,' Barbara pleads, and Jimmy gladly grants her request. 'You are a living joy to me, you are—especially this evening.' Torment and joy are seen to be inextricably interwoven in this relationship: the one almost as essential to its continuance as the other, and it is this state of passional delight and anguish that

175

the play celebrates, proposing that the mixture is triumphant always against whatever the odds that threaten.

Of all Lawrence's plays, this is the most obviously cut to the pattern of the traditional well-made play. Already by the end of Act I, we see that the design has been laid down. We have been given the exposition that tells us of the past, and the balance in which we must measure the possible outcome. The threat from outside must surely move progressively closer. We will have a *scène-à-faire*, and, as the lovers are successively shown surmounting progressively more dangerous obstacles, we know that the last act resolution will be a happy one.

Lawrence's dramatic originality in this play does not consist in the creation of a new form, but in the creative adaptation of an old one. Much of the humour arises from his skilful frustration of the expectations aroused by the conventional 'romantic' structure of his plot. Just as the scene with Sir William parodies the Victorian archetype of the scene in which the sinful woman is cast out of 'good' society, so the victory of the 'immoral' lovers casts scathing doubt on the moral system from which they are escaping.

There is too, a distinctly Shavian flavour and bite in the dialogue, though Shaw would not, perhaps, have ventured so close to the mainsprings of what is, despite the lightness of treatment, so obviously a passionate attachment between the two central characters. In many ways too, the manner of *The Fight for Barbara* reminds us of the comedies that Noel Coward was to write decades later, and brings to mind also the association that Catherine Carswell was to make between the dialogue of Coward and that of Lawrence in *Touch and Go*.[6]

To make these comparisons is not to belittle the achievement of Lawrence the dramatist, even in so slight a piece as this. In fact, in view of his high hopes of getting the play staged, one would feel rather that comparison with such masters of theatricality as Shaw and Coward could be seen as the highest of praise. It is hard to imagine Lawrence maintaining this particular mode of drama had he received for the play the recognition he so much

[6] In her discussion of *Touch and Go* in *The Savage Pilgrimage*, Catherine Carswell remarks that the scenes between the lovers, Gerald and Anabel, 'give one an odd foretaste of Noel Coward at his best.'

desired. Yet his particularly keen disappointment in Garnett's rejection of it points to a sense in which he evidently felt that it was written to meet the demands of a potential audience. That he could so well 'write to order', even though that order failed to materialise, must surely be a mark of credit to his dramatic craftsmanship.

8

Touch and Go

According to Catherine Carswell, Lawrence wrote *Touch and Go* in the spring of 1919 when he was living at Chapel Farm Cottage in Berkshire. (N.I. p. 488) May that year was hot and dry. Lawrence wrote that 'Summer has about exploded into leaf this year; violence is really catching'. He and Frieda, apparently relaxing in an away-from-it-all idyll of country life, were in fact 'waiting to be able to move'. *Women in Love* was still to be steered through the final traumatic stages towards publication, and Lawrence, having impatiently decided that he could not write the 'educational stuff' designed for *The Times Educational Supplement* (the series of essays entitled 'Education of the People' which was subsequently rejected and published only posthumously in *Phoenix* in 1936), put the finishing touches to his 'history book' (*Movements in European History*), wrote short stories, and the play *Touch and Go*.

Described by Lawrence's biographer, Emile Delavenay, as 'a curious sequel to *Women in Love*'[1] this play has generally been thought to have been written specifically for The People's Theatre Society under whose auspices it was published in 1920. There appears, however, to be considerable doubt as to whether Lawrence actually wrote the play with this end in view, or whether, having written it, it then happened to suit the purposes of Douglas Goldring's project.

Goldring's account of the episode[2] begins with his first meet-

[1] Emile Delavenay, *D. H. Lawrence: The Man and His Work*, trans. Katharine M. Delavenay, (1972), p. 249.

[2] A full account (from his own point of view) of the controversy over *Touch and Go* can be found in Douglas Goldring's autobiographical *Odd*

ing with Lawrence in the home of S. S. Koteliansky in Hampstead. Confessing himself at that time to have been a 'hectic idealist' still much under the influence of people and ideas long before rejected as phoney by Lawrence, Goldring admits that he himself had then given up writing anything except what the critics justly labelled 'propaganda'. His wife Betty (whom Lawrence admired for her 'silent quality' and thought should play the leading part in *The Widowing of Mrs. Holroyd*) was also politically involved and worked in what Lawrence described as a 'pamphlet shop' disseminating the ideas and literature of the 'advanced crowd' whom Goldring later came to distrust.

When he started the People's Theatre Society Goldring anticipated no difficulty in arranging for one of Lawrence's plays to be produced, but, according to his account, he had failed to reckon with his committee who flatly turned down *Touch and Go* as 'impossible of production'. Still convinced of the worth of Lawrence's plays, Goldring took the trouble to travel up to Altrincham for the 1920 production of *Mrs. Holroyd* and, like Catherine Carswell, was sufficiently impressed with the 'good amateur performance' to continue to press the case for the Society's presenting a play by Lawrence. His efforts, however, were fruitless, and he claims that the whole experience taught him never again to start anything from altruistic motives or to submit himself to the man-handling of committees.

Rightly or wrongly Lawrence took a very different view of the whole matter, though Goldring insists that the publication of his own play *The Fight for Freedom* first in what was to have been a series of plays for a People's Theatre was simply the natural result of the publisher having received his manuscript first. It was, as Goldring later felt, 'a great pity from every point of view that the series was not launched under the cloak of Lawrence's literary prestige'.[3]

From Lawrence's point of view it was something more than a pity. He was outraged that the play which he had been told was to inaugurate the series had to take second place, especially in view

Man Out (1935), and in his books, *Life Interests* (1948) and *The Nineteen Twenties* (1945). The relevant passages are conveniently to be found in Nehls, Vol. 1, pp. 490–496, and Vol. II, pp. 39–43.

[3] Douglas Goldring, *Odd Man Out*, p. 257.

of the fact that *Touch and Go* was, in his opinion, no 'pamphlet play' but a serious dramatic expression of social and political ideas highly individual to Lawrence himself, and certainly not a propaganda piece designed to promote a political platform of which he profoundly disapproved. Nevertheless, his letters to Goldring in 1920, after the publication of *Touch and Go* indicate that he at least made a show of swallowing his anger and accepting the latter's explanation of the publication muddle. The forgiveness appears to have been lasting, since Goldring also received a friendly and nostalgic letter from Lawrence some ten years later.

In July 1919 Lawrence wrote to his agent J. B. Pinker: 'A man called Douglas Goldring wants to do my play *Touch and Go* in a *People's Theatre Society* venture. It may not come to much, but the idea attracts me. Also, he wants to publish the play in a series of "Plays for the People's Theatre".' (N.I p. 490) By that time Lawrence had already written the play, and this letter clearly substantiates Keith Sagar's view that in 1919 Lawrence thought that, in Douglas Goldring, he had finally found his man to 'whip 'em in'.[4]

Excited by a further prospect of at last having a play properly staged, (especially, one must remember, in the light of the failed negotiations to mount a professional production of *Mrs. Holroyd*), Lawrence gladly accepted Goldring's offer to publish *Touch and Go*, and, according to Dr. Sagar, 'let Goldring have the play and its preface free' on the understanding that it would be the first in the series, and that it would be produced. This view of the matter would, of course, account for Lawrence's fury when the play was actually published second in the series,[5] as well as confirming that Lawrence's ambition to have a play produced was more important to him than any political considerations. The political tone of the play and its preface must indeed have come as something of a surprise to Goldring and his committee.

Printed together with the original 'paper-covered book' in 1920

[4] Keith Sagar, 'D. H. Lawrence: Dramatist', p. 176.

[5] Lawrence's disgust on this occasion is forcefully expressed in a letter to Koteliansky in which he writes: 'Douglas Goldring sent me his *Fight for Freedom*. A nice thing for my play to be following on the heels of such a shit: especially as, since I was purported to open the series, *I* have got a little "Preface" on "A People's Theatre".' *The Quest for Rananim*, p. 203.

and again together with the play in *The Plays of D. H. Lawrence* (1933), the preface to *Touch and Go* does not appear in the *Complete Plays* (1965).[6] It does, however, provide a very important gloss on the nature of the political commitment that we find in the play itself.

Only at a very superficial level can this preface be read as a doctrinaire statement of the conventional opposition between Capital and Labour. Lawrence indeed questions the very existence of these abstract concepts insofar as they eptomise for him the extremes of de-humanisation. Comparing the underlying human struggle going on between these abstractions in the twentieth century to that between the people and the king which underlay drama in the time of Shakespeare, Lawrence distinguishes between the 'merely mechanical' struggle which 'though it may bring disaster and death to millions, is no more than an accident, an accidental collision of forces' and the genuinely tragic dilemma where the struggle is between man and man, and 'The conflict is in pure, passional antagonism, turning upon the poles of belief.'

Read as an attempt to boost or promote the idea of 'A People's Theatre', the preface is a complete failure, and one can hardly wonder at Goldring's committee relegating it to second place in the series. Indeed it so critically undermines the very premises upon which partisan political theatre could be founded that one marvels how it ever came to be published—as it eventually was —under the 'label' of The People's Theatre Society. Whether or not Lawrence meant it seriously as a 'puff' for Goldring's high-minded venture, it is obvious that his temperamental resistance to the notion of dividing people into categories undercut any support that he may have felt was due to a theatre that proposed to set up in opposition to the contemporary 'establishment'. It was in the latter respect alone; that is, with the idea of forming some kind of 'alternative theatre', that Lawrence can be felt to have any kind of sympathy with a movement towards most of

[6] *Touch and Go* was originally published, together with its preface, by C. W. Daniel in London, and by Thomas Seltzer in New York, in 1920, and subsequently, in 1933, by Martin Secker (London) in *The Plays of D. H. Lawrence*, which also included *The Widowing of Mrs. Holroyd* and *David*. More accessible than these is *Phoenix II*, edited by H. T. Moore and F. W. Roberts, (1968), in which the preface to *Touch and Go* can be found on pages 289–293.

whose principles (as Goldring was later to discover and admit) he could hardly have been more bitterly opposed.

At the outset the preface takes the steam out of the high-sounding title, 'A People's Theatre' by pointing to the non-existence of the entity to which the title is supposed to belong. 'The name is chosen' Lawrence mocks, but 'the baby isn't even begotten; nay, the would-be parents aren't married, nor yet courting.' It is all, he implies, idealistic pie-in-the-sky, and he does not even put much faith in the as yet unrealised ideals. Deducing the kind of theatre that is being proposed from its title, Lawrence suggests the formula: 'Major premiss: the seats are cheap. Minor premiss: the plays are good.' Then he proceeds to demolish the political theory upon which the validity of such a formula would have to be based.

To have cheap seats would assume that the 'people' are poor. But, Lawrence argues, 'Appearances are deceptive. The proletariat isn't poor. Everybody is poor except Capital and Labour. Between these upper and nether millstones great numbers of decent people are squeezed.' As for the plays being 'good', Lawrence maintains, 'Any play is good to the man who likes to look at it. And at that rate "Chu Chin Chow" is extra-super-good. What about your *good* plays? Whose good? Pfui to your goodness!'

Ostensibly, of course, the rhetoric here is meant to represent the objections of the 'man in the street' to the proposal of a 'People's Theatre' with its failure to define even what it means by 'people'. But the voice of Lawrence becomes increasingly identified with that of the anonymous objector as he warms to his real theme: that people cannot be abstracted or categorised and made to represent concepts such as 'Capital' and 'Labour'. His metaphor is drawn from the stage, but applies more widely to life outside the theatre when he writes, 'Given a *rôle*, a *part*, you can play it by clockwork. But you can't have a clockwork human being'.

His protest then is not against any specific, topical social outrage, but against de-humanisation, and his plea is consequently not for some abstract ideal of a 'People's Theatre' but for a play which will truthfully illuminate the predicament of real human individuals, who are so much more than a 'whole bunch of rôles tied into one'. The crux of his argument rests on this element of humanity: 'Granted that men are still men, Labour v. Capitalism is a tragic struggle. If men are no more than implements, it is non-tragic and merely disastrous.' In Shakespeare's time, Lawrence identifies the comparable abstract, conceptualised struggle as 'people versus king'. Now, he says, 'A new wind is getting up. We call it Labour versus Capitalism.' The name changes, but the underlying struggle remains constant where it really counts—at the heart of men's living passions.

Defining the issue over which that 'old bull-dog, the British capitalist' and 'that unsatisfied mongrel Plebs, the proletariat' were currently wrangling as an obvious 'old bone' which is merely a pretext, 'a hollow *casus belli*', Lawrence calls for an open acknowledgement of what the fight is *really* about. If the contestants insist on pulling for grim life, they will at last tear the bone to atoms and bring the world down in débris upon themselves. But that result, he emphasises, would be disaster rather than tragedy, since the issue for which the bone stands represents only the mechanical, inhuman aspect of conceptual abstraction.

By contrast as we have seen, tragedy, in Lawrence's terms, arises when 'The conflict is in pure, passional antagonism, turning upon the poles of belief,' and for this, man must be involved to the depths of his being in the struggle. The 'bone' must therefore be recognised for what it is; a mere pretext representing accidental, contemporary issues. 'The essence of tragedy' Lawrence declares, 'is that a man should go through with his fate and not dodge it or go bumping into an accident. And the whole business of life, at the great critical periods of mankind, is that men should accept and be one with their tragedy.'

Having developed to this note of 'high seriousness' from the satirical mockery of the high-faluting notion of a 'People's Theatre' with which it opened, the preface has obviously gone far beyond any brief that it might have had to promote the programme of The People's Theatre Society. It is therefore with something of a bathetic bump that we come up against Lawrence's return to his opening subject at the end of the final paragraph. Here we find him returning to the very 'bone' that he has rejected when he writes that 'if we are to accept and be one with' our tragedy, we must open our hearts, and, 'For one thing we should have a People's Theatre. Perhaps it would help us in this hour of confusion better than anything.' If we are to respond to this suggestion with any enthusiasm, it must, in the light of the preface, be a response to a People's Theatre in which the tragedy of the individual transcends the accidental opposition of mechanical forces; a theatre in which people are seen to represent human individuals rather than issues of class. Above all, it must be a theatre in which the struggle between Capital and Labour is seen in terms of living human beings.

In Lawrence's ideal theatre, as outlined in the preface, characters are to be 'Men who are somebody, not men who are something'. Neither Capital nor Labour will be represented by a clockwork figure who is merely an 'assortment of parts' mechanically assembled into a role, but by individuals whose engagement in their struggle is seen and felt to engage the poles of their belief.

It is easy enough to point in Douglas Goldring's 'pamphlet play', *The Fight for Freedom* to examples of the mechanical approach to characterisation. Goldring's preface is, in any case, much more direct in its propaganda which issues the challenge, 'When is English Labour going to recognise its importance and start a theatre of its own?' There is no doubt here—as there is in Lawrence's questioning even of what could be meant by 'people' in the title 'A People's Theatre'—of the identity of the group that the proposed theatre would be designed to serve. Neither is there any ambiguity in the lay-out of the play.

The very characters have 'type-names', as in some latter-day morality drama. Samuel Slaughter, the villain of the piece, criticises artists as 'socialists—pro-German, even conscientious objectors'. Outspoken and very conscious of the new ideas for which she is a mouthpiece, Margaret Lambert—the slaughterer's sacrificial victim—'fails' because she accepts Philip who treats her as a person, rather than Oliver who enslaves her with his ideas. It is obvious too that Goldring is on the side of Margaret's sister, Eleanor. In his preface he writes, 'There are so many people in England particularly among the intelligentsia who "take up progress" or "take up socialism" as a change from taking up Jazzing or "art", and with the same essential frivolity! It is these who, when the red dawn breaks for which they profess to be sighing, will be the first to cry out in alarm. In England the Margaret Lamberts are many, and the Eleanor Lamberts are few.'

In Goldring's case, we at least get the play we have been led to expect from the preface. The case of Lawrence's play is much more complicated. We certainly do not get the 'pamphlet' over-simplifications of character found in *The Fight for Freedom*, but neither do we find the 'realistically' developed people, for the delineation of whom Lawrence has so often been praised as having a special gift. Far from naturalistic in its rendering of character, *Touch and Go* eschews that mode of providing character with psychological motivation. There is little, if any, of the kind of 'development' which guides our interpretation of behaviour within the play. Yet the characters are certainly very much more than 'ciphers', and by no means the assemblies of mechanical parts, against which Lawrence inveighs in his preface.

Rather than describe the characters of *Touch and Go* as artificial or mechanical, one would want to say that they are presented so as to be seen as all too human in their hopeless inadequacy to combat a system for whose existence they are all, in part, responsible. A producer would have a hard time presenting *Touch and Go* as a 'tract' in favour of either 'Labour' or 'Capital', but (in these days of familiarity with a mode like that of the Theatre of the Absurd) there should be no problem in bringing out the play's bitter sense of the stale-mate of values characteristic of the mid-twentieth century. Man has proved not to be 'perfectible'. Material prosperity is philosophically and culturally suspected as a snare and a delusion. Neither the 'haves' nor the 'have nots' are satisfied with their lot. Industrialisation has corrupted both workers and owners, and its hoped-for benefits are seen as barriers to the full development of human life. These themes of Lawrence's play are so familiar today as to be almost clichés, but, provided always that we do not look for another 'triumph of naturalism', it is striking to find them enacted in that play—written, as it was, close on fifty-five years ago.

It is easy to be led off the track by the apparent conflict between Lawrence's theory of characterisation in the preface and the practical treatment of character found within the play. Indeed the lack of 'rounded' character drawing has been generally regarded as a mark of the play's lack of any dramatic or artistic value. It has been persuasively argued that *Touch and Go* is a failure because in it Lawrence is attempting to expound an idea, instead of exercising his essential gift for observing people as they really are. It has also been held to fail insofar as 'we do not open our hearts when we are told to', as we do 'when we see on the stage living individuals going through with their fates as we saw them in *The Widowing of Mrs. Holroyd* and *The Daughter-in-Law*.' Keith Sagar who makes this criticism of *Touch and Go*[7] goes on to point out that 'there is nothing of comparable authenticity' in it; nothing comparable, that is to the 'authenticity' found in the 'colliery' plays. Here, of course, one would completely agree. The authenticity in *Touch and Go* seems, to me at least, to derive from a dramatic scheme of quite a different order from that of naturalism; a scheme in which the concept of character performs quite a different function.

Controlling this scheme, the elements of context and character here appear in quite a different relationship from that found to be characteristic of *A Collier's Friday Night, The Widowing of Mrs. Holroyd* and *The Daughter-in-Law*, where there seemed still to be a note of hope, in the irresolution of the endings, that character might be stronger than the context that threatened to mould and even crush it. In *Touch and Go*, the tragedy, undercut as it is by bitter irony, arises from the fact that the context proves too strong for all of those who struggle within it. In the 'colliery' plays, character inter-acted with context. We learned in them what people were like from the way in which they behaved within their milieu. In *Touch and Go*, we learn about the characters in relation to their failure to come to terms with their context; in terms indeed of their subjection to its domination.

By looking at the play in this light it becomes possible to reconcile the triumph of de-humanisation enacted within the play with the insistence in the preface that tragedy necessarily involves full 'passional' engagement at a personal, human level. Essentially a pessimistic play, again remarkably akin to John Osborne's *Look Back in Anger*, (significantly acclaimed as 'revolutionary' in 1956) Lawrence's play of 1920 plainly states that there are no longer any good causes, and it does so by illustrating the frailty of individuals in the face of a situation that has got out of range of human control.

It is for this reason, one might feel, rather than because of any

[7] Keith Sagar, 'D. H. Lawrence: Dramatist', pp. 177–178.

deficiency in the creation of 'living' characters, that *Touch and Go* differs crucially in its 'authenticity' from the more optimistic naturalism of the 'colliery' plays, in which people are seen as still having a chance—albeit a frail one—of achieving full humanity.

On the basis of what is known elsewhere about Lawrence's political philosophy at this time, especially perhaps from what is 'written in' to *Women in Love*, this may be felt to be taking altogether too tolerant a view of a play which turns out to be ambiguous in spite of what might, on that evidence from *outside* the play, be felt to be the dramatist's efforts to make it speak plainly. In the bluntest of terms it has been said that the play is badly and carelessly thrown together because Lawrence wrote it in the service of a cause to which he was fundamentally opposed. Even if that view were taken, however, an enterprising producer could, I believe, 'salvage' from the 'confusion' a play that could be felt to be bitingly true to the widespread political disillusion of the 1970's. Whether Lawrence 'intended' it or not, *Touch and Go* has the elements of a modern tragedy, presented in a mode that could be eminently congenial to a modern producer. Freeing the play from preconceptions about what is and is not 'Lawrentian', we might well find it to be altogether a better play than those critics who have viewed it only from a Lawrentian point of view have given us to believe. It is perhaps uncharacteristic of the better known Lawrence, the novelist, but that does not at all mean that it is uncharacteristic of modern drama—to the development of which, as we have seen, the less familiar Lawrence, the dramatist, was consistently sensitive.

Turning to the play itself, and looking at it—as we must— without reference to the 'fuller life' that Lawrence gave to the 'same characters' in *Women in Love*, the elements on which a fine modern production could be built emerge quite clearly. Beginning, as we did with the naturalist plays, with the structural components of time and place, we at once see that there is a striking contrast between the concrete definition of the earlier mode and the emblematic sign-system of *Touch and Go*. The setting scheme for the three Acts provides us with an excellent guide to the interpretation of this system. Act I Scene 1 and Act III Scene 2 (the first and last Scenes of the play) are set in the market place; the public forum in which the issues of the strike *and* of the relationship between Anabel and Gerald become *public* property. The only feature of this market place required by Lawrence's stage directions is 'a small memorial obelisk', monument to the slaughtered victims of a global conflict surrounding the local conflict dramatised in the play.

Act I Scene 2 closes in on Winifred's studio; the 'ivory tower' set high up 'over the outbuildings' of Lilley Close; a sanctuary significantly removed from the centre of the Capitalist stronghold in the Barlow house. Here Lawrence presents the personal hopes and frustrations of the artist, Anabel, and the emotional tangle of unresolved ideals that weave her inextricably into the web spun by the industrialised, mechanical society all around her.

At the centre of the play Act II is situated in the Barlows' drawing-room; the heart of the owners' power-house, where issues take on a semi-public tone, controlled by the dominant voice of Gerald. We will see, for example, the effect that this 'point of view' has on the way in which we respond to the militant agitator in this setting.

The intensely personal confrontation between Anabel and Gerald in Act III Scene 1 is set in a park surrounding the Hall which has been abandoned by the neighbouring coal-owning family (erstwhile partners with the Barlows in profiting from the industrialisation of the area), and is now given over wholly to administration of the collieries. Predicting the next phase in the owner/worker relationship in its representation of the complete divorce between employers and employees, this setting provides a symbolic 'double' for the problem at issue in the personal conflict between Gerald and Anabel; a problem which is left unresolved in this Scene on the outbreak of violence between Gerald and Job Arthur Freer.

Returning to the public forum of the market place for its final Scene, the play juxtaposes the Capital v. Labour conflict with the human issue in the climactic moment of the attack on Gerald which is 'unrealistically' but effectively—at least in the dramatic terms of this particular play—called to a halt by Anabel's long drawn out wail of animal pain and her plea: 'It's enough—he's a man as you are. He's a man as you are. He's a man as you are. He's a man as you are.' Violence is halted, but nothing is settled. There is no resolution and no suggestion that one can be found. Humanity's voice appealing for humanity can still, perhaps, call a brief halt to bloodshed—but nothing is changed. The conflict continues in a lower tone, but there is evidently no way out. Anabel takes no part in his return to the impasse. Her voice is silenced after the outcry which averts—for the time being—the crisis of violence.

Formally then, it can be seen that the play provides a ground plan for the enactment of a skirmish without issue one way or the other. There is no victory for either Capital or Labour, and a gloomy prospect of inevitable defeat for the real human beings enlisted on either side of the battle. The real enemy is seen to be outside the local flare-up, symbolised in the obelisk commemorating the war dead and in the de-humanised hall taken over as offices. Right at the heart of the matter too, the emotional lives of Anabel and Gerald are seen as stunted; incapable of overcoming in-built hostilities, and arbitrarily married into an uneasy truce in which the only positive element is the cry for survival for which Anabel's scream of defiance in the face of violence is the powerful stage metaphor.

In order to enact such an emblematic situation, psychologically motivated characters, realised in naturalistic performance would seem singularly inappropriate. What is required here is something more in the Brechtian style: the kind of performance in which the actor 'narrates' his character's part rather than becoming identified with the character whom he is portraying. There are clear guidelines for the creation of this alienated effect in the way in which character is presented within the text. Characters are seen as human beings constantly in danger of being dominated by the mechanical function that society is forcing them to perform. Like the Hall, the people themselves are being de-humanised. It is the intensity of their struggle against this process; their resistance to the final—and apparently inevitable—take-over that makes them somehow remote from full humanity. They are not yet the clockwork human beings that Lawrence, in his preface, refuses to believe in, but they are perilously close to being reduced to that condition, and the essence of the tragic quality in the play arises out of their desperate fight to remain human against overwhelming odds.

The veteran Socialist agitator Willie Houghton (most interestingly, in this connection, 'based' on Lawrence's real-life friend, Willie Hopkin), can, at the opening of the play, command only a tiny audience for his tired Sunday morning oratory, and, even among the small group of colliers who desultorily attend to him, hecklers outnumber supporters. Only in the final Scene, when blood lust has been aroused, does Willie attract a crowd whose violent inclinations he is shown to be singularly ill-equipped to control. A lifetime believer in social reform, Willie is seen at the height of the battle to be more in sympathy with the owners than the workers; to be hopelessly divided within himself about the nature of the values for which he believes he has always stood.

There is irreconcilable division too, in the presentation of the character of the more militant 'revolutionary', Job Arthur Freer who is first seen as unattractively surly in contrast to Houghton's sweet reforming reason. In the central Act, however, Freer is shown to be both devious *and* curiously attractive: a potential turncoat who represents the conventional go-between in the disputes of management and men, yet a human being with sensitive, if spoiled, potential. This division is manifested in action when the strike, brought about by Freer's meddling, breaks out accidentally, and the violence is shown to be a boiling over of frustration, rather than an organised demonstration of the will to be free. As a consequence, the play tells us, the strike fizzles out in ignominious indecision.

On the Capitalist side, the case is just as weakened by internal division. Now a worn-out invalid, old Mr. Barlow has stood by throughout his life, helplessly watching the growth of a system that began in his father's time and is being perpetuated in his son's. He can describe—as an *observer*—the stranglehold achieved by that system over the aspirations of individual men (including himself), but he is powerless to prevent its further growth, as his failure to influence his own son so clearly illustrates at a personal level.

Attracted to creativity, and the weak but persistent life-force of Anabel's artistic temperament, Gerald can only bluster about his refusal to be bullied and browbeaten by men whom he regards as being devoid of intelligence and sensitivity. His friend Oliver, who is so full of pious principle and well-intentioned theory, is seen, in the crisis, to be an ineffectual idealist, too out of touch with the realities of the situation to be instrumental in improving it. Symbolically Oliver's mouth is stopped by the rioting colliers, and his later pleas go unheeded.

Gerald's mother is a vicious and scheming megalomaniac who appears as almost a Gothic monster in her fierce tirades, directed equally against masters and men. In Mrs. Barlow indeed, the de-humanising division has gone to its extreme length in madness.

Winifred, an innocent and hopeful foil to the horrors, who seems at first to be little more, in terms of dramatic function, than an excuse for getting Anabel into the Barlow home and setting up a context for the artistic side of Gerald's nature, nevertheless represents a fearful foreshadowing of the divisive corruption that must erode the Barlow humanity in the conflict, that is seen within her between her dislike of Gerald's cold efficiency and her admiration of its effectiveness. Like Gerald, Winifred has 'rather a job between the two halves of myself', divided as she is between a search for humanity in the artistic life, and a recognition that her escape into that life depends upon her brother's creation of the system she professes to detest.

It is in Anabel that we find the 'touchstone' by which we are most reliably able to measure the values offered in each of the play's episodes, though this reliability is itself rendered ambivalent by the indeterminacy of Anabel's moral status. Characterised throughout as an 'outsider', and therefore belonging neither to the Labour nor the Capital faction, she stands as representative of the 'free' individual who has to some extent escaped the de-humanising forces of industrialisation. In turn, each of the key figures is set beside her, and finally it is she who saves Gerald's life, casting into doubt his confident prediction that the power of Labour is incapable of bringing about 'anything so positive as bloodshed'.

Clearly there is a very different relationship here between character and context from that which we found to be operative in the 'colliery' plays, where we saw that the structural interplay between person and place served to unify and integrate; to present a way of life so firmly interwoven with its social milieu that we necessarily perceived it as authentic and 'life-like'. To that extent indeed, Lawrence's naturalist plays exemplarily bear out Brecht's view that identification with the life portrayed on stage persuades an audience that such a way of life is unchangebale and inevitable. In *Touch and Go*, however, the interplay between character and context operates so as to *dis*-integrate lives from the milieu in which they are lived; to fragment and 'alienate' experience in order that we may look critically and from a distance at a social order which is desperately in need of a radical change.

In an overall view of the play we have already glimpsed this structural mis-fit between person and place, and noticed too that, in *Touch and Go*, both person and place have symbolic rather than naturalistic dimensions. Proceeding step by step through the action, we will see that this general impression depends on a continual disturbance of the 'naturalistic' surface of a play which is more concerned with life as it theoretically might be than with 'life as it actually is'.

The merest glance at the dialogue confirms that it breaks all the criteria that contribute to a naturalistic effect. Meanings are clearly stated. They do not depend for interpretation on their association with the context in which they are expressed. If there is an element that appears at first to be 'sub-textual' (as, for example, in the concealment from Winifred and Mr. Barlow of the relationship between Anabel and Gerald), it soon becomes apparent that this concerns only the level of plot development. The secrets will be revealed in due time. Since they have no bearing on the nature of those secrets, the elements of setting are free to operate symbolically in extending our understanding of the view of the Capital v. Labour situation taken by the play.

In terms of structure, the continuity of action is repeatedly broken up by interruptions—in complete contrast to the continuous flow of time characteristic of the naturalist mode. Act I, Scene 1 of *Touch and Go* exemplifies this episodic structure by being built up out of a series of such interruptions, each of which represents a separate and discrete unit of action without 'natural' consequence or development. Willie Houghton's speech is interrupted first by the hecklers, then by Anabel, and then by Job Arthur Freer. The arrival of Gerald and Oliver further *interrupts* the political argument by imposing constraints on both Job Arthur and Willie and, at the same time, *disrupts* Anabel's connection with the setting by questioning her very presence in the market place. The dispute between Willie and Job Arthur leads nowhere. Like the confrontation between Anabel, Gerald and Oliver which follows, it enacts a stalemate in which further moves are felt to be impossible.

Locked in opposition as they obviously are, Willie and Job Arthur should, we feel, be on the same side in the 'tug of war', just as Anabel should be allied with Gerald and Oliver. But the necessary human feeling for such alliances is shown in both cases to be singularly lacking. The 'system' has destroyed man's capacity for forming natural bonds of connection.

The absence of exposition in this opening scene contributes to the sense of disruption. For all practical purposes, Anabel might have arrived—as Oliver facetiously suggests—from the moon, on this Sunday morning scene. Any understanding that we may suppose formerly to have existed between her and Gerald would appear to have been shattered beyond repair.

Unexpected as her appearance is, however, Gerald regards it as deliberate, and accuses her of 'making a scene here in this filthy market place, just for the fun of it. You like to see these accursed colliers standing eyeing you, and squatting on their heels. You like to catch me out, here where I'm known, where I've been the object of their eyes since I was born. This is a great *coup de main* for you. I knew it the moment I saw you here.' At this point we are made abruptly to wonder whether the political argument has been merely a screen, behind which we are to observe the personal situation between Anabel and Gerald. Oliver's plea that the pair should withdraw to settle their dispute 'more privately' suggests that this is not the case. The two areas of dispute—between Capital and Labour and between Anabel and Gerald—overlap and are, at the same time, mutually exclusive. To see them juxtaposed, in the 'scene in the market place' which Anabel defiantly brings to an end, serves only to throw into relief the points of similarity and difference between these co-existent ruptures in the relationships between people.

This note will be taken up again in Act II when Job Arthur Freer is seen with Gerald in the Barlow drawing-room. But that central focus of the Capital 'camp' has to be reached by way of an ante-room, the arrangement of Scenes, as has already been noted, stressing the piecemeal and fragmentary nature of the situation which we are being persuaded to consider. In Act I

Scene 2, we enter the periphery of the Barlow world. Through Winifred's admiration of Anabel's work, and envy of the freedom and fame of living as an artist in Paris, we are directed to look upon the studio at Lilley Close as a possible escape route away from the grim reality of the industrial setting. Anabel's thrush with its beak lifted, singing 'makes something come loose' in Wilifred's heart. She feels 'as if I should cry and fly up to heaven'. Here the symbolism guides us to abstract from the scene an understanding that, only in theory can art provide that kind of release from the bondage of the world. It is futile to expect such a release in practical terms, through Winifred's father misguidedly insists on doing so, since, Winifred tells us, he is 'so glad you've come to show me how to work' because 'now I shall have a life-work and be happy'.

Winifred's optimistic idealism is, however, sharply brought down to earth by Anabel's reservation: 'Yes, till the life-work collapses.' Art itself cannot be sufficient. Winifred's studio is supported by the 'managing' aspect of Gerald which she and Anabel so much dislike, and by the wealth that Mr. Barlow has amassed in the past. The ivory tower is shown to be built atop a mountain of coal. In the face of this disparity it is indeed difficult to 'make things *balance* as if they were alive'. The relationship of the Barlow ménage to the colliery from which it draws its sustenance does not reflect this ideal balance which, for Anabel at least, is 'the secret of life . . . the inexpressible poise of a living thing, that makes it so different from a dead thing.'

Disturbing in its implications, the exchange between teacher and pupil is in turn disturbed by the arrival of Oliver, and the lesson spins off into a wild and improbable dance. Again we feel the disrupting effect of *non-sequiturs*, as the improvised ballet whirls itself to a close, and the mood changes abruptly to one of intimate confidence between Oliver and Anabel.

Here, most surprisingly, the play offers the exposition absent in the first scene. After the excitement of the dance, the anatomising of the liaison between Anabel and Gerald, complicated by the latter's attachment to Oliver, and finally broken by Anabel's passion for 'that Norwegian', is conducted with a perverse and icy calm. It is not, we see at once, a question of 'filling in' the characters' past life; of giving them a background which renders them authentically 'rounded' or 'real'. On the contrary, the recall of past passions in the cool light of the present, further serves to frustrate our expectations of a 'natural' development. By this time we have adjusted our view of the play to an acceptance of the past as a mystery. Its revelation here therefore provides a further jolt to our complacent 'consumption' of the ideas which are being offered for our consideration.

Mrs. Barlow's entrance provides yet a further jolt, making us re-shuffle our impressions in yet another order. Melodramatically frank, Mrs. Barlow makes us see that art can be regarded as a kind of madness as well as an 'escape' from the world. If Winifred is an artist as Anabel claims, it is, Mrs. Barlow insists, because 'All my children have the artist in them. They get it from my family. My father went mad in Rome. My family is born with a black fate—they all inherit it.'

Winifred's return with enthusiastic thanks for Oliver's present switches our point of view once again; this time to a modulation of the theme of violence *vis à vis* art via the metaphor of the marble wolf and goat. With a violence comparable to that portrayed in the sculpture, this line of thought is broken off by the arrival of Gerald and Mr. Barlow. To the latter the gathering in Winifred's studio is an image of homely peace and concord. Unaware of the hostility between Anabel and Gerald—and hence unaware of the irony in his son's comment that a studio is 'awfully nice you know; it is such a retreat', Mr. Barlow agrees: 'It is a sanctum the world cannot invade.' As audience at this point we, however, must be disturbingly aware of several levels of irony playing around the apparent 'peace' of the studio. In his doomed attempt to preserve the 'peace that passeth understanding' we watch Mr. Barlow trying to silence 'alarmist' reports of trouble brewing among the colliers, paralleled by Mrs. Barlow's witch-like incantations about the blackness of the local blood. Between Anabel and Gerald we are aware that there is little peace, and we know too, that Mrs. Barlow is unlikely to be of much help to her husband in his effort to cool Gerald's passion against the workers.

Challenging Anabel to play her part in this mêlée, Mrs. Barlow indeed stirs up further strife. Like Gerald, Anabel declares that she would 'never give the world my heart on a dish', but, unlike him, she wants this defiant independence to be reconcilable with peace. Her plea is drowned out by Mrs. Barlow's militancy. 'Between me and the shameful humble' the 'hulking half-demented woman' (as she describes herself) declares, 'there is war to the end'.

It is here that Gerald expresses his awareness of the division between the 'two halves' of himself; the one half defiant of the workers who rise up against him, and the other wanting peace. Neither the father nor the mother, from whom these two 'halves' are inherited, can consciously understand his dilemma. To Mrs. Barlow there appears to be only one course of action: to fight to the last drop of blood. For Mr. Barlow the slogan is 'peace at any price', however much his wife may blame him for sacrificing her and her children to the achievement of that goal. Even Winifred is drawn into the maelstrom that rages in her ivory tower as she protests, in support of her mother, that the colliers about whom her father was always worrying, 'didn't care a bit about you. And they *ought* to have cared a million pounds'. Though the Scene ends on Mr. Barlow's dismissive comment, 'You don't understand, my child', the effect of the pitched battle has been to whip up support for Mrs. Barlow's militancy against Mr. Barlow's earnest, but deluded, pacifism. Yet to say so much is not to overlook the powerful forces influencing us concurrently in the opposite direction. Mrs. Barlow is, after all, mad—and a singularly unsympathetic stage presence, even at this point in the play before her eaves-dropping activities have been revealed. Mr. Barlow is old and sick, as well as being an escapist who has been shown to shelve responsibility by buying his daughter peace with the proceeds of exploitation. It is hardly surprising that we have difficulty in deciding where our sympathies *should* lie.

Undermining the whole conflict too, there is a cutting edge of humour; a black and steely edge, admittedly, but one that effectively separates us off from these eccentric characters, and makes us reflect upon the real significance of the events so spasmodically and disconnectedly taking place before us. Are we really meant to be swept into an empathising concern for the immediate social consequence to these people of a strike, or are we not rather to feel that the central theme—symbolised in the improvised ballet of Anabel, Oliver and Winifred—is the irrelevance of the

Capital/Labour controversy to the issue of coming to terms with the modern world?

Mr. and Mrs. Barlow both belong to the past. Gerald, as Winifred has told us, is adapting their mode of life to the present by being 'good at electricity'; by bringing his expertise in up-to-date technology to bear on this further development of the Barlow-owned resources. Anabel's experience in Paris indicate that Winifred cannot escape from her inheritance by hiding her head in the clouds of 'Art'. As we see, Winifred is as much her mother's child as Gerald.

The question left unanswered at the end of this first Act is an abstract one: how is it possible to remain 'human' and 'alive' in the modern world? In the Barlow parents we have examples of failures to solve this question. Having sought spiritual peace for himself, and artistic escape for his daughter, Mr. Barlow is shown to have achieved nothing, since the responsibility for solving the problems of labour has merely been passed on to Gerald, and Art cannot be guaranteed to humanise Winifred. This is brought home by Oliver's accusation that Anabel has 'de-humanised' Gerald by her treatment of him in Paris. Fighting her rearguard action, Mrs. Barlow has failed equally in her attempt to maintain the past as a living force in the present. Only by the passing on of her militant spirit to her children has she succeeded, and in this respect we see that her success is the cause of continued suffering. At a parallel level we have become interested in the outcome of the impending strike which, in the event, will prove equally self-defeating. On both the private and public fronts, we are made to feel that the wrong battles are being fought; the wrong enemies locked in sterile combat.

Act I, as we have seen, is built up out of a series of episodes, the jerky, discontinuous effect of which prevents us from settling comfortably to consider the central issue from a consistent point of view. This process is repeated in Act II through the succession of encounters that take place in the Barlow drawing-room. As we approach and enter this heart of the Barlow stronghold, we learn more about the nature of the 'bone' over which the contestants wrangle. Though Gerald has been presented in a critical light in Act I for his 'coldness' and for his 'managing' skills, by means of which he has 'revolutionised the collieries and the whole

197

company', we discover that in doing so he is only perpetuating a state of affairs initiated by his 'peace-loving' father, himself a descendant of 'substantial farmers'. We know from Winifred that old Mr. Barlow would almost prefer to let the company die out—to let the pits be closed. But the process of modernisation for which Gerald is held responsible is, in itself, inevitable, as seen from the Barlow point of view that 'things must be modernised'.

A measure of personal peace, pleasure and a cultivated life are the rewards that can be enjoyed by those who concede the necessary for modernisation. The opening of Act II shows us this life, as the young people entertain Mr. Barlow with music and dance. The entertainment is, however, brief and uneasy, and its pleasurable aspect is undermined by Gerald's harsh irony as well as by the sense in which Mr. Barlow is deceived by the status of Anabel. The dance and the music are devices here for disguising the underlying emotional situation, just as they represent an escape from the truth of the social conditions by which they are surrounded.

At no point then, are we allowed unreservedly to admire the 'cultivated' Barlow way of life, any more than in Act I could we identify with either the reforming zeal of Willie Houghton, or the more subversive activities of Job Arthur Freer.

After the musical interlude, the play switches to a conversation piece in the manner of a Shavian debate, in which narration makes us focus on yet another vision of the central issue. Mr. Barlow states the case for the industrialist with a Christian conscience; Anabel questions his view that better conditions and higher wages would improve the lives of the men who work for him, and Oliver introduces the theme of the preface in his opinion that 'All our lives would be better, if we hadn't to hang on in the perpetual tug-of-war, like two donkeys pulling at one carrot. The ghastly tension of possessions, and struggling for possession, spoils life for everybody.'

Although Oliver continues to voice these Utopian themes, the scene does not, in fact, direct us to see his ideals as possible solutions to problems that are seen by the others as impossible of resolution. Indeed here, as in the climax of the final act, the ideals can be seen in *action* to be impossible of achievement in the given circumstances, even though, in theory, they are offered as 'true' and 'right'. Whatever Lawrence's convictions about these ideals may have been *outside* the play, the fact is that, in *Touch and Go*, his mode of presentation renders Oliver's voice as powerless in the context as are all the other voices with the exception of the life-saving cry of Anabel. It is in this sense, one might feel, that he has written a modern tragedy. In the debate at present under consideration, for example, Mr. Barlow's voice receives equal stress with that of Oliver, and it is through Mr. Barlow's account that we are directed to follow the course of industrial development from its apparently 'benevolent' beginnings through to the iron necessity for increasing efficiency which bedevils the present. Right from the start, Mr. Barlow admits to having seen the 'great disparity' between master and man as 'wrong', but he has not been able to make a fair adjustment, managing only to salve his personal conscience by giving to his men 'every private help that lay in my power'.

Gerald then, is offered, in this view, as the victim of a system which Oliver describes as being wanted much more by the poor than by the rich, because the poor are 'much more anxious to be rich—never having been rich, poor devils'. Mr. Barlow's experience comes over more strongly than Oliver's anti-materialist idealism by sheer weight of the emphasis in this scene on his narration of industrialism's history. As he recalls the great lock-out, of which Oliver's boyhood memories are so deceptively exciting, Mr. Barlow pin-points the moment at which it became impossible for the owners to continue their policy of liberal amelioration of the workers' lot.[8]

Inexorably developing, the industrial machine has now arrived at a point where both masters and men are its victims. Gerald has had to 'take it in hand', though his father cannot bear to see the 'men working against machines, flesh and blood working against iron, for a livelihood'. Above all, he fears the terrifying consequences of 'everything running at top speed, utterly dehumanised, inhuman'.

[8] For a comparative treatment of the 'same character' in the form of the novel, it is particularly instructive to look at the section on Gerald's father in the chapter entitled 'The Industrial Magnate' in *Women in Love*, (Penguin edition), pp. 240–241.

Anabel too is terrified of the 'unnatural' quietness that accompanies dehumanised labour. Even more fatalistic than Mr. Barlow, she concludes, 'Ah well, in death there is no industrial situation. Something must be different there', and her resignation strikes a more convincing note in the context than does Oliver's observation that sacrifice is not the slightest use, or his confidence that things can only improve if only people would be 'sane and decent'. In the crisis of the final Act, Oliver's political philosophy will be powerless, when Anabel's hold on emotional truth saves the day, and again we see that the form of drama allows for more to be said than the dramatist may have meant to say—at least, that is, if we take the view that Oliver is designed as a 'mouthpiece' for Lawrence's own ideas.

The total impotence into which the once powerful industrialist has declined is enacted for us, as the solicitous butler leads the tired Mr. Barlow off to bed, closing the episode in which his view of the situation has been dominant. Against the background of industrial history, the following episode between Anabel and Gerald then offers us a perspective in which to assess the effects of that history on an inter-personal relationship in the present. In Act I, Oliver's comment had drawn attention to the fact that Anabel's habit of going to church was a new one for her. Here Gerald comments further on her change of heart, and finds the search that she describes as being for 'something more dignified, more religious, if you like—anyhow something *positive*' rather repugnant and 'slightly sanctimonious'.

In Gerald's anger at this point, the issues of private and public strife are again juxtaposed, and again illuminate each other by virtue of their similarities and differences. Raging against Anabel's having 'impudently' left him alone in Paris, Gerald significantly uses the same term when he confesses 'I'm not only angry about that. I'm angry with the colliers, with Labour for its low-down impudence—' There is a sense then, in which the conflict between Capital and Labour and that between Anabel and Gerald are matched. Yet an important distinction emerges as Gerald continues—'and I'm angry with Father for being so ill—and I'm angry with Mother for looking such a hopeless thing—and I'm angry with Oliver because he thinks so much—' Most of all though, he is angry with himself for being himself. 'I was always that. I was always a curse to myself,' he concludes, refusing bitterly to accept Anabel's claim that this condition must be changed.

In contrast to the contest between Capital and Labour, the tragic quality of the irreconcilable conflict between man and woman is here presented in terms of 'pure, passional antagonism turning upon the poles of belief'. Where the former conflict is a futile wrangle, the latter is a fundamental antagonism which has to be come to terms with, if a living relationship is to grow between Anabel and Gerald. She must accept that there can be no change in Gerald. He will not 'get softer' in order to satisfy her need for a more spiritual quality in life. But, as the play will powerfully demonstrate, he will have reason to recognise the importance of her being intuitively in touch with the instinctive sources of life; sources which have been choked and overgrown by the process of mechanisation.

Once again an unresolved discussion is interrupted, in this case by Mrs. Barlow with her brazen admission of eaves-dropping and her advice to Anabel: 'Don't presume to be good to my son, young woman.' The melodramatic tone of Mrs. Barlow's speeches emphasises the absurdity of the situation, which is additionally pointed to by Gerald's mockery. 'Will you curtsey, Anabel?' he enquires satirically: 'And I'll twist my handkerchief. We shall make a Cruikshank drawing, if mother makes her hair a little more slovenly.'

The fantasy which has been lurking in the corners of the Barlow *ménage* here takes complete command. Very aptly, the allusion to *Alice in Wonderland* provides a reference for the quality of nightmare confusion in which the emotions of the participants become entangled. Beating her son savagely about the head with her fan, the mother furiously dismisses the would-be intruders, Oliver and Job Arthur Freer. Like Christiana Crich in *Women in Love*, Mrs. Barlow refuses to have her husband's 'people' in the house, but, where in the novel this revulsion is treated with tragic intensity, it is, in the play, displayed as an absurd enormity, comparable to the irrational violence of the Duchess in *Alice*, who speaks roughly to her little boy and beats him when he sneezes.

The taking up of this refrain renders Gerald's mother into a grotesque, whose wild defence of her son's virility in turn satirises his claim to Anabel that he must be allowed to remain unchang-

201

ingly 'cold' and 'hard'. We are not moved by the passion of the mad mother, but disquieted by her surrealism into a recognition of the violent repression that poisons the very air of Lilley Close. Like the Duchess' kitchen, the Barlow drawing-room steams with the boiling over of pent-up frustrations. Even the wondering Anabel; the 'Alice' curiously present at so weird a spectacle, becomes caught up in the heady atmosphere, as she accepts Gerald's challenge to take a poker to him, and echoes his apostrophe to courage.

At the height of Gerald and Anabel's excitement, Oliver and Job Arthur return, and again we experience the frustration of a scene being deflated just as we felt that it was about to reach its climax. Again, in this way, the possibility of a resolution that might have been arrived at in that climax, is snatched away from us, and we are made to take new bearings on the altered situation.

Job Arthur's amazement at, and disapproval of, the high-spirited 'charade' provoke us to uneasy laughter. He is reluctant to accept Gerald's offer of a drink, and is solemnly dignified when the master mocks his lack of social poise. Job Arthur is 'a white-faced fellow' woefully ill-equipped to 'trample' (as Mrs. Barlow puts it) in the owners' private rooms. Yet he is invested with a sinister power as he evades Gerald's sophisticated thrusts at his inept language, and parries the rapier wit of his master with a blunt but effective repartee of his own.

When, for example, Gerald pokes fun at the well-worn slogan 'United we stand', Job Arthur cites the 'three thousand colliers standing up for thirty-odd office men', and the more powerful image obviously goes to Job Arthur for all his fumbling with words like 'love' and 'funny'. It would certainly go against all the textual indications here to present Job Arthur as a complete buffoon. Gerald may be given the edge when he says, 'There's nothing they can do, you know, that doesn't hit them worse than it hits us', but his confidence is held up for serious criticism by Job Arthur's refusal to acquiesce to the proposition that 'Labour is a great swarm of helplessly little men'. Against the dangerous over-confidence thus revealed in Gerald's sweeping over-simplifications about the weakness of Labour, Job Arthur is allowed to speak simply and directly of the courage that Labour will show when the opportunity occurs, and, although Gerald continues to try to out-talk him, the balance remains fairly held between the degrees of conviction invested in their respective 'representative voices'. Job Arthur is, in fact, awarded an important point, when Gerald is drawn by his opponent's taciturn refusal to capitulate into a tirade in which he goes too far and is defeated by Job Arthur's observation: 'Perhaps you see now why you're not so very popular, Mr. Gerald.'

Oliver and Anabel form an on-stage audience for whom this scene is played. Like us they must weigh up the envy of Gerald's position, inherent in Job Arthur's deferential acceptance of a rich man's bounty, against his stubborn refusal to concede Gerald's superior strength. Like our own impressions, Oliver and Anabel's are ambivalent. Oliver can confess to a dislike of Job Arthur, but he must base that feeling on a wider knowledge of the man than has been given, in the immediately past encounter with Gerald, to Anabel and to us. She, in fact, finds Job Arthur's capacity to 'sun himself' in the overawing setting, 'like a cat purring in his luxuriation', rather commendable. 'It shows a certain sensitiveness and a certain taste' she finds, thus justifying her liking for Job Arthur against Oliver's distaste. Job Arthur's status *vis à vis* Gerald is equivocal, and is made even more so when the latter returns to exult in his victory over a handicapped adversary. Again Anabel rebels against the crowing victor. 'How pleased you are, Gerald! How pleased you are with yourself! You love the turn with him' she exclaims. The men may mock at the ineffectuality of the British working man, but Anabel, who sees Job Arthur as an individual, will have none of their mockery, and the play enlists us on her side. When Oliver generalises vaguely about the British employer being equally 'beside the point of life', Anabel fiercely declares that the working man may, in the event, have something more positive to offer than this vague and patronising philosophy, and she refuses to take any further part in what, for her, has become a pointless discussion.

After her exit the two men are allowed an opportunity to criticise her unrelenting morality, but their unity is also broken. Like Anabel, Oliver objects to Gerald's mood, and leaves him abruptly to smile to himself as the curtain falls.

Keith Sagar has objected that *Touch and Go* fails to ring true, and his judgement is certainly supported by the play's failure to secure our unquestioning assent at those points where it seems most intent on doing so. Where we feel that we are meant to take a clear line—one way or the other—we are constantly prevented from making a decisive choice, as at the end of this Act where we appear to be being directed to agree with Anabel and Oliver, though it is Gerald who is left smiling. It would seem likely therefore, that what we experience as a pressure to opt for one side or the other, is a response to the play's indeterminacy, which gives equal weight to both sides of the controversy, while implying that a solution, not yet grasped, eludes both parties. This, at any rate, is the *effect* of the play's consistent balancing of alternatives, both in the public sphere of Labour and Capital and in the private conflict between Anabel and Gerald. There is no clinching argument which 'rings true' on behalf of one side or the other.

This impression is certainly confirmed by the final Act, between the two scenes of which Gerald and Anabel are quite arbitrarily married. We observe here that no time is specified in the stage directions, and contrast this with the precision of such instructions in the naturalist plays, where even the hours were meticulously laid down. We notice too, that the whole concept of setting functions throughout at an emblematic level, in a stylised, circular pattern that moves from the market place to the studio, the drawing-room, the park and back into the market place, pointing to the concepts that are thematic and away from the notion of 'real' people in a 'real' time and place.

The disquieting subversion of exposition conventions, noted in Act I, and the lack of 'psychological' preparation for such major events as the marriage of Gerald and Anabel are all of a piece with this design, in which we are formally prevented from identifying with the individuals, and are directed instead to make a cool and critical appraisal of the issues that control their lives.

So, in Scene 1 of the final Act we see the conventional and expected love scene between Gerald and Anabel subverted by its overlap with the rumblings that presage the outbreak of the strike.[9] What we had been led to expect here was either a com-

---

[9] The contrast between the form of *Touch and Go* and that of the 'naturalist' plays is well illustrated by a comparison of the strike, as it is seen to function here, with the way in which a similar social disruption was seen to function in *The Daughter-in-Law*. cf. Chapter IV, above.

plete breakdown in the relationship between the erstwhile lovers, or a complete reconciliation—either of which would conform to a conventional narrative pattern. In the event, there is no decision either way, nor does either of the alternatives play a vital part in the further development of the play. In effect, the arbitrary marriage, which certainly does not follow 'naturally' from the meeting in Act I Scene 1, directs us, in the crisis, to see Anabel as formally aligned with the Capital faction, but, emotionally, still capable of acting with the degree of humanity that saves the situation.

The presence of Anabel and Gerald, walking together through the park at the opening of the Scene, is in itself surprising, after the quarrel on which the previous Scene ended, and again we feel the play's avoidance of logical causality. We are not, it transpires, being asked to reflect on the quality of a possible relation between the lovers, but on what their uneasy present relationship will have to do with the strike, when it occurs.

Gerald and Anabel's conversation brings to our attention the background image of 'a low Georgian hall, which has been turned into offices'. The old park, in which the hall stands, is, as Anabel observes, still beautiful. Bereft of its owners, who could not bear to be so near the ugliness of the pits, the hall still retains its stateliness, and the beauty of 'an eighteenth century aquatint'. Yet, as Gerald remarks: 'Stateliness is on its last legs.' The beautiful old world—a world in which, it will be noted, the values of property and a benevolent property-owning class went unchallenged—is now undermined by damp, and buzzing with inky clerks. Aesthetically pleasing as it may have been, the past—here emblematised in the hall—is now merely a hollow shell in which those same inky clerks are, even now, plotting as Job Arthur has warned, 'to get a bit of their own back'.

From Gerald, Anabel wants the admission that they have needed to go through the sufferings and mistakes of the past in order to arrive at a more hopeful present, and she insists that they must now plan for what is to follow. Gerald refuses to accept her vision of development and continuity. In the past, he argues, they have gone the way they *had* to go. Now they are in the park where he, at least for the time being, is happy. If Anabel could only be as sure as he is that he loves her, as she says she loves him, they could, as he wishes, 'both be happy at the same moment'. 'But', as he continues, 'apparently we can't.' Happiness cannot be made, but must be waited for, 'like a dispensation', and, unlike Anabel, Gerald is prepared to go through more of the 'real process' of hate while the dispensation works itself out.

Charged by Gerald with keeping something back; 'some sort of female reservation—like a dagger up your sleeve', Anabel flies out against his selfishness, and contrasts his self-deceiving complacency with her own honesty. 'I *have* changed, I *am* better, I *do* love you—I love you wholly and unselfishly—I do—and I want a good new life with you' she asserts hotly, only to be met with the coolness of Gerald's response: 'I wish you'd make up your mind to be downright bad.'

Framed as it is in a setting which symbolises for us the structure of social development, this scene between Anabel and Gerald is necessarily indecisive, in that we cannot sympathise wholly with either of their claims. Is the growth of industrialisation as inevitable and inexorable a process as Mr. Barlow's narrative, and Gerald's acceptance of the 'facts' of his life suggest, or can it be changed by the kind of act of faith which Anabel's insistence on 'something positive' proposes as an alternative? The play continually defeats our efforts to opt for one side or the other.

As the first of the clerks passes by the couple, Anabel's faith is seen to be shaken by her sensing of an atmosphere of fear. Yet she remains hostile to Gerald, and feels that he has 'come to sit here just to catch them, like a spider waiting for them'. Respectful to a fault, the clerks themselves bear out Gerald's suspicion that they have uneasy consciences over the strike, and so strengthen our sympathy for the masters' adoption of an inevitably predatory role.

The movement of feeling is enacted here through Anabel, as she is swayed from her initial disapproval of Gerald's cold dislike of his men to an understanding of his feelings towards them. 'The attitude of them all is so ugly' she concedes. 'I can quite see that it makes you rather a bully.'

Breffitt, the chief clerk and cashier—'one of father's old pillars of society'—also denies the office men's responsibility for the agitation, showing himself up as the hypocrite that Gerald's epithet calls to mind. According to Breffitt, the trouble has been stirred up by 'a set of loud-mouthed blatherers and agitators' like Job Arthur Freer. Breffitt, for one, believes that such men 'deserve to be hung—and hanging they'd get, if I could have the judging of them'.

Neither Gerald nor Anabel are impressed by this self-righteous show of indignation which, in Anabel's terms, puts Gerald in a fury. Though Breffitt's case for the office workers' rise may strike us as reasonable—as it does Anabel—his character is presented so as to align us with *both* Anabel and Gerald against him.

We are not, however, allowed to take sides so easily for long. Resuming her argument against Gerald's 'stupid obstinacy' in refusing to grant the office men their rights, Anabel provokes him into an outburst against the strikers whom he sees as 'vicious children who would like to kill their parents so that they could have the run of the larder'. The workers, we are told, would win Gerald's respect if they fought bravely, but he predicts that they will not, and bases his prediction on his conviction that the present state of affairs is inevitable and universal. There is no place in the world where one can escape. 'It's the same wherever you have industrialism—and you have industrialism everywhere, whether it's Timbuctoo or Paraguay or Antananarivo.'

Anabel's spirited contradiction, 'No, it isn't: you exaggerate' wins a measure of our assent at this point, but our view of the situation is once again changed by the appearance of Job Arthur Freer 'suddenly approaching from the other side.' Even in so small a matter as this stage direction, we note the symbolic design of Lawrence's play, as the effect of Job Arthur's approach from a direction opposite to that taken by the clerks, shifts our sympathy once more towards Gerald and all that he represents.

In the confrontation between Gerald and Job Arthur, both men are stripped of humanity and presented as mere ciphers for 'that old Bull dog the British capitalist' and 'that unsatisfied mongrel Plebs, the proletariat', wrangling over a particularly hollow '*casus belli*'. As the Bull dog, Gerald ferociously seizes Job Arthur by the scruff of the neck and shakes him, while the 'mongrel' snarls viciously back that he and his comrades will rid the parish of the vermin that 'lives on other people's lives'. Bull dog Gerald retorts by kicking Job Arthur to the ground—and threatening to kick him out of the park. Horrified (as we are surely designed to be) by this enactment of the de-humanisation of which we have been *told* so much, Anabel begs 'Don't say any more, you, Job Arthur. Come away Gerald. Come away—come— do come.'

Foreshadowing the crisis of the final scene, it is Anabel's plea that averts further violence, here saving Job Arthur, as it will later save Gerald. Reluctantly the attacker turns away from his victim, exclaiming: '*That* a human being! My God!—But he's right. It's I who go. It's we who go, Anabel. He's still there—My God! a human being!'

Our sympathy here with Gerald's vehemence is tempered by the knowledge we have been given that Job Arthur can also be a 'human being'; a sensitive music-loving man whom Anabel has admired for his appreciation of the fine things of life. Gerald too is, as Winifred has put it, 'good at bottom'. But, in the power of the industrial machine, both are subject to the dehumanising forces that make men behave like savage animals. Anabel's faith in an alternative positive force seems fragile indeed, yet it is she who, twice in this Act, is seen to stave off a fatal outcome to the wrangle over the bone.

Having set the archetypes of his preface in motion, Lawrence brings the play swiftly to its climax back in the market place which is once again dominated by the obelisk, commemorating the wasted lives of men sacrificed to preserve what has been shown to be a squalid *status quo*. Now that the strike is under way, Willie Houghton has an unwontedly large audience. But it is with Job Arthur that this mob's sympathies are seen to lie, not with Willie who has 'fooled for thirty years' and got them no further.

With his rabble-rousing phrases, so much despised by Gerald in the previous Scene, Job Arthur whips the men into a fury. Their blood lust is up. They will get rid of the Capitalist vermin: 'drop 'em down the shaft—sink 'em—ha' done wi' 'em—' Willie is powerless to calm them with his warning that 'You'll be far less free with Job Arthur for your boss than ever you were with Gerald Barlow.' Confirming the alignment that has been made throughout the play between Capitalists and liberal *reformers*, Willie goes on to avow his own allegiance to the masters: 'For I'd rather die with somebody who has one tiny little spark of decency left—though it *is* a little tiny spark—than live to triumph with those that have none.'

Interrupted by the arrival of Gerald, Anabel and Oliver in their motor car, the enraged mob breaks out into violence, surrounding the car and dragging its occupants out into the square. It is at this moment of crisis that Anabel announces her marriage to Gerald, only to be howled down by the abuse of the strikers. Together with Oliver, Gerald and the now equally hated Willie Houghton, she is bundled as a prisoner into the space cleared before the obelisk, where Job Arthur stands as self-appointed inquisitor.

It is to Gerald—the figure-head of the Capitalist camp—that the interrogation is addressed, and, though he is evidently in danger, the Master holds firm to the 'policy' which Anabel has condemned as 'stupid obstinacy', and refuses to acknowledge the right of three thousand men to an answer to their 'straightforward question'. Eager for the kill the men press forward, forcing the prisoners to kneel. Only Anabel, we notice, 'kneels quietly—the others struggle.'

The men have no use for Oliver's high-sounding ideas, and brutally stop his mouth. Their attention is concentrated upon Gerald who turns aside Anabel's plea that he should put an end to the violence. Obscenely roused, the men turn their scorn upon Anabel, but Gerald will not be moved even when Anabel ignores the mockery and pleads with him again to give the men an answer. Impatiently, 'The crowd surges and begins to howl—they sway dangerously—Gerald is spread-eagled on the ground, face down.' Job Arthur forces the men back, but thwarted of an answer, he fulfills Oliver's vision of him as a Judas and releases the mob to wreak its fury on the obdurate Gerald.

Once confident that Labour could never achieve anything as positive as bloodshed, Gerald is now perilously close to paying with his life for the stubbornness of his policy. It is only Anabel's cry that saves him; the cry for humanity that reaches to the spark of humanity which is flickeringly alive in the hearts of the miners—just as much as Willie had declared it to be in Gerald's.

Defying Mrs. Barlow's command to be hard with Gerald, and subverting his own determination to remain defiant to the last, Anabel averts disaster, thereby vindicating the faith she has consistently maintained in a positive alternative to the hollow strife of the present. That it is a fragile and tenuous faith, all too easily vulnerable to extinction, is dramatised by the uneasy anti-climax on which the play ends.

After her moment of triumph, Anabel speaks no more. Her faith has been shown to work its small miracle and return to obscurity. Released from immediate danger, Gerald, prompted by Oliver, attempts some degree of rapprochement with the men. But his stand is taken from the same angle as that for which Breffitt was discredited in the previous scene; simply, that is to say, by shifting the blame on to Job Arthur. It is Oliver on whom the burden of arbitration most heavily rests. His plea for 'a new state of things'; for a new arrangement in which 'money flowed more naturally, so that it flowed naturally to every man according to his needs', may be taken to be the didactic statement of the play—though it can clearly be felt to be doubtful of realisation. All that can be hoped for towards the achievement of Oliver's Utopian goal is, *Touch and Go* tells us, an extension of the flow of humanity between human being and human being, as it has been climactically dramatised in Anabel's life saving cry.

Within the play, neither Gerald nor the strikers are shown fully to have been reached by this appeal to their spiritual humanity. Gerald indeed takes up Oliver's theme from the coal-owners' point of view by promising to 'cry quits' on the attack that has been made upon him, and expressing his willingness to work for a new way of life, on terms that sound dispiritingly close to those that he has always maintained as his own. We are given to feel that further outbreaks of violence cannot be far off, as the strikers jeer at Gerald's unconvincing claim, 'I don't care about money really.' 'No, because you've got everything' a voice from the crowd is heard to cry, as Gerald, resuming all his masterly airs, calls for his coat and orders the strikers to step out of the way, as the Lilley Close party moves towards the car, and the final curtain falls.

Declaring that the preface to *Touch and Go* 'reveals all the symptoms of a vague political ideology bordering on what became Fascism', Emile Delavenay dismisses the play itself as 'of little, if any, dramatic or artistic value'. Yet its very ambiguities and ideological tensions seem to me to refute such a dismissive view. Wrestling with a similar problem in the novel, *Kangaroo* (1923), Lawrence certainly puts words with a distinctly Fascist tone into the mouth of the quasi-autobiographical Somers. In his sympathy with the cause of the nationalist Diggers, it is Somers, for example, who states unequivocally, 'The real sense of liberty only goes with white blood. And the ideal democratic liberty is an exploded ideal. You've got to have wisdom and authority somewhere, and you can't get it out of any further democracy.'[10] Somers' excesses, however, are criticised, not only by the developing action of the novel, but also by the scepticism of Harriet, who challenges her husband's faith in the Australian nationalist movement, to which he inclines to ally himself. 'You know quite well,' she says, 'you say yourself life doesn't *start* with a new form. It starts with a new feeling and ends with a form.'[11] In *Touch and Go*, Lawrence has found a form for the feeling that criticises political dogma. The specific political 'message' of the play may appear to bolster élitist ideals, but, in the action of the play, these are shown up, together with the revolutionary ideals to which they are opposed, as being impossible of realisation. At the distance from which the form of the play requires us to view the cases made by both Capital and Labour, we are able to exercise a critical judgement—and find both sides of the contest wanting in the vital spark of humanity which, in Lawrence's terms, can alone promise hope for the future.

[10] *Kangaroo* (Penguin edition), p. 102.
[11] Ibid., p. 111.

9

Altitude and Noah's Flood

After *Touch and Go* Lawrence abandoned his experiments with dramatic form for a number of years. More than ever a wanderer and a voluntary exile, he was continually in search of the new and unspoilt worlds of whose existence—like Gerald Barlow—he never seems fully to have been convinced. Dampened by rejection after rejection, his enthusiasm for the theatre became engulfed during this period in a tide of momentous events. Only when he at last found himself in an environment which—impermanently as it turned out—appeared to offer the peace for which he had been seeking, did he return to the writing of plays.

It was in New Mexico in 1924 and 1925 that he resumed this contact with drama, tentatively at first, as the unfinished fragments, *Altitude* and *Noah's Flood* indicate, but most confidently in the end with the accomplished achievement of a radically new form in the Bible play, *David*.

While *Noah's Flood* may be regarded as a false start on the way to *David*, *Altitude* is an altogether different case. Written in a bouncy lighthearted manner, highly untypical of the later Lawrence, it is a thinly disguised satire of the 'artists colony' gathered around the Lawrences on Mabel Dodge Luhan's Taos estate. Often enough elsewhere, Lawrence 'used' people he knew as the basis for his fictions, but seldom as openly as he does in this unfinished play, which he could certainly not have imagined to be publishable in its incomplete and unrevised state.

Although highly critical of his friends' foibles, the satire in *Altitude* is not cruel. It could, in fact, very easily be seen as the start of a script for an elaborate charade in which the various characters 'send up' their own idiosyncracies—though what we

212

know of some members of the 'cast' from memoirs and other accounts[1] may make it seem rather surprising that they were prepared so readily to poke fun at their own respective 'philosophies' of life, even in the form of a private entertainment.

That it was originally designed as a private entertainment—an amusing charade among friends—is confirmed by 'Spud' Johnson's introduction to the first scene of *Altitude* which he published in *Laughing Horse* in 1938. The opening lines, it would appear, 'were scribbled on the back of a candy box one evening in Mabel Dodge Luhan's living-room, and the various guests made suggestions about the characters and speeches'. It was not, however, 'until several years later that the company knew that Lawrence had actually finished one scene and started another'.[2]

Even without this background information, we can see just how little Lawrence has done to render 'life' into dramatic fiction in this fragment of a play, by comparing its text with other accounts of the time in Taos. In the first place we see that many of the characters are not even disguised by so much as a change of name. The Mabel of the play is obviously Mabel Dodge Luhan, patroness of the arts and owner of the Taos property, who married in 1923 the Pueblo Indian, Tony Luhan, who also figures as a character in the play. Equally transparently, Ida is modelled on the actress Ida Rauh, for whom the role of Michal in *David* was originally designed. So close are the incidents of the play to what we know of the everyday life of the colourful characters on the Taos ranch, that the husband who telephones Ida at the end of Scene 1 is even given his real-life name of Andrew, and it is most inter-

---

[1] e.g. Dorothy Brett, *Lawrence and Brett: A Friendship* (Philadelphia, 1933) and Mabel Dodge Luhan, *Lorenzo in Taos* (New York, 1932). Generous extracts from both these memoirs can conveniently be found in Edward Nehl's *D. H. Lawrence: A Composite Biography*, from which quotations for the present study have been taken.

[2] Quoted by F. Warren Roberts in his *Bibliography of D. H. Lawrence*, pp. 286–287. Willard Johnson began publishing and editing the *Laughing Horse* in the Spring of 1922 in California, while working as a journalist and also attending classes at the University of California. Edward Nehls notes that Johnson's own account of the magazine's history can be found in *The New Mexico Quarterly*, XXI, No. 2, Summer 1951, and also gives a bibliography of Lawrence's contributions to the *Laughing Horse*. (N.II, p. 502)

esting to note again here that the real Andrew Dasburg recalls of Lawrence at this time that: 'No one enjoyed himself more playing charades than he.' (N.II p. 197)

As a model for the dramatised Clarence, we have the screen writer Clarence Thompson who had been introduced to Mabel Luhan by a Mrs. Alice Sprague—who herself joined the Taos party while Clarence was a member of it in the early summer of 1924. Described in Dorothy Brett's memoir of the period as a 'tall, good-looking, delicate featured young man in white, with his shirt sleeves rolled up to his shoulders and wearing many Indian rings and blankets', (N.II p. 516) the real life Clarence Thompson obviously bore a very close resemblance to the Clarence of *Altitude* whom Lawrence's stage directions call upon to appear in 'rose-coloured trousers with much jewellery', though the concern of the dramatised Clarence for the effect made by his pink trousers may, of course, be considered as being among the fictionalised exaggerations of the high-spirited 'charade'.

In Mabel Dodge Luhan's memoir of the same period, there is also a description of Alice Sprague, at the time of her visit to Taos, which again accords meticulously with Lawrence's dramatised version of the character of the same name. According to Mrs. Luhan, Mrs. Sprague was 'one of those who determinedly see only the best in anyone'; one who, in the face of all the confusions that must have complicated the lives of this gifted group of people, 'continued to smile and smile and to consider Lorenzo an avatar, and Clarence a potential genius'. (N.II p. 517) Even the white muslin dress, in which Lawrence costumes the Alica Sprague of the play, conforms with the portrait 'from the life' drawn by Mrs. Luhan.

Based just as obviously on the American poet and 'little' magazine editor, Willard 'Spud' Johnson, the Spud of the play is presented with considerable affection, and is indeed credited in the play's second scene with views on love and marriage that sound remarkably close to Lawrence's own. For a more artistically distanced version of the 'same' character, it is revealing to compare the Spud of *Altitude* with Bud Villiers of *The Plumed Serpent*, and to notice, in the scene at the bull-fight, for example, that the character in the novel is rendered with a rather sharper pen.

Entertaining as it is to us for the light it casts on Lawrence's attitudes to his Taos companions, *Altitude* is also immensely interesting for its unfinished status as a rough draft in dramatic form. As we have seen from the closeness to life of many of its characters, the fragment seems to be only partially and perfunctorily removed from the 'life' on which we would want to describe it as being based. Like *The Fight for Barbara*, much of it could presumably be described as 'word for word true'. Yet, even in the unfinished play, there is evidence of deliberate artistic shaping, and clear signs that the random experience of everyday life has been schematised in accordance with a dramatic design. Though founded on speeches suggested by the 'characters' themselves, the symmetrical line-up of opposing opinions in the text of the play strongly indicates that this degree of schematisation was the result of Lawrence's working over (without his friends' knowledge) of the material they had each contributed. It would appear too, that, in the summer of 1924, the various inhabitants of the Taos estate were living in a group of neighbouring cabins, so the situation of the play, in which they are all actually living under the same roof, also suggests an element of designed arrangement of the 'facts'.

As important as the fictional adjustments of dialogue and setting, is the choice of a situation (the failure of the cook to arrive) which allows us to measure *in action* the attitudes of the conveniently juxtaposed participants to the practical tasks about which they so much enjoyed theorising. Proud as we know him to have been of his ability to cope in such moments of domestic crisis, Lawrence indulgently mocks, in the play, the comparative helplessness of Mary who makes a symbolic occasion out of the trifling upset, and uses it as an illustration of the role of 'Woman' in the fundamental issues of life. Mabel too, is teased for being intent only on ensuring that she herself is minimally inconvenienced by the 'crisis'. More practical Spud gets on with the job in hand, but Clarence enlarges the '*contretemps*' into a 'calamity', while Ida accepts the situation with calm amusement, and the benign Mrs. Sprague hovers helplessly.

Though these varying degrees of helplessness or practicality differentiate between characters, it is the opposition between the white people and the Indians which marks the crucial design.

Mabel, in fact, compares the several reactions to the domestic *contretemps* with the contrast between Indians and white people in the audience at an Indian dance when, 'The Indians are like glowing coals and the white people are the ashes.' Ida and Spud object to her over-simplification, and the small incidents of the play—Indian Joe's reluctance to chop wood, for example, also criticise the romantic view expressed by Mabel and to some extent shared by Mary.

Having presented Mabel to us as rather pretentious and selfish in this opening episode, the play then proceeds to show her up as something of a hypocrite. Doyenne of this artistic circle, she evidently subscribes to a more conformist way of life than that to which she pretends. Her objections to Clarence's pink trousers, and her view that they are 'alright indoors. But not to go down to the Plaza' set up a further series of oppositions in which Ida supports Clarence, assisted by Mary who, however, changes sides in the dispute when she hears the combined verdict of the Indian servant Joe and Mabel's husband Tony to the effect that the trousers are unsuitable for the public appearance of a white man. Though Mrs. Sprague (characterised in real life, it will be remembered, for her capacity to see good in everyone and for her uncritical attitude towards her protegé, Clarence) praises the lovely colour of the trousers, Clarence is nevertheless reduced to parting with his 'glory', and to exchanging the vibrant life-enhancing pink of his offending trousers for dull but respectable grey. While he is making this change, the talk turns to the 'rightness' of the Indian and we see, in Mabel's idealised view of the Indian as 'having something that the white people have not' a direct contradiction of her behaviour over Clarence's trousers.

Theoretically Mabel wants to be adventurous; to make something significant happen among the 'group of more or less remarkable people, in a remarkable place, at a remarkable altitude', but in practice she will not even allow one of those remarkable people to wear a remarkable garment. In general philosophical terms, Mabel wants everyone to feel fine and to make 'everybody around you feel wonderful', but, at a practical level, the play tells us that she cannot even take the trouble to get a banging door fixed in order to achieve peace of mind for one of her guests.

In the second Scene—largely between Spud and Elizabeth on

216

the topic of love, marriage, fun and freedom—Lawrence begins further to develop this contrast between what his characters *say* they want and what they actually do in order to achieve it. More evidently a sketch on which to base further revisions even than its predecessor, this final scene of the unfinished play nevertheless shows that the opposition between ideal and reality must have been designed as a central structural feature, and that the adjustments we have seen to have been made between the life actually going on around Lawrence in Taos at the time of writing and the events of the play, have all been made with that central design in view.

It is perhaps stretching the available material too far to come to any serious conclusions about what is so evidently an enjoyable and extrovert diversion as the fragment of *Altitude*. It seems just, however, to maintain that Lawrence's preoccupation with the corruption of modern life—both among white people and among the Indians—is clearly present beneath the satirical surface of this latter-day impromptu. With the fragment of *Noah's Flood*, we can even more confidently observe this central theme being given the fully serious treatment that was to be developed on the grand scale in *David*.

Though there is no evidence to support a view that Lawrence actually discussed theatrical form with *avant garde* experimenters of the middle and late 1920s, this subject must surely have come up in gatherings such as we have seen portrayed in *Altitude*. As can be seen from the few extant pages of *Noah's Flood*, Lawrence was evidently casting round for a radically new form in which to present his Biblical epic. As we shall see, the form into which he eventually chose to present *David* bears close resemblances to that which, under Brechtian influence, we have come to be familiar with as 'epic' theatre. There was also a precedent for the episodic form of Lawrence's play in the silent cinema which has, from its beginnings, tackled subjects in a manner recognised today as epic, though overlooked in its own time. We cannot, of course, reliably conclude that these early masterpieces of the cinema had any direct influence on the form taken by *David*. From all the evidence it would appear that Lawrence himself was consistently hostile—at least at a conscious level—to the cinematic medium, and we can be quite sure that the critic of the

1927 production of *David* was not praising the play when he referred to its 'cinematographic' form.

Nevertheless we can see from the structure of the Bible play that new concepts of form comparable to, if not drawn from, those being developed in the theatre and the cinema of the 1920s are skilfully put to work in the presentation of Lawrence's epic subject. There may be no more than a coincidental connection between his first choice of subject and the film version of *Noah's Ark* which appeared in 1929 though, as we have seen, Lawrence was at the time familiar with representatives of the film world (like Clarence Thompson) and was obviously aware of the activitie of Hollywood—even though, according to his friends, he thoroughly disapproved of them.

Less a matter of conjecture is Lawrence's own preoccupation with the Noah theme. As long before as 1917 he had put forward 'Noah's Ark' as a possible title for the novel that was to become *Women in Love*, and in 1924 (the year in which the undated fragment was most probably written) his essay on *Books*[3] deals extensively with the relevance of the Noah story to the state of twentieth-century society. In that essay Lawrence maintains that, 'catastrophe alone never helped man. The only thing that ever avails is the living adventurous spark in the souls of men.' Christianity, Lawrence claims here, has done its work as the inspiration for that spark of adventure. 'If I had lived in the year 400' he writes, 'pray God, I should have been a true and passionate Christian. The adventurer. But now I live in 1924, and the Christian venture is done. The adventure is gone out of Christianity. We must start on a new venture towards God.'

Like *The Plumed Serpent*, *David* is an imaginative effort to get that new venture under way. In the novel, Lawrence already had a form that he was accustomed to fitting to the new feeling. It was a form, however, which necessarily proclaimed the 'new venture' in a complex way to the individual consciousness of a solitary reader. For the play a new form had to be forged, and we can understand the feeling that led to this form if we read 'Indians and Entertainment'[4] in which Lawrence describes his view of the relationship between entertainment (or drama) and audience in

---

[3] In *Phoenix*, pp. 731–734.

[4] In *Mornings in Mexico*, (Penguin edition), pp. 52–64.

the white world, as it contrasts with that found in the world of the Indian. Fundamentally it is a question, Lawrence claims, of the difference between individual and universal consciousness. The white spectator is defined as a 'little god'; 'a little individual consciousness lording it, for the moment, over the actually tiresome and inflexible world of actuality'. For the Indian 'There is no God looking on. The only god there is, is involved all the time in the dramatic wonder and inconsistency of creation. God is immersed, as it were, in creation, not to be separated or distinguished.' It follows therefore, in terms of Lawrence's pantheistic metaphysic at least, that 'The Indian is completely embedded in the wonder of his own drama. It is a drama that has no beginning and no end, it is all-inclusive. It can't be judged, because there is nothing outside it, to judge it.' On the stage, as the audiences of his time knew it, Lawrence says 'we see ourselves: we survey ourselves: we are the gods above our own destinies'. At a safe distance, 'aloft in plush seats' in the auditorium, 'we are creatures of pure consciousness, pure spirit, surveying those selves of clay who are so absurd or so tragic, below'.

It was this relationship between spectator and entertainment that Lawrence's new form was designed to change; the relationship that he defined as characteristic of Western theatre from 'even the earliest form of Greek drama'. As drama has evolved since that time, Lawrence believes that 'we ourselves become the gods of our own drama. The spectacle is offered to us. And we sit aloft, enthroned in the Mind, dominated by some one exclusive idea, and we judge the show.' We judge it, yes, but we also identify with it. We play—as Lawrence puts it—at 'being Mrs. Paradiso'. And it is here that Lawrence's idea of theatre finds common ground with that of Brecht. According to both dramatists, it is the convention of identification with the action on stage that prevents the spectator from being moved to take the action in life that will change his own world. The changes that Lawrence saw as necessary were, needless to say, very different from those envisaged by Brecht. But the essential shift that dramatic form had to make, in order to destroy what Lawrence describes as the 'soothing and satisfying' effect of self-recognition and empathy, was common to both. Only by shattering the spectator's comfortable expectations of theatrical experience, and disrupting the traditional relationship between audience and play, could a radical shift in consciousness be achieved.

The connection suggested here between the dramatic theory and practice of Brecht and the work of Lawrence in *David* may seem perverse, if not indeed positively misleading, since for Lawrence the ideal of theatrical performance was one in which 'There is no division between actor and audience. It is all one', while the opposed concept of a necessary critical distance between actor and audience was crucial to Brecht. As fundamentally opposed in the matter of their dramatic aesthetics as in the view each took of the direction mankind must take in order to be 'saved', Brecht and Lawrence nevertheless both chose epic form as their medium. Both also took the view that the revolutionary change in an audience's mode of perception could only be achieved by disrupting that audience's expectation of a particular kind of relationship between spectator and play. To this extent then, it can be seen as inevitable that their idea of a new form had to be as different as possible from the prevailing norm of theatrical performance, and that both saw a complete break with the conventions of naturalism as central to their method.

Insofar as Lawrence is concerned, the form he chose for *David* is one that deliberately creates in an audience those 'misgivings about destiny' which make 'you sit rather uneasily in your seat', and it is a form so very different from the conventional theatrical experience of its own time that we can hardly wonder at the failure of the Stage Society to realise it with any degree of success —especially as the producer had to work without benefit of the author's presence at rehearsals. As will be seen in the following chapter, Lawrence knew well enough that his presence at rehearsals was essential to the proper realisation of the new form he had created. Letters of exhortation simply were not enough, though we can clearly see from them what Lawrence had in mind. When, for example, he writes to Robert Atkins (who was to produce the play), 'If one can only get that feeling of primitive religious passion across to a London audience. If not, it's no good' (N.II. p. 524) we recognise (as Lawrence himself must surely have done) that his experience with his own work for the theatre had conditioned him to accept the inevitability of failure. More importantly we see too that the driving force—the 'feeling'—behind the new form of *David* is the achievement of a new state of consciousness in which the audience will be at one with the play, as in the experience of a religious ritual.

We have no means of knowing what made Lawrence decide that the 'Noah' story would not suit this purpose. We can see though, why it appealed to him in the first place, as an appropriate allegory for his new philosophy from what he has to say about the Noah myth in the essay on *Books*, where we read: 'It's no good leaving everything to fate. Man is an adventurer, and he must never give up the adventure. The venture is the venture: fate is the circumstance around the adventurer. The adventurer at the quick of the venture is the living germ inside the chaos of circumstance. But for the living germ of Noah in his Ark, chaos would have redescended on the world in the waters of the flood. But chaos *couldn't* redescend, because Noah was afloat with all the animals.'

We can also tell, from the unfinished first scene of *Noah's Flood*, that Lawrence had begun to flesh out the bones of the Bible story with a motif of insurrection. Three conspirators plot to overthrow the power of Noah—the authority of 'the Old One and his demi-god sons'—by stealing the secret of fire. Devoid of psychological motivation or characterising 'background', the three men are anonymous, representative only of varying degrees of superstition and rebellion. There are Miltonic echoes in the tone of this revolt, as the rebels resolve no longer to accept the word of the 'demi-gods', and to seize for themselves the secret knowledge that will set them free. Representative too of the sickness of modern society (as Lawrence saw it), the three anonymous dissidents are united in their belief that, if they can only harness the energies of the world and understand its physical mysteries, they will be masters of the universe. They will, as the First Man proclaims, be 'Men, masters of fire, and free on the face of the earth. Free from the need to answer, masters of the question. Lo, when we are lords of the question, how humbly the rest shall answer. Even the stars shall bow humbly, and yield us their reply, and the sun shall no more have a will of his own.'

Though the language sometimes stumbles close to absurdity in its effort to capture a spare, primitive quality, the imagery of rebellion is well sustained, and the rhetoric of the debators dis-

221

turbingly persuasive. One can only hazard guesses as to why Lawrence gave up this promising start and turned to the story of Saul and David as an alternative source. Perhaps he felt that an emblematic treatment of the deluge and its consequence would be too close to the medieval miracle play model, making it appear that his call for the creation of a totally new religious consciousness was simply a plea for the revival of an old one. Or perhaps the personal appeal to him of the David story over-rode all other considerations. In the light of our present knowledge we can be certain only that the choice of the David theme was integrally bound up with his purpose to write, *for the stage,* a play which would shake spectators out of their complacent ways of seeing into awareness of alternative modes of consciousness.

10

David

More than one meaning can be read into the statements that Lawrence made about some of his dramatic works. As we have seen, this ambiguity has led, during his lifetime and since, to a serious misunderstanding of his attitude to drama. On the subject of *David*, however, Lawrence's own voice is totally unambiguous. In the June of 1925, he wrote to his agent, Curtis Brown: 'I expect by this time you have had the MS. of the play, *David*. It is a good play, and for the theatre. Someone ought to do it.' (CL p. 845)

Brown disagreed with Lawrence, as the latter explains to Alfred Knopf, to whom the MS. of *David* had been passed on. 'I don't want it published, unless it is produced' Lawrence insists, as he explains to Knopf that 'Curtis Brown thinks it would be better if it appeared first as "literature". Myself, I am a bit tired of plays that are only literature' Lawrence continues. 'If a man is writing "literature", why choose the form of a play? And if he's writing a play, he surely intends it for the theatre. Anyhow I wrote this play for the theatre, and I want the theatre people to see it first.' (CL p. 845)

The terms used here allow of no doubt as to the destination Lawrence planned for *David*, though, as things turned out, he was disappointed of his hopes, and the play did appear first as 'literature'. In spite of the fact that he was not always so unequivocal about his plays, there would appear to be adequate evidence to suggest that he saw all his dramas as he saw *David*; that is to say, as 'for the theatre'. Though it was at one time commonplace to describe Lawrence as a 'formless' writer, it is now widely recog-

223

nised that he unerringly opted for the appropriate form.[1] As early as 1911, he had stated of *The Widowing of Mrs. Holroyd*, 'I wrote it for the stage', and for all his tactful reservations about himself as a dramatist, we have seen too, that he was all the time convinced of the stageworthiness of his plays, and of the fact that 'an audience might be found for some of my stuff, if there were a man to whip 'em in.' When he chose the form of a play then, we must surely credit him with intending it for the theatre.

Lawrence was also keenly aware that *David* would require a particularly sensitive 'whipper in' if its effectiveness in the theatre was not to be lost. In his letter to Knopf he testifies to this awareness when he writes: 'Curtis Brown says it is not a "popular" play. But damn it, how does he know even that? Playgoing isn't the same as reading. Reading in itself is highbrow. But give the "populace" in the theatre something with a bit of real feeling in it, and they'll respond. If you do it properly.' The proviso is, of course, all-important.

Curtis Brown had also objected that Lawrence's play called for a whole company of Forbes-Robertsons to do justice to its long, poetic speeches. Totally disagreeing with this contention, Lawrence felt that 'there might be a whole company of better men'. Star actors, brought up in the tradition that his play so fiercely rejects, were just what Lawrence did *not* want. Heatedly he declares to Knopf, 'there's many a nigger could play Saul better than Forbes-Robertson could do it. And I'd prefer the nigger. Or men and women from that Jewish theatre.' To get the right 'feeling' for his play Lawrence wanted actors raised in a totally different tradition: 'Jews or Italians or Spaniards or Celts . . . not Teutons or Scandinavians or Nordics: it's not in their blood—as a rule.' We may deplore the racial distinctions made here, but in essence we can see that Lawrence is calling, as he did in 1913, for a revolt against the 'bony, bloodless theatre' of the 'rule and measure mathematical folk'; for a production of his play that would break every tenet of the established English convention and speak directly—from blood to blood.

Right up to the time of the play's first production in May 1927,

[1] See, for example, Frank Kermode's *Lawrence* (1973) for a discussion of 'form' in relation to Lawrence, with special reference to the 'metaphysic' in the novels and in their 'doctrinal doubles'.

Lawrence's letters show him doubting that this essential feeling could be captured—or even remotely understood—without the benefit of his advice at rehearsals. After the disastrous 1926 production of *The Widowing of Mrs. Holroyd*, he began indeed to feel that even his own presence would be of little avail. The producer of *David* evidently shared the author's doubts, and the production—much to Lawrence's irritation—was repeatedly postponed.

In the August of 1926, he had written to Mabel Dodge Luhan, 'We shall be in England for a week or two. The stage society is giving a couple of performances of *David* in Oct. or Novem. I should like to see the first rehearsals anyhow.' (N.III. p. 88) A month later, things were no further advanced, and Lawrence wrote impatiently to Koteliansky: 'We'd (then) stay here at least a week, and longer if it were necessary for the play. . . . But how long do they think I'm going to wait in England for them.'[2] Delays evidently became too protracted, and the Lawrences left England. By October, there was still no sign of the production materialising, but Lawrence, by then in Florence, remained much concerned about it. 'I haven't heard any more from those Stage Society people, so don't know if we shall come to London in December, for the play' (N.III. p. 116) he wrote to his step-son, and, in the same month, expressed his continuing concern about the play in another letter to Koteliansky: 'I sent off the music to *David* the other day. . . . Wonder if they'll make anything of the play, anyhow. I don't feel very sanguine.' (CL p. 942)

In the event, as we have seen, the production of *The Widowing of Mrs. Holroyd* preceded that of *David*. Despite his anger at the critics, and his disappointment over what he heard from friends about that production, Lawrence remained reservedly hopeful about the Bible play. In the January of 1927, he wrote again to Koteliansky: '. . . now I think *David* is being put back until April, so that I should not need to come to England before the end of March. The later the better, for me, in the hopes of spring.'[3] To another friend around the same time he confessed: 'I feel an infinite disgust at the idea of having to be there while the fools nimble-pimble at the dialogue. They ruined *Mrs.*

[2] *The Quest for Rananim*, p. 296.
[3] Ibid., p. 306.

Holroyd by trailing out the last scene all wrong. Why should I bother about them.' (CL pp. 963–4)

When April came around, the long delays had obviously worn Lawrence's patience even thinner. Appearing to despair of the play's ever being staged, he writes: 'I heard from Mrs. Whitworth that *David* is now due in May . . . the producer also shirked it: so I don't know whom they'll get, and don't care much. It feels forever so uncertain. I don't think I shall come over.' (CL p. 973) Yet, two weeks later, his interest had again revived—perhaps out of satisfaction at having finally received a definite date for the production—and he writes: 'I hear *David* is on May 22 and 23— and they urge me to come. I suppose they'll make a mess of it without me. So I shall pretty well have to come.'[4]

Continuing, through the spring of 1927, to be torn between a desire to assist with the production, and a reluctance to involve himself in an enterprise that he feared was bound to end in disaster, Lawrence was finally prevented from travelling to England by a further bout of illness. Though his predictions before the event indicate that he had not hoped for much in the way of success for the play, his anger at the critics was, nevertheless, bitter. 'They produced *David* last week,' he writes to Mabel Dodge Luhan. 'I heard the audience was really rather enthusiastic, but the press notices are very unfavourable. It's those mangy, feeble reviewers; they haven't enough spunk to hear a cow bellow.' (CL p. 982)

The friend from whom Lawrence had heard about the production was Koteliansky, to whom he writes: 'I was very glad to hear about *David* from you. It seems to me just as well I wasn't there —you can't make a silk purse out of a sow's ear. But if ever the thing is regularly produced, I'll come and see what I can do: though I doubt if it would be much. Actors haven't enough *inside* to them.' (CL p. 979)

It is clear enough from this, and other letters that Lawrence did not himself seriously regard his play as a 'sow's ear', and that his disappointment in the failure of a project, into which he had put so much of himself, was profound. It is clear too, that he despaired of finding, in a theatre that had been consistently hostile to

[4] Ibid., p. 312.

what he was trying to do, a company that could free itself from tradition sufficiently to do justice to his pioneering modes. Not content with creating a wholly *new* form for *David*, he also concerned himself with the realisation in performance of that form. As we shall see when examining the play in detail, it is conceived as a total, enveloping experience; a fictive world, existing in and for itself, and supported in so doing by being based on what a hostile critic of the 1927 production described as the 'most well-known book in the English language'.

Towards this totality Lawrence contributed not only the play, with its verbal and visual symbolism, but also the music with which it was to be accompanied. Of this music he writes to Robert Atkins (the producer): 'It is very simple, needs only a pipe, tambourines and a tom-tom drum. I hope it will do.' (N.II. p. 524). It is this same letter which ends with Lawrence's verdict on the likely fate of his own play, if it were not done 'properly': 'If one can only get that feeling of primitive religious passion across to a London audience. If not it's no good.' As Lawrence had feared, the production singularly failed to get across any kind of passion to its London audience, and, in that sense certainly was 'no good'. The last experiment with drama had failed—and there were to be no more.

Despondently Lawrence writes 'finis' to his career as a dramatist in a letter written in the October of 1927 to Max Mohr, a German physician and playwright who held out some hope of producing *David* in Berlin. In the self-deprecatory tone which has come to be so familiar to us in Lawrence's letters about his plays, he begins: 'It's awfully nice of you to take so much thought and trouble for *David*. But don't you bother too much about it, you'll hate it and us in the end. I know the translation is very unsatisfactory: my sort of German, which, like your English, must go into a class by itself. And of course the whole play is too literary, too many words. The actual technique of the stage is foreign to me. But perhaps they—and you—could cut it into shape. I shall be very surprised if they *do* play it in Berlin. The public only wants foolish realism: Hamlet in a smoking jacket.' (CL p. 1016) The derisive tone of that final image gives away something of Lawrence's game. As we have seen from the letters to Curtis Brown and to Knopf, Lawrence very strongly felt that the play was *for the stage* and not 'literary' at all. Significantly in this respect his letters take no account whatever of the reviews of *David* when it came out in book form in 1926. His handing over of the 'cutting' and 'shaping' of the play to Dr. Mohr does, however, indicate the extent to which he had given up all hope of reaching a public with his exciting and revolutionary ideas of what was possible in the theatre. The then existing technique of the stage was indeed foreign to him—and he had no desire to learn its language. What he *had* wanted to do was to replace that technique and language with a new and startling dramatic voice of his own. But, since no one would listen, that voice was permanently stilled.

The sad tale of the fortunes of *David* during Lawrence's lifetime is particularly poignant in view of the fact that the play was a work very close to Lawrence's heart. In her memoir, Frieda Lawrence recalls the almost fatal illness that struck her husband down as he was completing *The Plumed Serpent*. At the time the Lawrences were living in Oaxaca and the local native doctor was, according to Frieda, 'scared at having anything to do with a foreigner and he didn't come'. Lawrence himself thought he would die. But 'at last slowly, slowly, he got a little better' and managed the 'crucifixion of a journey' to Mexico City where Frieda was advised by the doctors to 'take him to the ranch; it's his only chance' and warned her that: 'He has T.B. in the third degree. A year or two at most.'

Under this sentence of death Frieda watched over her husband at the ranch as he gradually recovered from the most recent attack. 'As he got better he began writing his play *David*, lying outside his little room on the porch in the sun. I think in the play he worked off his struggle for life. Old Saul and the young David —Old Samuel's prayer is peculiarly moving in its hopeless love for Saul—so many different motifs, giant motifs, in that play.'[5]

As Frieda observed, there are indeed 'giant motifs' in the play, not least among them being the motif of David and Jonathan— the archetypal image of friendship between man and man to which Lawrence had aspired so unsuccessfully in his own life, and to which he had referred so often in his novels and stories. Greater even than this, perhaps, is the motif of man's relationship with the unknown; with that ultimate mystery to which mankind has

[5] *"Not I, But the Wind . . .*", p. 143.

always given the name of God. To Lawrence himself though, the chief of the play's giant motifs must have been the 'feeling of primitive religious passion' without the communication of which to an audience the play must be condemned, in its author's own terms, as 'no good'. Even if we did not have corroborative evidence for Lawrence's dramatic preoccupation with that 'passion' in *David*, we could still see, in the structure of the play itself, that it represents a supreme effort to realise the theatrical possibilities of religious ritual. As we can glimpse too, from a comparison of this major work with the surviving fragment of *Noah's Flood*, the element of conflict that is essential to the primitive religious passion of *David* lies in the recurrent paradox which makes men reject and corrupt the very power which they regard as God-given.

The opening scene of *David* bounds into life—almost literally with a clash of cymbals—and we are faced at once with an image of impassioned conflict. The maidens celebrating in triumph are beautiful, young and regal. The daughters of Saul; Merab and Michal, chant their victory anthem with delight. But their words are savage: vanquished King Agag is a bound and helpless prisoner, guarded by warriors with spears. Can it, the scene asks us, become these princesses to gloat over Agag's misery, or is beauty in fact being desecrated as the maidens spit upon the captive king and heap abuse on him?

Yet the words of the chant tell us that it is not an 'unjust' victory that is being celebrated. Nor is Agag a martyr to be pitied. It is the vengeance of God on the Amalekites—who stab their enemies in the back and 'killed our women,, and the weary ones, and the heavy footed, in the bitter days of wandering'— that has been brought about by the armies of Saul.

Only in the taking of spoil and the rejoicing in the rewards of battle is Saul defying the Divine decree. Towards the end of the Scene, Samuel will appear to remind Saul of that commandment, and of the consequence of his disobedience, but the play has already, in its opening moments, enacted the enormity of Saul's offence in the image of youth and beauty exulting over the spoils of victory.

Mercy for the vanquished is not called for here. The God of the Old Testament is an avenging God, and Saul has opposed His will by sparing life rather than by slaughtering—though it is plain that he has acted out of avarice, rather than compassion. At once then, an audience is faced with a conflict at odds with the Christian ethic.

To read the episode as it is narrated in I *Samuel* xv. requires a modulation of those Christian sensibilities. Typically among the key events of the Old Testament, the ethic proposed is incompatible with that of the New. For Christian writers who choose the Old Testament as their source, the dilemma has been recurrent, and one is reminded again of Milton and the controversy that still rages over whether or not he successfully overcame the problem of 'dramatising' this God of wrath and vengeance.

Lawrence's interest here obviously takes quite a different direction. His object is not to comprehend the fierce religious consciousness of the Old Testament within the compassionate consciousness of the New. Indeed we might regard this element of the vengeance ethos as a cardinal factor in his rejection of the Noah story in favour of the episode dramatised here. Throughout the history of Western Christianity, the Noah story has become absorbed into the teachings of the church, so that its element of the wholesale slaughter of the sinful has become less emphasised, while the survival of the good has gained prominence. Noah, we might say, has become acceptably Christianised, while the God who punished Saul can only be rendered morally acceptable by a view of the Bible which accepts everything as Divine writ, and rationalises only to the extent of claiming that even the most savage vengeance was just in the context of its own time.

In terms of the play, Lawrence's choice of subject is therefore designed to bring his audience face to face with this crisis of faith; to make them vividly aware of the incompatibility of the edict to wipe out the Amalekites with their (professed) Christian morality, and to make it impossible for them to evade the 'feeling' that there are modes of consciousness quite alien to those which our society holds to be universal. Thus the 'primitive religious consciousness' is actively foregrounded from the outset.

Saul's daughters, despite their ugly taunts, are beautiful and graceful. Only when they wrangle over the spoil do they become morally suspect, and the scene shows us that this defect is a consequence of the corruption that Saul has brought upon his people by failing to carry out God's commandment. The God of

Flame, to whose will Saul surrendered when accepting his destiny as king, has been defied. Stubbornly setting his individual will against the will of the Unknown, Saul must inevitably fall from grace.

Most vividly, the close of the scene dramatises the conflict between the consciousness of the play and that of its audience, when Samuel, to whom Saul has been praying for restitution and forgiveness, slays the captive Amalekite king in the name of God.

What we notice in this opening scene is the dramatist's refusal to 'modernise' his subject by giving his characters a dimension of psychological motivation that might make them—in the terms of the tradition he was rejecting—seem 'human' or rationally understandable. We are evidently not meant to 'understand' the play in that way. Saul and David are not to be seen in the conventional perspective of 'foolish realism' as biblical 'Hamlets in smoking jackets', but as larger than life, emblematic figures. We must accept the experience whole, as it strikes us in the superhuman terms of its concrete dramatic imagery, and not look for the sub-textual nuances that might interpret the action for us in present-day terms. We are being prevented from standing outside the play and judging; from taking up that point of view which Lawrence regarded as definitive of the relation between spectator and play in the Western tradition of theatre.

We note too that, though Lawrence has eschewed character development in the naturalistic sense, he has nevertheless taken considerable liberties with his source. Michal, Merab and their maidens are pure invention.[6] Yet it is upon the effect they make that an audience's response must depend, so that the moment of the slaying of Agag, which is taken almost literally word for word from the Bible, may achieve its full force as an act of Divine justice.

In complete contrast to the whirling excitement and bloody climax of the first scene, the following episode withdraws into the privacy of Samuel's room for its profoundly contemplative and poetic rendering of the conflict raging within an individual

---

[6] Michal and Merab do, of course, figure in the Bible narrative, and, in that sense, are not invented by Lawrence. The part played, particularly by Michal, in enacting and personifying Lawrence's themes, is, however, pure invention.

mind. The prophet's prayer is not only moving (as Frieda Lawrence felt it to be) in its 'hopeless love for Saul', but also structurally and thematically definitive. In the penultimate scene of the play, where Saul, among the prophets at Ramah, briefly rediscovers the bliss of the union of his spirit with the consciousness of the Unknown, we will hear Samuel declare to David that 'the Lord is all things': to Saul, 'a tall and rushing flame'—to David, a 'God in thine own likeness, or as a brother beyond thee who fulfills thy desire'. As we have seen from Lawrence's philosophy in 'Indians and Entertainment', the concept, from which he sees it as necessary for Western society to free itself, is that of regarding mankind as being judged by an unseen Other. And it is the split in consciousness arising from this concept that he condemns as destructive for its division of man into 'good' spiritual and 'bad' instinctive elements. Somehow, man must be restored to a totality; to a reunion of soul with body in a unified consciousness. It matters not that the form of the Mystery to which a man submits his own individual will may differ from one age to another, as we see symbolised in the play in the different Mysteries with which Saul and David unite to find their wholeness.

As he prays, we see Samuel tormented by the split between his love for Saul, the man, and his knowledge that 'Saul has crawled away from God.' Through the intensity of his prayer, we see him finding strength to submit completely to the will of the Mystery in which he finds his prophetic wisdom. Abandoning his own will to be compassionate to Saul, he rejoices that 'I sink like a stone in the sea, and nothing of my own is left me. I am gone away from myself, I disappear in the deeps of God. And the oracle of the Lord stirs me, as the fountains of the deep. Lo! I am not mine own.'

Objections to the unsuitability for the stage of this scene on the grounds that it is too 'literary' must surely be over-ruled by the intensity with which the soliloquy dramatises the conflict within Samuel's soul. Against the violent physical action of the first scene, with its range from the triumphal dance to sacrificial murder, we have here the inward range, from the heartbreak of divided loyalties, through supplication, to the calm and settled obedience of a resolved soul. In all but the most naïve terms, Samuel's soliloquy is taut with action, moving as it does from despairing doubt to a willed resignation. Throughout the prayer too, it is implicit that, though Samuel speaks alone, he hears the voice of God, and that his resolution is achieved in response to that voice.

If we look at the verses out of which this struggle of a tormented soul is constructed,[7] we see that Lawrence has expanded his source into the moving prayer of Scene 2 on the basis of a single phrase: 'nevertheless Samuel mourned for Saul', and that the direct speech of the Lord to Samuel commands him to cease mourning and proceed to the anointing of a new king. In his dramatisation, as we have seen, Lawrence has made this voice implicit in the emotional movement of Samuel's prayer. The prophet's mourning is an act of disobedience and, in the play at least, we must be made to feel that it is inevitable for him to find, in the resources of his own consciousness, a way of coming to terms with his individual impulse and a way of surrendering to the will to which his life is dedicated. 'Tell me, and I will do it' he prays, and, being answered, obeys absolutely the voice which he has heard.

Yet there remains a profound ambiguity about the nature of the 'voice' to which Samuel submits his own individual consciousness, and, in the following scene, we see this ambiguity further developed in the context of a social and more everyday life, far removed from the prophet's sanctuary. The setting for this scene is 'an open place in the village' and our eyes must be led first to the 'old man on a roof calling aloud and kindling a signal fire.' We are entering into the life of a community which, though complete in itself, must maintain contact with other human communities.

It is in this setting that we are confronted with the dialogue between Jesse and Eliab. 'We live our lives as men, by the strength of our right hand. Why heed the howling of priests in linen ephods, one or many?' Eliab challenges his father. Like the men who plot to rob Noah of the secret of fire, Eliab proclaims the supremacy of the will of man. Like them too he is proved wrong by events. It is the boy David, not his eldest brother, who will be anointed king, just as the plotters would, we know, have been obliterated in the deluge.

[7] I *Samuel* xv. 35, xvi. 1.

It is not enough, Lawrence uses the Bible to declare, to trust in the strength of man; to put faith in the will of the individual. Yet, as his chosen story so powerfully illustrates, it is the individual who triumphs against the many, when once he has surrendered his own will to that of the Unknown. The might of Saul's armies will be impotent against the champion of the Philistines, while David, delivered into the hand of the Lord, will defeat him in single combat.

Inside Jesse's courtyard, the scene that follows remains very close to its source in the matter of action, as Samuel, in response to the voice of God (rendered in the play by Samuel's asides), successively rejects the sons of Jesse as they are brought before him, fixing his choice finally on David. Eliab's scepticism and doubt are untouched by the ceremony of anointing. Yet it is in this ceremony that the play surely calls for our recognition of the surrender of will required of a leader of men. Samuel's speeches during this ceremony are entirely Lawrence's invention, and again we hear most emphatically the re-iteration of the phrases that could be felt to be the play's thematic leitmotif. 'Thou shalt be a master of the happenings among men' Samuel pronounces, asking of David to 'Answer then. Does thy soul go forth to the Deep, does the Wonderer move in thy soul?' As the anointing solemnly confirms David as the chosen one of God, Samuel continues. 'The Chooser chooseth thee. Thou shalt be no more thine own, for the chosen belongs to the Chooser. . . . Henceforward thou art not thine own. The Lord is upon thee, and thou art His.'

This ceremony of choosing, and of the chosen one's surrender to the will that reaches to him out of 'the whirlwind of the whole world's middle', is set for us within the context of the sacrificial feast, and again, as in the moment of Samuel's killing of Agag, Lawrence directs us to the elemental nature of primitive religious passion through a close association with the blood of sacrifice.

After the anointing, the Bible simply records that 'the Spirit of the Lord departed from Saul, and an evil spirit from the Lord troubled him'. In the play it is given to Michal to report this to her father, when Saul furiously interrupts the maidens at their play, and threatens to kill his younger daughter. As in the opening scene, Lawrence adds a whole new narrative element to his source with the expansion of the role played by Michal. It is through her that we have seen the corruption consequent upon Saul's failure utterly to destroy the Amalekites, and here in Scene 5, it is through the threat made upon the life of Michal that we are made to feel the presence of an evil spirit.

As Michal, Merab and their maidens enliven their spinning with gossip and riddles, we learn that David has come to Gilgal, and that already there are signs that he has attracted the attention of the king's younger daughter. Older and wiser Merab fears that her father will be enraged by the wild laughter of the maidens in the courtyard, and her fears are fully justified when Saul furiously threatens to run Michal through with his spear for her wantoning and ribaldry. The frightened Merab and the maidens steal away from the king's wrath, but bolder Michal remains to try to soothe her father who savagely rejects her words of comfort, and damns her for a witch.

It is here that Michal reports what the people are saying of Saul, and pleads that 'I would only help thee with the Lord, as Jonathan helps thee against the Philistines'. Innocent of the blasphemy for which Saul curses her, Michal draws upon herself the fury of the evil spirits who break into the soul of Saul; into the 'empty place' left since the Lord abandoned him. Saul himself commits the blasphemy when he likens the killing of Michal to Samuel's killing of Agag, and it is only the intervention of David and Jonathan that prevents him from putting the commands of the evil spirits who possess him into effect.

David alone, however, can find words to bring Saul to his senses and restore him to a less troubled humour. We notice here, that Lawrence has held back the information that David has been sent for by Saul, because the king had heard that the boy had power to calm troubled spirits, and we see that this retardation has the effect of making David's power *in action* the more wonderful. Michal too rejoices in her father's recovery, and dares to ask 'Why not laugh as you used to laugh, Father, and throw the spear in sport at a mark, not grip it in anger?' Rescued from the grip of the evil spirits, Saul responds with affection to his daughter's plea, and laughs at her pert dismissal of David's compliments.

As we watch the king mellowing before the respectful wisdom of David's words, we see, in the shapes of the king and the king-to-be, the transference of authority that has taken place. Though the old king still commands, it is the anointed youth whose spirit prevails, and David, we know, is delivered into the hands of the Lord.

In the dialogue between Jonathan and David on which this scene ends, Lawrence puts into David's mouth this declaration:

> There are two motions in the world. The will of man for himself, and the desire that moves the Whirlwind. When the two are one, all is well, but when the will of man is against the Whirlwind, all is ill, at last.

When we look at the play as a whole, we can see that an aspect of this declaration is illustrated in each of the key episodes. All goes ill in Scene 1 because Saul's will has opposed that of the Whirlwind; for Samuel in Scene 2, things move from ill to well as the prophet rediscovers harmony with the desire of the Whirlwind. In Scenes 3 and 4 we are shown the contrast between the overlooked Eliab who knows only the will of men, and the chosen David who feels the Whirlwind within him as his 'soul leaps with God.' Saul, in the present scene, has acted out the evil that occurs when a contrary motion rejects the will of the Whirlwind, leaving a void to be filled up with manifestations of ill, and, even at the point of making his declaration, David himself is torn between his own will to return to his father and the hills where the sheep are in Bethlehem, and the certain knowledge that all can only be well if he overcomes that individual desire and submits himself to the 'flame of Hope'.

Significantly, David's declaration arises out of Jonathan's questioning of Samuel's slaying of Agag. As we have repeatedly seen, Lawrence's chosen subject cannot evade this un-Christian element of human sacrifice, and, to Jonathan's objection that he 'would not willingly have drawn the sword on naked Agag', David must be able serenely to comprehend the murderous act in his submission to the Whirlwind will. Indeed, his declaration of faith leads to the corollary: 'So all is decreed ill that is Amalek. And Amalek must die, for he obstructs the desire of the breathing God.'

Loath to appear presumptuous or vainglorious, David, the anointed of God, must be seen to be learning that the greatest joy is to submit his individual will to the will of the Whirlwind, and, in that submission, he rests confident that the love between Jonathan and himself is true.

Through David's actions, the play illustrates the miracles that can be wrought through such a surrender. On the other hand it offers, in the invented portrait of Michal, the image of a spirit that is stubbornly resistant to submission. Like Jonathan, Michal is not vouchsafed the vision of the Thunderer. In this way, both of Saul's children are seen to be dispossessed of the glory that their father has thrown away. Both too find their glory through David. In Jonathan this acceptance of fate is shown to be resigned and composed, but Michal struggles against her fate, wilfully opposing her female individuality to both human and divine decree. 'As for me' she complains (in Scene 6), 'I am sad, I am sad, I am sad, and why should I not be sad? . . . I don't know whether the Lord is with me, or whether He is not with me. How should I know? Why should I care? A woman looks with different eyes into her heart, and, Lord or no Lord, I want what I want.'

It is to Michal, in her state of spiritual defiance, that the account of the Philistine giant who terrorises her father's army is brought by an anonymous soldier. Though she has denied the spirit of God in herself, Michal—whom David loves—is shown to partake unwittingly of that spirit in her challenge that, if Goliath 'were a mountain, I would prick him with my needle', and in her insistence to the wounded Jonathan that 'some man should think of a way' to defeat the giant who shames all Israel.

This scene of pure invention focuses attention on the range of David's unconscious influence. Michal knows only that she loves the man, but his love for her in return endows her with the power to foreshadow events. She sees the overthrow of Goliath in terms of human victory—and it is the man she loves whom the Lord chooses to 'think of a way' to defeat the giant. The elaborate ritual of witchcraft, to which Michal calls our attention, fails her, but David's love makes her an effective 'seeress'. We may observe here too, the Lawrentian philosophy of 'sex relations' which again puts a Miltonic emphasis on woman as the passive vessel, through whom man's destiny is revealed.

In dramatic terms, this scene prepares most effectively for the acting out in Scene 7 of David's victory over Goliath. This is undoubtedly the most familiar episode in the David story, and it is therefore particularly interesting to observe how Lawrence handles it in relation to the predominant theme of his play; a theme which differs crucially from that of the Old Testament narrative. As we have already noted, the dramatist leads up to the combat scene with a scene drawn from his own imagination; a fictive episode for which there is no biblical parallel. In Michal's practice of witchcraft, we have seen that her father's accusations had some justification. But we have also seen that her spells and charms are cast in vain. Partly of the house of Saul, and tainted with the ill that must befall that house, Michal is also partly David's. Like Michal's spells, Saul's attempt to regain power and eradicate evil by slaughtering the soothsayers is shown to fail. In both cases, magic is seen to be an instrument of the individual will; a human device designed to bring about the individual's desires. In both cases too, magic is powerless against the will of the Whirlwind.

It is by submitting to that greater will that David triumphs, and it is *this* aspect of his victory over monstrous odds that is emphasised in the dramatised version of his battle with Goliath. Apart from some filling out of the encounter between David and his brothers, we note that the play keeps very closely in Scene 7 to the events recounted in I *Samuel* xvi., up to the moment when Saul accepts David as the champion of Israel and insists upon sending him forth armed. This incident, so central to Lawrence's view of the story, is seized upon and developed for all its symbolic value as an enactment of the contrast between Saul's faith in the strength and devices of man, and David's in the deliverance of the Lord. To the accompaniment of Goliath's distant taunts, David asks of his king, 'Shall thy servant go in armour clad?', to which Saul asks in return, 'How else canst thou keep thy life?'

Since there can be no question of suspense here, we must attribute the holding back of the action for the elaborate tableau of arming to Lawrence's emphasis on Saul's loss of faith. Willing to hand over to David the sword which is the symbol of his temporal power, Saul is reluctant to allow David to venture forth armed only by the power of the Lord; that power which Saul once knew, but which has now been withdrawn from him.

As with our knowledge of the Bible story we know he must

do, David defies Saul and refuses the armour. The scene of the battle between the armed Goliath and the 'uncovered' shepherd boy is then rendered for us through the narration of the spectators. It is, of course, a very wise piece of dramatic strategy to keep the battle itself off-stage, since the encounter is so securely impressed on our imaginations that the enactment of it would inevitably disappoint our expectations. To everyone for whom the Bible is (as the critic of the 1927 production described it) 'the most well-known book in the English language', the combat between David and Goliath is surely one of 'the most well-known' scenes. It is therefore all the more effective in the play, that David and Goliath are heard but not seen, and the strategy also provides for the gradual emptying of the stage, as David's brothers and the soldiers hasten away to be in at the kill, leaving Saul alone to comment on the moment that confirms his own doom and the inevitable ascendance of a new king in Israel.

Desolate in the knowledge of his failure, Saul (as in the biblical source) forgets the identity of the youth who has arisen to save him, realising only that his own day is done, and that of the young champion of Israel, rising. In the second of his two soliloquies here, Saul is magnificently given rhetoric which combines narration of the scene before him with a revelation of the resilience of individual will. Brought to the point where he recognises the loss of his God-given power in his admission, 'I have lost the best. I had it, and have let it go,' he turns to mortal tactics by directing suspicion on the shrewdness and cunning of his supplanter.

With its stress on the clash between individual will and submission to the consciousness of an unknown force, the play here exploits the biblical view of Saul as a treacherous enemy of the Lord's anointed by showing the king's cunning to be, at every turn, outmanoeuvred by David's faith and innocence.

In appearing to glorify the youth by making him the leader of his hosts, it is clearly shown that Saul's promise to David 'not to hasten thee to they confusion' is peremptorily broken. David's response: 'Honour me not to my confusion' provides a verbal link with that promise from the previous scene, reminding the audience that Saul is seeking here to destroy the young man who is to succeed him. Saul imposes his will on David as he was unable to do in the case of arming him to meet Goliath. Again the play calls upon our fore-knowledge of the outcome, by enlarging upon David's unwilling acceptance of the heavy charge laid upon him. Unconsciously he is fulfilling the decree of the Whirlwind, which will ensure his victory and frustrate the schemes of Saul. This unconscious submission to destiny is made manifest in David's open-hearted confession to Jonathan, and is affirmed as just in the sealing of the bond of divine friendship between the two.

The covenant of faith made between David and Jonathan, and the exchange of garments which symbolises that covenant, occupies two verses at the beginning of I *Samuel* xviii., immediately after the slaying of Goliath. Transposed in the play to the moment when David is forced to accept Saul's treacherous offer of leadership, it serves Lawrence's theme the more effectively by illuminating once more the conflict between 'good' and 'bad' faith with which the dramatist is consistently concerned.

Resolved to 'rest in the Lord', David nevertheless pleads with Jonathan to stand by him, and their friendship is blessed by the mutual surrender of self-will. Emblematically clad in Jonathan's robes, David *becomes* the prince, and the sacrifice is willingly accepted by Jonathan who closes the scene with his own expression of surrender to the will of a God 'who hath not revealed himself unto me'. As the Lord's anointed, David must learn to commit himself to that will, but Jonathan's faith is shown to be equally strong in that he abandons himself freely to the fate decreed for him—without expectation or knowledge of the glory of possession by the spirit of the Lord.

After this intensely private scene of personal commitment, the stage surges to life in the courtyard of Saul's house in Gilgal, where Merab and Michal once again lead their maidens in a triumphal dance. Exultant, as on the occasion of the defeat of the Amalekites, the princesses beat out a primitive chant of victory in which David is lauded far above Saul. Lawrence's composition of the music for this scene, and his emphasis on that music's primitive simplicity, underline the contrast between the mood of the celebrants and that of the heroes whose exploits they are celebrating. The victors themselves do not join in the celebraion. As the procession, the arrival of which is watched for by 'men-servants gazing into the distance', approaches the waiting people, the princesses and maidens keep up their singing, but 'the men pass slowly into the gate without response', as the servant-men silently carry the spoils of battle past the curious eyes of the singers. Clearly this is designed to be seen as a victory of a different order from that celebrated in the first scene.

The following scene, within the gates of Saul's house, testifies to the nature of the difference. Saul is angered by the women's glorification of David. As in I *Samuel* xviii. 8, we are shown in the play that 'Saul eyed David from that day forward.' In the play, the king's suspicion is presented in terms of his jealousy of his successor's enjoyment of the spirit with which he himself was once blessed. Again, it is through Michal that this point of view is rendered. Merab, she sees, will not be David's bride, and, though her elder sister protests that she does not want David and will not see him 'climb above her', Michal predicts that the king's promise will again be dishonoured.

In Scene 11 her prediction is proved true by Saul's curses upon David, and by his private withdrawal, in the presence of Adriel and Abner, of publicly made promises. Though Abner warns that 'It is a bad thing . . . to let this jealous worm eat into a King's heart, that always was so noble', Saul cannot heed the warning. The evil spirit has entered into him and he can only plot resentfully against 'the supplanter'. Saul's tragedy is to have heard the voice of the Thunderer and to know: 'I hear it no more, for It hath closed Its lips to me.' Instead of that voice, he now hears other, evil voices, prompting him in the night of his spirit.

At the very centre of the play's passionate, religious 'feeling', Saul is portrayed as a man who has known and lost the greatest good; the divine gift which is the understanding of what it means to surrender judgement, and to be at one with the motion of the Whirlwind. That gift having been lost through his own disobedience, Saul (very much like Milton's Satan) heroically summons up the torments of the damned in his diabolic vision of the future of mankind, when 'God shall be gone from the world. Only men there shall be, in myriads, like locusts, clicking and grating upon one another, and crawling over one another.'

Wherever Lawrence's language may be held by critics of the play, to stumble, it is surely not in this daemonic prophesy, in which Saul foretells the future with what Abner describes as 'The spirit of the Underearth'. In its imagery of darkening locust clouds and apocalyptic serpents, Saul's tirade summons up a monstrous vision of corruption and decay; of evil in its most virulent form, defiantly opposing good.

It is in the emotional force with which this tirade is charged that we see the formal purpose of Lawrence's insistence on the 'primitive religious feeling' at the play's core, and understand fully the effect he was seeking in casting his characters as archetypes, rather than as psychologically motivated 'real' people. At one level, we understand that Saul is describing his own tragedy; his own vision of a personal future eaten up by monsters for whom he has himself made room.

Yet, much more than this, his speech is representative of a larger destiny, and prophetic on a universal scale of the future awaiting a Godless race, intent only on the mechanical fulfilment of their tiny, individual wills.

At this moment of Saul's desolation, David is once again shown as the psalmist, gradually restoring the king from the grip of the evil spirits under whose power he has been conjured to make two attempts on the life of the Lord's anointed. In the grip of those spirits, Saul has been endowed with the 'soft, swift suddenness of a great cat', as he leaps round and hurls the javelin 'which David as swiftly evades'. Released from their power, he emerges wearily from his trance, and briefly regains his stature as king by renewing his promises to David. Here too, we see the dramatist manipulating the familiar incidents of his chosen subject to provide yet a further example of the abstract theme in concrete terms of stage action. More than ever here, we see that Lawrence is not seeking simply to bring the Bible story to dramatic life, but is *using* it to illustrate his own interpretation of the crucial issues at stake in an ethical philosophy that can redeem mankind.

With its mockery of the deceived David, the opening of Scene 12 lightens the tone, and prepares for Saul's offer of Michal in marriage. After the stark opposition of good and evil, represented by David's overcoming of the evil that had possessed Saul, this lightening is evidently necessary in order that the human desires of David the man can be brought into focus. Once again having disgraced the name of king by having married Merab to Adriel and broken his word to David, Saul is not redeemed by making the offer of Michal—which is also hedged about with treachery. In Lawrence's terms, however, Saul's dishonour unwittingly works to the delight of David who longs for the king's younger daughter with a longing that is next to his longing for God.

In David's prayer, Lawrence presents this longing for Michal as holy; as a passionate desire that fulfills the spirit of the Lord in David, as is made specific in the plea: 'So Thou bringest us together in Thy secret self, that it may be fulfilled for Thee in us.' As we have seen throughout the play, Michal is characterised in Eve-like terms, though nowhere more patently than at the moment of her acceptance of David, as he overcomes her resistance to his seeking her, not for himself alone, but 'for the Lord's own self in me'. As so often in the play—and not only, one feels, because of its biblical diction—the associations with Milton are inescapable. Pert and teasing as she is, Michal stands to David as Eve to Adam: 'He for God only, she for God in him,' and the relationship is one that is strongly ratified by the spirit of Lawrence's play. It is a relationship that we know from other works to be fundamental to Lawrence's 'philosophy of sex relations'. It is for David to submit to the will of the Lord—to surrender his consciousness to the voice of the Thunderer—and for Michal to surrender herself to that Voice by way of submission to David.

Michal's submission is seen to be troubled by fears of her father's treachery. Even in her attainment to glory by way of love for David, she is still the daughter of Saul and subject to the ills that he has brought upon his house. Those ills are realised as Saul once again goes back on his word, and makes it a condition of the marriage that David must pay for his bride with the lives of a hundred Philistines.

Having once more evaded the king's treacherous plot to kill him, David is seen at the beginning of Scene 13 praying to an image in his room in Gilgal in the words of Psalm V, the burden of which is a plea for redemption from the transgressions of enemies. In Michal's words of comfort to her husband, we are given confirmation of the desolation that has, in fact, consumed the greatest of David's enemies. Not only has the spirit of the Lord departed from Saul, but this children have also forsaken him, and, like the love of Michal and Jonathan, the loyalty of the people has also been transferred from Saul to David. Yet, deserted and alone, Saul still strikes horror into David, who must fly into the wilderness. Michal can provide no lasting refuge for David from the vengeful wrath of her father; only a delight, a bliss and a 'forgetting' into which—with the Lord's blessing—he can briefly escape from his fears.

The role of Michal is certainly no easy one, calling as it does for an actress who can, at one and the same moment, be seductress and saviour, and who can command an audience's belief in unswerving devotion to David while she retains all the characteristics of a daughter of Saul. For a role that makes comparable demands in emotional range one thinks inevitably of Shakespeare's Cleopatra who is 'superhuman in her humanity'.

We see how essential it is for the duality in Michal to be portrayed for us, when the servant calls attention to the characteristics of Saul in his daughter, as Jonathan arrives at dawn to rouse David from his 'marriage sleep', and warn him of Saul's further plot upon his life. In this scene and the next, Saul's irreparable loss of the 'greatest good' is enacted in his children's risking of their lives in order to protect David. Yet there remains a strong sense in which they are both concurrently shown to be conscious of belonging to the house of Saul, and of being aware that they and their children have been supplanted by the choice of David as king as much as their father has been.

Jonathan has already expressed this conflict of loyalties, and will do so again as the play ends with David in exile. Yet we may note particularly in the play, that Jonathan comes in person to David's house to warn him of imminent danger. Sister and brother—both children of Saul—unite to save David's life, and are prominently seen to do so. So much the more telling then, in action, is Saul's rage at the close of Scene 14 when he prophesies that 'David shall pull down Saul, and David shall pull down Jonathan; thee, Michal, he will pull down, yea, and all thy house'.

We see here how the dramatist has elaborated Michal's deception of her father, by inventing her prayer to the household gods and foregrounding the dialogue between the voice of the captain and the voice of the servant as she delays the search. These retardations highlight the rage of Saul, which must be felt by the audience as savage, when he discovers that his victim has fled.

It is in contrast to the intensity of that savage rage that we must feel the mood of Saul on his arrival among the prophets in the penultimate scene of the play, when his lust for revenge is transmuted into deep despair in the presence of the Spirit that rules over the holy place.

Anticipating Saul's arrival, Samuel strengthens David for the struggle that lies ahead of him. While Saul lives, David must flee and flee again, never to rest secure in the promises of his king. David yearns for peace with the house of Saul, but Samuel reminds him that he cannot now escape from his own kingly destiny. Only at the bidding of God could David pronounce the words of abdication that Samuel offers him. He cannot repeat them 'for Saul's sake, and for Jonathan's, and for Michal's and for peace'. Of his own free will David surrenders yet again, saying 'The Lord shall do unto me as He will', and entering into a life of exile.

As Samuel blesses the King-to-be, a tumult is heard among the prophets who have gathered expectantly aloft on the pyramid that dominates this setting. Saul and his men have been sighted, and David must 'go forth into the fields, as a hare when the hounds give mouth'.

Chanting rhythmically, the prophets prepare to receive Saul, whose first words of peaceful greeting must appear strikingly at odds with the company of armed men gathered about him. But, 'beginning to come under the influence of the chant and to take the rhythm in his voice', the vengeful Saul leaves the search for the fugitive to his men, and moves slowly forward towards the brightness upon the hill, in which he recognises the glory of the Lord whom he has lost.

Like his king and master, one of the soldiers is caught up in the spirit of brightness, and cries 'The sun is in my heart. Lo! I shine forth', inspiring Saul to cast off his kingly garments and seek the peace of the Lord's blessing.

Feeling his death upon him, Saul prophesies once again the degeneration and decay that will follow David's succession, but here the prophecy carries the weight of an absolved spirit. Here at least Saul is at one with the Lord, as he was in the days before his fall from grace. Samuel has foretold that Saul will pursue David all the days of his life, and he has prophesied too, that

David and his house will live by cunning. The regeneration of spirit, vouchsafed to Saul out of his renewed submission to his God of Flame, will pass away, leaving him in even deeper despair. But, received into the company of prophets he is seen, at this moment, to be reminded of, if not received back into, the glory that was his before his fall.

Moving finally to the exiled David, alone and hiding in the wilderness, the play shows the future king, cast into despair in his turn. As Samuel has foretold, Saul's wrath has been rekindled against his successor, and Jonathan brings the news to the exile in the manner described in I *Samuel* xx., 35–41. Recognising the prearranged signal, David cries out against the fate that has been ordained for him: 'This is put upon me, I have not chosen it! . . . Let me come to Gilgal and die, so I see thy face, and the face of Michal, and the face of the King. Let me die! Let me come to Gilgal and die!'

Only the bond of friendship, the divine covenant that is between him and Jonathan, supports David in his grief, and, heroic as he has been shown to be in the fulfilment of his destiny, he is nevertheless overshadowed as the play closes, by the heroism of Jonathan, who must remain with his father and the 'starstone of despair', yearning after David, but destined too to wait and watch 'till the day of David at last shall be finished, and wisdom no more be fox-faced, and the blood gets back its flame'.

It is to Jonathan—the king's son who has not directly heard the Voice of the Thunderer, nor been called to serve the will of the Whirlwind, as his father and friend have been—that the final words of the play are given. Unlike Saul and David, Jonathan is not a divinely appointed leader of men. His role, like ours—the form of the play suggests—is to watch and wait.

Throughout the play, we have seen that the moral balance rests upon the declaration made by David in Scene 5:

> There are two motions in the world. The will of man for himself, and the desire that moves the Whirlwind. When the two are one, all is well, but when the will of man is against the Whirlwind, all is ill, at last.

The 'feeling' that animates both this declaration, and the dramatic treatment of the biblical narrative, are entirely Lawrence's. We see very clearly then, that the play is by no means a straightforward attempt to bring to dramatic life what is *there* in the chapters of *Samuel*. On the contrary, it is an original work which takes our familiarity with the biblical account for granted, and uses it as a foundation on which to build a completely new structure of feeling.

In going through the play, we have found the surrender motif to be thematic. Yet it is never completely unambiguous. Saul's tragedy is to have known what it was to have been at one with God, and to have lost that glory by his own fault. His is the greatest descent from bliss to bale. But David's assumption of that bliss does not free him from sorrow. Before David's anointing, Eliab says, 'It is a hard thing, to be the Lord's anointed,' and Samuel adds, 'For the froward and irreverent spirit, it is a thing well nigh impossible.' Moreover, it is shown in the play, that the glory David himself speaks to Jonathan of experiencing in the hand of the Lord, fails to sustain him in exile, when it is Jonathan who urges him to pursue his destiny.

It is all too easy to explain away these pervasive mysteries, and smooth out the disturbing ambiguities in the play, by following the clue that Frieda Lawrence provides, when she writes: 'I think in the play he worked off his struggle for life.' Taking this clue as a guide to our interpretation of the play, we could quite readily trace, in *David*, an allegory of Lawrence's own personal commitment to the 'will of the Whirlwind', seeing, in Saul, a personification of the tired old European culture which, in Lawrence's view, had turned its back on the mainsprings of creativity, and disobeyed the voice that spoke to it out of the instinctive and primitive sources of passion. Thence we could see in David (whose name Lawrence himself bore), a portrait of the Artist who has heard that voice, and knows that he must follow its decrees— even if obedience means submission to a lifetime of exile. Obviously there are marks of such a pattern to be found in the play,[8] just as there are signs in it of Lawrence's philosophical preoccupations, in the treatment of the love between David and Michal, and—even more importantly—in Saul's despairing vision of man-

[8] In his chapter on *David* in *Adventure in Consciousness: The Meaning of D. H. Lawrence's Religious Quest* (The Hague, 1964), pp. 136–150, George Panichas interestingly develops the implications of such a pattern.

kind's dehumanised destiny. But, to consider the play only at this personal, 'Lawrentian' level would be considerably to minimise its epic dimension, and to lose almost completely the force of its episodic, non-narrative form, which is surely designed to draw the spectator out of the constraints of his own individual consciousness into participation in an experience that partakes of the universal.

To use the personal level, (as Lawrence so evidently does) as one layer of a complex and imposing structure; as the basic stratum of personal and particular experience, out of which the conceptualised form of a philosophy organically grows, is, however, to become conscious of the close interweaving within the play of intense individual feeling with a more comprehensive and universal form, in which that individuality is willingly subsumed. In that form, 'There is no God. There is no Onlooker. There is no Mind. There is no dominant idea. And finally, there is no judgement: absolutely no judgement.' The way in which Lawrence saw Art as being shaped out of the particular and personal experience of life (as he expressed it in *Kangaroo*), is perhaps even more relevant here, than it was in *Touch and Go*. The 'life' of *David*, as we have seen, 'doesn't *start* with a new form. It starts with a new feeling and ends with a form.' And, for the nature of the 'feeling' in the biblical play, we have Lawrence's phrase, 'primitive religious passion' to guide us in the direction towards which a fine modern production might aim.

Lawrence's Plays and the Critics

Very often, when one comes to study the critical record of any work of literature over a long period of time, one learns more about the critics themselves—their attitudes both as individuals and as 'men of their time'—than about the work being criticised. This is, at all events, very true of Lawrence's plays. Criticism always takes second place to the work itself, often falling far behind the new directions taken by writers of genius. Yet, as has been seen throughout this account of Lawrence's drama, the response of critics can hold back a genuine talent, and even divert it into paths quite different from those which it had been the author's original 'intention' to follow. Because of this necessary interaction between creativity and criticism, it seems appropriate to place an account of what has been written about Lawrence's plays at the end of this study, where, in the light of what has already been recounted of the history of these plays, it can be seen in chronological perspective.

Hardly any attention at all was given to *The Widowing of Mrs. Holroyd*, the first of Lawrence's plays to be published (in 1914). The attitude to it then is perhaps best summed up in a tiny notice in an American magazine which describes the piece as 'A psychological play involving sex, with a very sordid setting. Written with insight'.[1] Even in that fragment of a response, however, we can read a whole world of social and cultural hostility to drama which involved sex in a sordid setting, redeemed as it might be by being written with insight. It would have taken a brave spirit to stage such a play at that time, especially as the play in question did not appear to embody the kind of social thesis that, in a Shaw or a Galsworthy, might have been felt to justify

[1] *The Independent* (New York), 25 May 1914, p. 324.

the bringing in of elements so controversially daring as sex and a working-class setting.

By the time of the publication of the text of *Touch and Go* in 1920, Lawrence had, of course, become a figure of some importance among contemporary writers, and the centre of considerable notoriety as a result of the proceedings launched against *The Rainbow*. Reviews of the second play to be published are therefore understandably coloured by expectations of particular Lawrentian preoccupations in the matter of political philosophy and the treatment of the relations between men and women.

The critic of *The Spectator*[2] was uncompromising in his view that Lawrence's play was the kind that the average manager would react to by saying ' "I am driven to the average musical or 'straight' comedy because this is the sort of stuff you highbrows give me. Here is black-and-white proof of what we managers have always said. It is impossible to have ideas without being dreary".' The critic who puts these words into the 'average manager's' mouth insists that his own objections do not arise out of a personal antipathy to Lawrence's ideas, but to the fact that they are dramatised in the play 'with greater length than clarity'. Holding that 'the worst foes of ideas which are right and just are not those who oppose them, but those that set out such ideas in an unattractive way' he claims that the ideas in Lawrence's preface are praiseworthy: 'But when we turn to the play itself we know it is a sort of performance (I will not say entertainment) through which none but the earnest could sit.'

Describing *Touch and Go* as 'a play with an obscure plot and an enigmatic love affair', the critic of *The Times Literary Supplement*[3] declares that 'the strength of the play lies in its picture of colliery life' and the 'strong impression of reality' which this creates. Here he is admiring the feature of Lawrence's work which has always been most accessible; that gift for re-producing the 'real' which we have seen to be so powerful in the naturalist plays, and for which those who otherwise dislike Lawrence's work always manage to find an appreciative word. Much more remarkably this same critic sees, at least in the final scene of *Touch and Go*, in the treatment of the mob that comes close to murdering

[2] 28 August 1920, p. 279.
[3] 13 May 1920, p. 304.

250

Gerald, 'an excellent piece of crowd psychology which should prove even more effective in the theatre than in the printed page'.

For all the force of that suggestion, however, the first criticisms of Lawrence's drama 'in the theatre' were delayed until the 1926 production of *The Widowing of Mrs. Holroyd*. By this time the controversy over Lawrence's stature as a writer had become even more heated, as is demonstrated by the contrast between *The Times'* review, which concludes that the play is 'stagnant and tormented; it lies like a burden on the mind' and the more sympathetic viewpoint of H. H. in *The Outlook* where we read, 'not a sentence is spoken but serves to intensify the situation and absorb the spectator's concern'.[4]

Very interestingly it is at this point that commentators, not noted for their general sympathy with what Lawrence had to say or with the way in which he had to say it, begin to discriminate between the straightforward clarity of the early 'realist' writing and the more opaque 'metaphysics' of post-1914 Lawrence. As we have seen, Desmond MacCarthy, reviewing the production of *Mrs. Holroyd* in *The New Statesman* under the headline, 'A Poet's Realism',[5] admires the play for the way in which it dramatises Lawrence's philosophy of sex relations without recourse to 'preaching and obscure exposition'. In the play which, he points out, is an early work, MacCarthy writes that 'Mr. Lawrence has austerely kept his gift for lyrical expression within the bounds of naturalism'. Again, as with *Touch and Go*, it is the mastery of the art of re-producing life in the form of drama for which the play receives the largest measure of praise.

Even Ivor Brown, who felt the play to be dramatically unsatisfactory because of the way in which—as he saw it—Lawrence evaded the issue posed by the situation he had created, remarked upon the quality of life that the drama conveyed. 'In this play', he writes, 'Mr. Lawrence has shown himself a tantalizing dramatist. He has also suggested how well he might have written since if he had stuck to the life which he knows instead of plunging into the theory which is clamorously acclaimed by people who have been educated beyond their intelligence.'[6] The praise is, to say the

[4] 24 December 1926, p. 629.
[5] 18 December 1926, p. 310.
[6] *The Saturday Review*, 18 December 1926, p. 767.

least, back-handed, and it is little wonder that Lawrence was stung by it to report to Maria Huxley, 'They played my *Widowing of Mrs. Holroyd* and I believe they hated it, and somebody says I ought to write about the class I come from, I've no right to enter into the Peerage—people educated above their class, etc.!' (CL p. 955) Interestingly it was the taunt Lawrence evidently felt to be aimed at his working-class background that hit hardest. He does not seem to have objected so strongly to Brown's more serious criticism that 'It is a good situation, from which the dramatist has bolted in a way disastrous to his piece'. The play's failure to answer the question posed by its triangular situation, with Mrs. Holroyd poised between Holroyd and Blackmore, is seen here not as a triumph of naturalism, but as a mis-handling of potentially tragic drama. Perhaps Lawrence was right not to take issue with an objection framed in terms so totally uncomprehending of the mode in which the play is written.

Yet again, in the enthusiastic review given to the production in *The Nation and Athenaeum*,[7] it is Lawrence's 'failure' to conform to current expectations of drama that accounts for critical disappointment. At the outset, the reviewer is all admiration. 'The first two acts of this play are extraordinarily good. The bare life is filled with that astonishing vitality that Mr. Lawrence can put into his best work. This is not realism, but reality, shorn of everything irrelevant to the emotional issue. These acts, crisp yet weighted, have that real literary quality which comes of fidelity to the truth imaginatively grasped: they are dramatic and moving. But since we were thus wrought up to the level of tragedy,' he concludes, 'the collapse of the third act was desolating.' The critic here shares the 'blame' between Lawrence and the producer, but it is clear that the real question concerns the 'appropriate' development of the situation that Lawrence had worked up so successfully in the first two acts. Complaining that 'photographic, not imaginative, realism obtruded itself' in the 'disappointing' third act, the review ends by recommending the 'immensely interesting, even exciting, evening' afforded by the production of *Mrs. Holroyd*, and looks forward to the forthcoming production of *David* which 'reads like a masterpiece' and

[7] 18 December 1926, p. 422.

represents, in this reviewer's opinion, an enormous stride forward in Lawrence's literary competence over the earlier play.

This high opinion of *David* on the page was shared by Edward Sackville-West who declares, in a review of the text of the play in *The New Statesman*[8] that 'It would be hard to beat *David* for sobriety, for the deliberate and well-managed archaism of its diction, for clarity of thought and beauty of detail'. Comparing the play favourably with Gide's *Saul* on the same subject, Sack-vills-West goes on to define *David* as an 'austere drama' characterised by 'subtlety and depth of restrained feeling'. For all his preference though, this critic feels that we can scarcely imagine *David* on the stage, whereas Gide's play 'should be effective enough'.

Bonamy Dobrée's review of the play in book form re-iterates this admiration for the language of *David* which is 'never excessive, but it burns like a great smokeless flame'.[9] Once again it is felt that, though Lawrence's play is 'far more profound' than Gide's, it is *Saul* which is the more 'stageworthy' of the two.

That such a view accurately represented contemporary taste was borne out by responses to the play when it was produced. The drama critic of *The Times* then felt 'bound to say that the result is neither drama nor poetry. Truth to tell, this unending insistence on the verbal symbols of mysticism grows wearisome long before the last of the sixteen scenes.'[10] This critic could not find any answer in the play to the question of what purpose the dramatist had in mind in making use of the biblical story. Feeling that 'it is fatal to the play if this question remains unanswered,' this critic concludes that the filling out of the story of Saul, rather than that of David, with 'the peculiar intensity of language he (Lawrence) invariably uses—the sort of language he cannot help using' is a complete failure in dramatic terms: 'Flames of life and love and spirit, if they are meant for the theatre at all, need to be illustrated in common or uncommon action; merely to speak of them in dark hints conveys nothing.' Clearly the man who could write that, had not been touched by the spirit of

---

[8] 10 July 1926, pp. 360–361.
[9] *The Nation and The Athenaeum*, 24 April 1926, pp. 103–104.
[10] 24 May 1927, p. 14.

'primitive religious passion' which Lawrence knew so well had to be 'got across' if the play were to succeed.

In *The Nation and Athenaeum* the pseudonymous critic 'Omicron' did not even find the language of *David* a redeeming feature. 'What on earth', he asks, 'is the good of a twentieth-century writer striving to imitate the style of the early seventeenth? The result can only be a tedious Wardour Street diction frequently interlarded with quotations from the most well-known book in English.'[11] Even though he hesitated to blame the author for the 'fiasco' of the production, this critic notes, in the producer's defence, that the play 'lacked all dramatic movement' which 'no doubt made it very hard to produce'.

These reviews of the production of *David* in May 1927 were the last responses to production of his drama that Lawrence was to read. He regarded them as 'impudent', but, discouraging as they must have been to him in his low and rapidly declining state of health, they did not defeat his fighting spirit. On the contrary, he regarded their 'impudence' as a stimulus to fierce defiance of the 'eunuchs' who found his play dull. Retreat was not for him. 'My business is a fight, and I've got to keep it up', he wrote, defying the disdain that had greeted what was to be his last endeavour to write for the stage. (CL p. 980)

While respect and admiration for the novels began to build up in the decades after his death, there were still few who came forward to defend the achievements of Lawrence, the dramatist. A notable exception was Sean O'Casey who, as has already been seen in the chapter on *A Collier's Friday Night*, deplored the neglect of a potentially great English dramatist in his review of the publication of that play in 1934. Apart from this fiery defence by a fellow dramatist, and the production in London in 1936 of Walter Greenwood's adaptation of *The Daughter-in-Law* under the title of *My Son's My Son*, nothing further was heard of Lawrence's plays until 1961, when a version of *The Widowing of Mrs. Holroyd* on television won approving notices from the critics. *The Times*, for example, headed its review, 'Lawrence play skilfully adapted to Television' and reminded its readers that 'Like almost all the notable English novelists to emerge in the ninteen-hundreds, D. H. Lawrence tried his hand at drama, and

[11] 28 May 1927, p. 261.

on at least three occasions, but few who have read his novels are familiar with his plays in print, and even fewer can have seen them performed'.[12]

It was a report of this television production that first interested Peter Gill in Lawrence's plays and led to his 1965 Sunday night production without décor of *A Collier's Friday Night* at the Royal Court Theatre. So vividly had the play fired Gill's imagination that spectators were able to discern and admire—even without décor—the shape of a play which firmly delineated an aspect of family life which *The Times*' drama critic aptly characterised as 'the economics of affection'.

Despite this measure of recognition, two more years were to elapse before Peter Gill was able to build on the experience of that Sunday night success with the full-scale production of *The Daughter-in-Law* which took the London theatre critics by storm. In his review of that production, Irving Wardle reminded his readers that 'Peter Gill's beautiful production two years ago of Lawrence's first play, *A Collier's Friday Night* exploded in one night the idea that Lawrence the dramatist could safely be ignored'.[13] Suddenly, in the March of 1967, the truth of that 'explosion' became common knowledge. After long decades of almost complete neglect, Lawrence's dramatic genius had at last become apparent, thanks to the emergence of a producer sensitive to the long overlooked theatrical possibilities of Lawrence's 'colliery' plays. The man who could 'whip 'em in' had at last come upon the scene, and, as Lawrence had foretold way back in 1913, there was, under such a man's direction, no lack of an audience for his dramatic 'stuff'.

With well-deserved justice, Peter Gill enjoyed a large share of the critical acclaim awarded to this 1967 production, and to the D. H. Lawrence Season which followed in the spring of 1968. Without him the plays would no doubt have remained mere literary curiosities, interesting only to scholars as the minor works of a major writer. It was by bringing the plays to life in the theatre: by reviving them in every sense of the word, that Gill put an end to the persistent myth of Lawrence as a mere

[12] 24 March 1961, p. 18.
[13] *The Times*, 17 March 1967, p. 13.

dabbler in drama, and established him once and for all as a major English dramatist of the twentieth century.

Interestingly enough, the details and structures which have been described in this study as fundamental to Lawrence's writing in the naturalist plays were, as has been seen, among the elements attributed by the drama critics to the skill of the producer, and it is a measure of Gill's sensitive response to the essentials of Lawrence's drama that he realised, in production practice, precisely those features that are intrinsic and integral to Lawrence's texts.

Representing a recurrent theme in the critical response to these productions is Harold Hobson's observation that they 'revealed a dramatist of outstanding talent who, though famous in other connections, has been unaccountably neglected on the stage'.[14] Derek Malcolm combined a similar recognition of Lawrence's stature as a playwright with the opinion that the achievement of Peter Gill and his company would be 'recognised as the definitive versions of these supremely reticent, yet extraordinarily eloquent slices of strict naturalism'. At the end of his review Mr. Malcolm formulated the question that was in all minds at the time: 'Had Lawrence seen Peter Gill's productions, what else might he not have written?

Summing up the critical reaction to the 1968 D. H. Lawrence Season, which included *A Collier's Friday Night*, *The Widowing of Mrs. Holroyd* and *The Daughter-in-Law*, B. A. Young recommended without reservation that 'no one who cares about the theatre can afford to miss a single one of them'. Here then was full recognition for at least one aspect of Lawrence's drama; that aspect of 'high', 'close' or 'strict' naturalism which has here been described as having close affinities with the dramatic mode of Chekhov.

As an immediate consequence of the 1967 success of *The Daughter-in-Law*, interest was aroused in the remainder of Lawrence's dramatic output which had recently become conveniently available with the publication of the *Complete Plays* in

[14] In *The Sunday Times*. This, and the following reviews of the 1968 Season of plays by D. H. Lawrence at the Royal Court Theatre, London, can conveniently be found, collected in *The Critic*, 8 March 1968, pp. 10–12, and 22 March 1968, pp. 9–11.

1965, and, in August 1967, *The Fight for Barbara* became the second of Lawrence's plays to achieve a full-scale professional production in the English theatre. Unfortunately the play suffered —through not fault of its own—from coming so close on the heels of the naturalistic triumph of *The Daughter-in-Law*. The comparative coolness of the reception accorded by the critics to Robin Midgley's production of *The Fight for Barbara* could well be held to have had much to do with the fact that the critics were expecting more of the same kind of experience, to which they had reacted with such astonished admiration, when confronted with the life-like quality of *The Daughter-in-Law*. As we have seen in studying the plays, it was inevitable that such hopes should be doomed to disappointment. The general tone of that disappointment is conveyed in Harold Hobson's comment that 'In recent days enough has been seen of Lawrence's unfamiliar stage work to suggest that there was in him a considerable dramatist. This production will not confirm that impression'.[15]

Persuaded, perhaps, by his enthusiasm for what had been generally hailed as the life-like authenticity of *The Daughter-in-Law*, Mr. Midgley concentrated on that aspect of *The Fight for Barbara* which Lawrence had described to Garnett as 'word-for-word true'. Overlooking the shift that we have seen in the play away from the naturalistic mode, and pinning his production to what has here been described as the misleading factor of its close resemblance to the lives of Frieda and Lawrence at the time of writing, Mr. Midgley presented his version of the play as an extension of the Lawrence biography, thereby confirming views of Lawrence's drama such as that expressed by Robert Lucas, who maintains of *The Fight for Barbara*, that 'The play has no literary value, but it has some interest for the biographer'.

As a curtain-raiser, Mr. Midgley offered stage readings of a selection from the writings of D. H. Lawrence, Frieda Lawrence, Ernest Weekley and others under the title, 'Men and Women'. Since the actors and actresses who read these letters and other documents, subsequently played the characters, supposedly 'based' on the people whose real life writings they had read, the play which followed inevitably became a mere commentary on the real life records; 'a fictionalised account' as Robert Lucas calls it,

---

[15] *The Sunday Times* 13 August 1967, p. 21.

'of his (Lawrence's) own flight with Frieda'. As a consequence, the tragi-comic distancing of the play *from* life; that 'framing-off' which has here been held to distinguish it from the plays in the naturalist mode, was almost completely lost. The time, it appears, was not then ripe for the discovery that Lawrence had been a master of more than one dramatic mode.

Significantly, Philip Hope-Wallace described the play itself as 'static', and found the real life material, arranged by Robin Midgley, much more interesting than the fiction. Not all responses were quite so dismissive though, of Lawrence's fictive creation. Irving Wardle, for example, found that the play was 'essentially a duet for the lovers, and on those terms, autobiography blazes up into art'. Conceding that 'the actual language has not worn well', he maintains that 'no matter how volatile the emotion, it is always anchored in hard detail', and concludes that 'one index of the play's quality is that it consists mainly of hostility, but leaves one in no doubt that the relationship (between Barbara and Jimmy) is built to last'. Mr. Wardle's favourable review[16] (which appeared under the heading 'Forgotten Play Shows Power of Genius'), was, however, an exception, and renewed acclaim for further revivals of Lawrence's plays had, as we have seen, to await the 'trilogy' produced by Peter Gill in March 1968.

On that occasion it was the hostile reaction that was exceptional, and even the rare expression of disapproval was tempered, as in the case of Eric Shorter's review in *The Daily Telegraph*, with admiration for the 'unquestionably authentic atmosphere' of the plays. In *The Daily Mail*, Peter Lewis observed that 'Lawrence's plays . . . are all on one note and I don't like them, but the desolate, inexorable note sounds like a tocsin'. Despite his personal reservations about the plays, Mr. Lewis, like most of his colleagues, was also unstinting in his praise of Peter Gill's 'finely understood production' (of *Mrs. Holroyd*) which he found 'as real as life itself'.

Apart from some doubts about the relevance of the naturalist mode to the more 'liberated' modes current in the English theatre of the late 1960s, there was little but praise for the D. H. Lawrence Season of 1968. Ronald Bryden summed up the general response most succinctly when he drew attention to the fact that

[16] *The Times*, 10 August 1967, p. 5.

Peter Gill's productions 'disprove conclusively the belief that Lawrence's writing for the stage was too "literary" for performance.'[17] In his summing-up of the Season, Benedict Nightingale too was representative in his opinion that 'The plays are remarkable for their refusal to pin down characters for approval, parody or condemnation. There are no villians and no heroes; no fools and certainly no wise men; only a number of people, usually rather self-righteous and invariably maladroit, trying to sort out the problems they continue to create for one another. There is continual action, reaction and re-reaction; they are the least static plays one could imagine. In short they are tremendously alive.'[18]

It was not until 1973 that Peter Gill followed up this enormously successful Season with his version of *The Merry-go-Round* which once again won high praise, much of which was again lavished on the naturalistic aspects of the play. As we have seen, Mr. Gill made certain adaptations to Lawrence's text, replacing, for example, the exotic Polish cleric, Baron von Ruge, with a probably more credible upper-class English vicar, whose attempts to minister to the awkward Hemstocks are just as summarily dealt with by that recaltricant family as they are in Lawrence's original. As a result of the adaptations, which are perfectly justifiable in the practical theatrical terms upon which they were made, the movement made by Lawrence outside the bounds of strict naturalism did not appear as abrupt as it does in a reading of the text, though Mr. Gill skilfully made sure that sufficient of the movement remained to make it clear that this was not 'just another instalment' of the previous episodes that he had presented in the lives of Lawrence's mining communities. That this development in Lawrence's dramatic style was firmly registered in the production is vouched for by remarks like Michael Billington's that *The Merry-go-Round* is 'more of a theatrical hybrid than the Court's earlier Lawrence trilogy: a comedy laced with pain and passion'.[19] Irving Wardle pin-points the development too in his

---

[17] The three reviews cited can be found in the relevant numbers of *The Critic* (see Note 14 above). Mr. Bryden's is reprinted from *The Observer*.

[18] Benedict Nightingale, 'On the Coal Face,' *Plays and Players*, May 1968, pages 18–19–21 and 51.

[19] *The Guardian*, 8 November 1973, p. 10.

observation that, in this play, 'Lawrence sets his ruling obsessions in comic perspective',[20] and by his recognition of the fact that the comedy is framed by, and based upon, truth; on that total sense of reality so characteristic of Lawrence's particular brand of dramatic naturalism.

Following the trail blazed by Peter Gill's re-creating genius, other Companies have seen the possibilities in the plays that he retrieved from obscurity, and have produced them with great success. Notable among such productions in England was Michael Wearing's of *A Collier's Friday Night*, presented during the Nottingham Festival in 1972 at the Playhouse. An outstanding feature of that same Festival was the *Young Bert Lawrence* exhibition, the organisers of which contributed so much to the recognition of Lawrence, the dramatist. No one who went from the exhibition, where attention was drawn in such a lively way to Lawrence's dramatic interests, to the performance at the Nottingham Playhouse of a play which so finely demonstrates the fulfilment of those interests in drama that 'really works in the theatre, could have been left in any doubt whatsoever that Lawrence was a playwright to be reckoned with. Nor was it possible to experience the combined impact of exhibition and production without being keenly—and regretfully—conscious that the failure of his contemporaries to recognise Lawrence's potential deprived the English theatre of a dramatist who might well have been among its greatest of glories.

Touch and Go, The Married Man, The Fight for Barbara and *David* still await the revitalising treatment that has restored four at least of Lawrence's plays to the 'classic' repertoire. Each of these very different plays will need an approach sensitively keyed to the major shifts in style and mood that have been seen here to be such remarkable features of Lawrence's enormously varied dramatic output. Now that prejudices against Lawrence as a dramatist have been thoroughly rejected, it should not be long before someone comes forward to give a production of *Touch and Go* that will do justice to its emblematic counterpointing of relationships at a personal and at a social level. From among the talented band of directors currently at work all over the world, we may also, surely, soon expect a fast-moving, farcical treatment

[20] *The Times*, 8 November 1973, p. 13.

of the whirling kaleidoscope of couples in *The Married Man*, and a cool and distanced presentation of the delicately poised tragi-comedy of *The Fight for Barbara*. Most difficult of all to present will be *David*. Yet here again, directors—and audiences too, for that matter—much more familiar with the techniques, conventions and terms of 'epic' theatre, should now be able to rediscover, in this play's majestic shape, the force of the structuring principles that so completely eluded the brave producers of the 1927 version.

In looking closely at the plays, as I have tried here to suggest might usefully be done, it may be agreed that they reveal the multi-faceted talent of a major dramatist whose gift was not allowed to flourish. Certainly I would submit that the growing recognition of that talent, demonstrated in the record of critical response assembled in this chapter, powerfully supports such a view.

Deprived of contact with the centres of dramatic activity, Lawrence nevertheless moved in his drama through a range of forms which reflect, and indeed prefigure the directions in which the drama of this century has developed. Pre-dating the acceptance of 'high' naturalism by some twenty years in the achievement of his 'colliery' plays, Lawrence proceeded, in *The Merry-go-Round*, *The Married Man* and *The Fight for Barbara*, to anticipate the mannered and satirically distanced 'black' comedy that was to emerge in the 1960's. Still pressing forward with his own experiments, he created in 1920 a form for *Touch and Go* which, in many ways, is more radical in its rejection of established conventions even than the so-called 'revolutionary' outbursts of the 'angry young men' of the mid 1950's. Finally, in *David*, he attempted an epic form so far in advance of its time that it was —understandably—misconceived in its first production and remains dauntingly 'difficult' today. There can be few dramatists of this, or any other, century who can be felt to have attempted more or ranged more widely.

Whatever happens next in the continuing story of the bringing to light of Lawrence's plays, it is certain that we can never go back to the time when these plays were written off as 'dull' or 'formless'. The experience of some of the plays on stage has brought us a long way from the point at which a critic could write, with confident authority, that Lawrence had 'no gift for drama', and few would agree wholeheartedly today with the once definitive opinion that Lawrence's plays 'have little, if any, dramatic or artistic value.' Now that a taste has been established for some of these plays, it would seem that Michael Billington speaks for many discerning theatregoers when he writes, at the end of his review of *The Merry-go-Round*: 'Personally I shall not rest until the Court gives us the remainder of the Lawrence output.'

While profoundly agreeing that it is to the Royal Court Theatre, London, and to Peter Gill, that our greatest debt is due, for repairing the omission of so many generations of managements and producers, one might broaden Mr. Billington's plea to a more general request that all of Lawrence's plays should be looked at with attention by everyone who has the best interests of the English-speaking theatre at heart. And in that 'everyone' I would want to include not only the essential 'men of the theatre' who can bring the plays to living realisation on the stage (where Lawrence himself would so dearly have loved to see them), but also all those students, scholars and general readers, for whom the development of theatre is a matter of literary and cultural consequence.

Bibliographical Note

All quotations from the plays are taken from *The Complete Plays of D. H. Lawrence* (London: Heinemann, 1965; New York: Viking Press Inc., 1966, ᶜ1965).

As all the standard bibliographies of Lawrence pre-date this edition, the information they give is chiefly of interest in regard to the various manuscript and typescript versions of the plays, full details of which can be found in F. Warren Roberts, *A Bibliography of D. H. Lawrence* (Soho Bibliographies, London: Rupert Hart-Davis, 1963).

With reference to the plays, the most useful of the many biographies of Lawrence is *D. H. Lawrence: A Composite Biography* edited by Edward Nehls, in three volumes (Madison: University of Wisconsin Press, 1957, 1958 and 1959).

Unless otherwise indicated, the place of publication of all newspapers and periodicals cited in this study is London, and the publication date of books cited in footnotes is the same for London and New York.

Much of the existing criticism of Lawrence as a dramatist can be found in the introduction to editions of the plays, a complete list of which (in chronological order of publication) is given below, together with details of other critical work directly relevant to Lawrence's drama.

Bibliography of the Plays of D. H. Lawrence

The Widowing of Mrs. Holroyd, with an introduction by Edwin Björkman. New York: Mitchell Kennerley, 1914; London: Duckworth, 1914.

Touch and Go, with a preface by D. H. Lawrence. London: C. W. Daniel, 1920; New York: Thomas Seltzer, 1920.

David, London: Martin Secker, 1926; New York: Knopf, 1926.

The Plays of D. H. Lawrence (The Widowing of Mrs. Holroyd, Touch and Go with the preface, David). London: Martin Secker, 1933.

The Fight for Barbara (under the title, Keeping Barbara). Argosy (London), Vol. XIV, No. 91, December 1933, pp. 68–90.

A Collier's Friday Night, with an introduction by Edward Garnett. London: Martin Secker, 1934.

Noah's Flood. In Phoenix: The Posthumous Papers of D. H. Lawrence, ed., Edward D. McDonald. London: Heinemann, 1936; New York: Viking Press Inc., 1936, pp. 811–816.

Altitude (Scene 1 only). The Laughing Horse, No. 20, Summer 1938, pp. 121–123.

The Married Man. Virginia Quarterly Review, XVI, Autumn 1940, pp. 523–547.

The Merry-go-Round. Virginia Quarterly Review, XVII, Winter 1941, Supplement, pp. 1–44.

The Complete Plays of D. H. Lawrence (The Widowing of Mrs. Holroyd, David, The Married Man, The Daughter-in-Law, The Fight for Barbara, Touch-and-Go, The Merry-go-Round, A Collier's Friday Night, Altitude, Noah's Flood). London: Heinemann, 1965; New York: Viking Press Inc., 1966, °1965.

The Widowing of Mrs. Holroyd and The Daughter-in-Law, with an introduction by Michael Marland. London: Heinemann Educational Books, 1968. (Includes a glossary of Dialect and Mining words.)

Three Plays by D. H. Lawrence: A Collier's Friday Night, The Daughter-in-Law, The Widowing of Mrs. Holroyd, with an introduction by Raymond Williams. Harmondsworth: Penguin, 1969.

Note: An edition of the complete plays was also produced as part of a D. H. Lawrence collection by Heron Books (London, 1969). This edition has an introduction by Malcolm Elwin and original illustrations by Patrick Rixson.

Critical work on the Plays of D. H. Lawrence

Gray, Simon. 'Lawrence the Dramatist', in D. H. Lawrence: A Critical Anthology, ed. H. Coombes. Harmondsworth: Penguin Education, 1973, pp. 453–457. Reprinted from New Society (London), 21 March 1968.

Panichas, George. Chapter on David in Adventure in Consciousness: The Meaning of D. H. Lawrence's Religious Quest. The Hague: Mouton, 1964, pp. 136–150.

Sagar, Keith. 'D. H. Lawrence: Dramatist', The D. H. Lawrence Review, Vol. 4, No. 2, Summer 1971, pp. 154–182.

Waterman, A. E. 'The Plays of D. H. Lawrence', D. H. Lawrence: A

Collection of Critical Essays, ed., Mark Spilka. Englewood Cliffe, N.J.: Prentice-Hall, 1963, pp. 142–150.

Williams, Raymond. 'D. H. Lawrence: "The Widowing of Mrs. Holroyd" ' in *Drama from Ibsen to Brecht*. Harmondsworth; Penguin, 1973, pp. 292–296. (Originally published London, 1968).

Index